GPs AND PURCHASING IN THE NHS

GPs and Purchasing in the NHS

The internal market and beyond

BERNARD DOWLING
Centre for Health Planning and Management
Keele University

Routledge
Taylor & Francis Group

LONDON AND NEW YORK

First published 2000 by Ashgate Publishing

Reissued 2018 by Routledge
2 Park Square, Milton Park, Abingdon, Oxon OX14 4RN
711 Third Avenue, New York, NY 10017, USA

Routledge is an imprint of the Taylor & Francis Group, an informa business

Publisher's Note
The publisher has gone to great lengths to ensure the quality of this reprint but points out that some imperfections in the original copies may be apparent.

Disclaimer
The publisher has made every effort to trace copyright holders and welcomes correspondence from those they have been unable to contact.

A Library of Congress record exists under LC control number: 99075447

ISBN 13: 978-1-138-63436-7 (hbk)
ISBN 13: 978-1-138-63434-3 (pbk)
ISBN 13: 978-1-315-20544-1 (ebk)

Contents

List of Figures

List of Tables

Preface

The introduction in 1991 of a quasi-market into Britain's health service was commonly perceived as the most radical change to the service since it began. The reform established a system in which the purchasing function was performed by health authorities and those general practices that joined the fund-holding scheme. Yet while this change clearly altered the organisational structure of the service (the purchaser-provider split), its impact on the services received by patients was less clear. A reason for undertaking this research was to resolve this problem in the context of one service, elective surgery (though the project compared the performance of the purchasers within the quasi-market, not that system with its forerunner).

Whilst the literature (prior to this study) lacked any direct comparison of the performance of health authorities and general practice fund-holders as purchasers, there was much controversy about the equity implications of the system. Most notably this focused upon alleged differences in the waiting times for hospital services of patients registered with fund-holding and non fund-holding practices. However, such allegations were based on anecdotal evidence and open to contradiction.

The research on which this book is based moved that debate beyond a reliance on anecdotal evidence and for one service, elective surgery, redresses the lack of evaluation in the relative merits of fund-holders and health authorities as purchasers. The performance of health authorities and general practice fund-holders were tested by comparing the waiting times of patients who had their elective surgery commissioned by each purchaser type. To do this, the waits of fund-holding and non fund-holding patients for operations covered by the fund-holding scheme were compared at four public providers over a four-year period.

Another important aim was to ascertain why any tendency towards waiting time differences occurred. A series of hypotheses were tested, including the generosity of fund-holders' budgets, contrasts in the surgical case mix of each population, plus variations in the way fund-holders and health authorities performed their purchasing roles. In discussing the policy implications of the study, the book then addresses how public sector quasi-markets can work in the contexts of both equity and efficiency.

Acknowledgements

This book firmly has its origins in my doctoral research at the London School of Economics. Looking back, my studies actually progressed more rapidly than I was initially expecting and for that I must pass much credit to Howard Glennerster and Julian Le Grand. I was extremely fortunate to be able to call on their guidance and expertise throughout the project and my sincere thanks go to them both for their advice, support and encouragement. I am also indebted to Calum Paton for his invaluable help towards transforming a doctoral thesis into this book.

Beyond such academic support the research was, and could only have been, completed with the crucial help of a large number of people. I must thank as a group all the general practitioners, hospital consultants, plus the trust, health authority, and practice managers who spared their time to be interviewed or partake in less formal discussions for the research. Much gratitude also goes to the practice staff who facilitated the checking of medical records against the details for some of the patients included on the computerised database that was a central element of the study. Thanks are also due to numerous managers from the West Sussex Health Authority for their assistance in providing me with the data required for the successful completion of the project.

Appreciation is also due to my employers during the whole of the research period, the Victoria Road Surgery in Worthing. My need to regularly take impromptu leave in order to undertake research was always accepted without question. The Economic and Social Research Council funded the research project (grant number: R00429534090), and I take this opportunity to thank them for that financial assistance. I also acknowledge the *British Medical Journal* for granting me permission to use the material from a couple of articles I had published through them as a central feature in this book. Details of these can be found in the bibliography.

Last but not least, mention must be made of my partner, Chris. In order to free my time for studying she took on a far greater proportion of domestic responsibilities during the project, including the care of our children, than could reasonably have been expected. I shall always be grateful for her help.

1 The 1991 Reforms: Questions, Background and Rationale

The reforms to the National Health Service (NHS), introduced by the government of the United Kingdom (UK) in April 1991, were widely judged as inaugurating the most radical changes to the service since its inception in 1948.   Even so, they were still representative of an international trend during the last decade or more when health care reform was commonplace (Wagstaff *et al.*, 1993).   For whilst the Thatcher regime was perhaps one of the most noted advocates of market mechanisms in welfare provision, their reforms to the NHS reflected a pattern of change that can be seen to various degrees almost everywhere in Europe (Baldock, 1993; Brommels, 1995; Saltman and von Otter, 1995).   Indeed, there is room for states to learn from each other's experiences (Ham, 1996a; 1997a), even though the precise pattern of the changes in different countries have been specific to each individual nation (Kane, 1995).

The central characteristic of the UK reforms was a division of the organisational structure of the service, or at least the part relating to the procurement and provision of secondary care for patients, into separate purchaser and provider functions to create a more competitive climate.   In brief, the treatments received by patients from service providers were to be purchased on their behalf by health authorities and those family doctor general practices which elected, and were eligible, to participate in the fund-holding scheme.   An important reason, alongside concerns about cost containment and the tradition of centralisation in the NHS, why patients had the purchasing function performed for them derives from the economics of health care that stresses poor consumer knowledge.   They are not generally considered to be knowledgeable enough to make appropriate clinical decisions themselves (see Strong and Robinson, 1990).

The reforms, and in particular this dual-purchasing configuration for the services covered by the fund-holding scheme, generated a mass of literature in which a number of issues have been discussed in an almost confrontational manner.   Perhaps the most contentious debate concerned the implications of the system for equity between patients represented by

health authorities and fund-holding practices. Most notably this focused on
disputed assertions that fund-holding patients benefited from shorter
waiting times for the hospital services covered by the fund-holding scheme
than did non fund-holders. It is this issue that provides the principal focus
of this book.

QUESTIONS

The research on which this book was based had two primary functions.
First, to fill the gap in knowledge regarding the question of whether fund-
holding patients were given quicker access to hospital services, specifically
for elective surgery.   Second, to establish the reasons why any such
contrasts existed. After all, health authorities were far larger purchasers
than fund-holders, even when such practices are taken as a block.[1] It might
thus be expected that hospitals would have been more reliant on the custom
of the local health authority for their financial viability than on their
business with fund-holding general practitioners (GPs).   This could
presumably have given health authorities a stronger negotiating position
with providers than that enjoyed by the practices.

Indeed, this understanding led Glennerster *et al.* (1994a) to declare that
the earlier admission of fund-holding patients was an implausible strategy
for hospitals because it would mean them discriminating against the largest
purchaser.   Proposals that fund-holders were more able than health
authorities to gain shorter waiting times for patients therefore seems to
represent something of a paradox. As well as demonstrating whether and
why providers pursued such a strategy, the dilemma will also be addressed
by explaining the nature of purchasing leverage and examining hospital
behaviour in the post-1991 NHS.

TERMINOLOGY

In the literature the system introduced in 1991 tends to be referred to as
either an internal market or quasi-market. Pietroni (1993) inferred that the
market was said to be internal because it operated within the public health
care system of the UK. However, purchasers could buy services from both
public and private providers, and the reforms may thus have increased

---

1.   In 1995/96 fund-holders in England and Wales purchased just 7 per cent of the value of
     all NHS hospital and community services. Even in the area most densely covered by
     such practices the health authority still retained 71 per cent of the available resources
     (Audit Commission, 1996a).

competition for the private sector as well (see Propper and Maynard, 1990). This engagement of the public and private sector in a competitive relationship led Butler (1992) to question the appropriateness of the phrase 'internal market'.

Le Grand (1991a), using what might thus be a more suitable term, distinguished a quasi-market from a conventional market because it differs in one or more of three ways. First, many of the organisations competing in the market may not be seeking to maximise their profits. Second, payment for services could be centralised away from the purchaser or otherwise made in the form of vouchers rather than cash. Third, agents might act on behalf of the consumers of the service, patients in the case of the NHS.

But for any talk of the post-1991 NHS, the 1997 general election result has made the use of words like 'markets' and 'purchasing' less fashionable now, at least with the new government, than under the former administration. Yet the actual purchaser-provider split, or should one say the separation between commissioners and suppliers, looks here to stay for the foreseeable future. Moreover, since the study concerns events prior to the 1997 election, the use of the traditional language of the quasi-market period is continued in this book. Therefore, while doubts have been raised about the technical correctness of calling the system an 'internal market', because of its widespread use it is utilised interchangeably here with the phrase 'quasi-market'. Similarly the term 'purchase' is sometimes substituted by the word 'commission', and such expressions are also used without distinction.

Another small matter to briefly explain at this juncture is the use of a hyphen when the term 'fund-holding' and its derivative phrases are used in the book. The only exceptions are the times when direct quotations are cited from other works and the authors had not used a hyphen in this way. Such use of the hyphen is very rare in the academic literature and in lower status official publications like the 'Executive Letters' and 'Health Service Guidance' documents produced by the NHS Executive. However, in the higher status governmental literature, including 'Statutory Instruments' and 'Acts of Parliament', a hyphen has been used. As such, the use of a hyphen when referring to the fund-holding scheme can be seen as technically correct, despite its infrequent usage.

EQUITY: PAST AND PRESENT

Although equity became such a contentious issue since the 1991 NHS reforms, there is nothing new about attention being devoted to this topic. It has long held a prominent place in the literature about the health service. This is not surprising, as the creation of the NHS under Attlee's administration can be seen as an attempt to secure greater equity in health care (see Bevan *et al.*, 1980; Mays and Bevan, 1987). Indeed, despite Pereira's (1993) claim that precise specifications of equity objectives were often disregarded, Whitehead (1994) saw such aims as inspiring the original design of the NHS. Moreover, the accent given to equity in governmental publications before the last election (see NHS Executive, 1995a; Department of Health, 1995a) shows it has continued as a seductive goal across the broad range of the political spectrum. In short, equity is closely related to concepts like justice and fairness (see Le Grand, 1991b; Donaldson and Gerard, 1993; Le Grand *et al.*, 1992), making an equitable service synonymous with a just or fair one.

This of course raises the question as to what a fair or just health service would actually look like. Wagstaff and Van Doorslaer (1993a) felt the essence of an equitable service was for payments to be progressive and primarily related to the ability to pay rather than the amount of care received, with access to services being available to those requiring them in quantities relative to their need. Similarly, others saw equity as implying things like the same treatment for those in equal need, with the extent of people's treatment correlating with their degree of need (for example, see Evandrou *et al.*, 1992; Harrison and Hunter, 1994). Such interpretations also encompass two other definitions of equity. Horizontal equity occurs when persons with a matching capacity to pay make identical contributions and those in equal need receive the same level of treatments. Vertical equity transpires if people in differing need obtain appropriately dissimilar treatments and those of unequal ability to pay make suitably disparate payments (see Appleby, 1992).

Yet in truth, the measurement of need and treatment is a complicated process (see Illsley and Le Grand, 1987) and the extent to which the NHS has matched the two concepts is uncertain (Le Grand, 1993). Still, the achievement of equity has traditionally been approached from a couple of angles. First, by trying to equalise the distribution of health care by social class. Second, by attempting to balance the geographical spread of resources through budgetary allocation and financial incentives to doctors (Le Grand *et al.*, 1990; Barr, 1993).

Equity by social class

Despite doubts as to whether it is the best tool for gauging inequality, differences in health across the population are commonly measured by comparing the mortality rates of different social classes (see Illsley and Le

Grand, 1987). That was the health indicator used when the high correlation between material deprivation and ill health was most famously identified in the *Black Report* (Black *et al.*, 1988), first published in 1980. This comprehensive review concluded that disparities in health between social classes at that point had not declined since the early 1950s. Regardless of any criticisms concerning the methodology used for the report, the broad argument that deprivation and poor health are linked has not been seriously challenged, and was reiterated more recently by Subner and Bruce (1993).

The perceived links between deprivation and poor health led to calls that health policies should be widened to include measures which counteract poverty (Townsend, 1987) and reduce inequalities in income and housing (Rutten, 1993). Such ideas also reinforce the claim of Culyer (1993a) that the health of individuals is unlikely to be determined just by the distribution of health care alone. However, Arblaster *et al.* (1996) made the point that some interventions can be made by health care agencies to lessen inequalities in health.

Also relevant to social class and the definition of vertical equity is the burden falling on different segments of the population for funding the NHS. Judgements that the UK tax system is only mildly progressive in terms of financing health care (for example, see O'Donnell *et al.*, 1993; Van Doorslaer and Wagstaff, 1993) comply with Wagstaff and Van Doorslaer's (1993b) claim that pro-rich inequity has almost certainly existed in Britain. Indeed, it seems that this tendency may be representative of the position in some developing countries as well, even where the state has shown a concern for promulgating equity (see Baker and van der Gaag, 1993). Moreover, an earlier study pronounced that the more affluent sections of society have better utilised the health care available through the NHS, even though it is the deprived classes who may be in most need of its services (see Le Grand, 1982).[2]

Equity by geographic spread

The second traditional approach in the attempts to achieve equity in health, the nature of the geographic spread of resources, can be linked to the claim of Maynard (1993a) that the equal distribution of health care resources does not ensure a reduction in health inequalities. This also mirrors the verdict of Culyer and Wagstaff (1992) that achieving greater equality of health in the community requires an unequal distribution of medical care. However, the precise arrangements required for the equitable location of health care

---

2.   This hypothesis was later challenged (see O'Donnell and Propper, 1991; Powell, 1995), both articles prompting replies (see Le Grand, 1991c; 1995).

suppliers has remained open to question, and Mohan (1987) argued that more effort was still needed to amend any geographical and spatial inequalities in the level of health care provision in different areas.

New and Le Grand (1996) saw the allocation of NHS resources on a geographical basis as addressed by the introduction in 1977 of a methodology known as RAWP (Resource Allocation Working Party). The fundamental aim was to identify the health care needs of the population in each of the geographic regions of the NHS (Powell, 1998). Decisions were then made annually as to how much actual allocations should be adjusted to move such areas towards their target share, as indicated by the RAWP formula (Department of Health, 1989a). These targets were based upon a calculation of what was required to provide the national average service to patients in each of the regions (West, 1988).

Although this venture moved regions closer to their RAWP targets, that success was qualified by criticisms that the system gave too much weight to planned service developments, like opening a new hospital, and historic patterns of service use that took little regard of efficiency. The Thatcher government felt this caused a weak relationship between the allocations to health districts and the number of patients in those areas (see Department of Health, 1989a), and thus abandoned RAWP in favour of setting health authority cash limits on a weighted capitation basis. This was founded on a 'needs' based formula using rather elaborate population statistics. Subsequent work has taken place to try and make it more robust (see Carr-Hill *et al.*, 1994; Smith *et al.*, 1994).

In sum, the conventional past interest in equity pertaining to the NHS has mainly tended to concentrate on social class and geography. But however meaningful these factors are the quasi-market reforms had significantly, if not completely, altered the nature of the equity debate. It was largely diverted towards another two issues, cream skimming and the two-tier service. And even though more than eight-years have now passed since the changes were implemented and a new system has since been introduced, it still seems fair to say that many of the questions raised in the literature about these subjects, particularly concerning the latter, have remained unanswered. Both topics will now be discussed.

Cream skimming

Anxieties were evoked that the system introduced in 1991 might have induced what is commonly known as 'cream skimming', the act of discriminating against expensive users of the service for financial gain (see Matsaganis and Glennerster, 1994a). Such conduct has also been called 'risk selection' (see Ham, 1996b) and 'adverse selection' (see Scheffler,

1989). The contention was largely based upon conjecture built on two linked grounds: that GPs participating in the fund-holding scheme might have blocked the entry of people on to their practice list who they either perceived as likely to be expensive, or removed those existing patients who actually were costly. Such suspicions have partly arisen due to experiences with health maintenance organisations in America (see Scheffler, 1989), from where much of the literature on this subject comes (for example, see Wilensky, 1988). They could also have gained validity from the suggestion of Crump *et al.* (1991) that random variation in patients' needs may have put individual fund-holding practices at financial risk.

Moreover, O'Reilly *et al.* (1998) found evidence that fund-holding practices in Northern Ireland removed patients from their lists at a higher rate than non fund-holders had. Yet they acknowledged that such decisions were infrequent, concluding that a fund-holding practice with a list size of 5,000 patients would, relative to non fund-holders, remove just one extra patient every five years. The inference from this might be that the trend could have reflected the additional workload and pressures arising from participation in the fund-holding scheme, rather than financial gain.

In line with that view, there is no firm evidence that 'cream skimming' happened in the NHS internal market (see Glennerster *et al.*, 1994a; Ham, 1996b; Le Grand *et al.*, 1998) due either to the financial mechanics of the fund-holding scheme, medical ethics, or a mix of both. Two examples may explain how the financial mechanics of the scheme nullified the prospect that fund-holders would 'cream skim'. Firstly, the scheme ended with them only paying the initial £6,000 of an individual patient's treatment in a single year (see NHS Executive, 1994a), with costs above this figure met by health authorities. This form of insurance should theoretically remove much of the incentive to turn away high cost patients. Secondly, fund-holders customarily had much of their hospital services budgets set on the basis of past activity levels. If the period used for recording this activity was typical, high cost practices should have got larger budgets that were adequate for the care needed by expensive patients.[3]

---

3. Matsaganis and Glennerster (1994a; 1994b) argued that this funding methodology might not have provided sufficient motivation for fund-holders to enhance hospital efficiency in the longer-term. They suggested a capitation formula, weighted for chronic health factors, would have given enough resources for expensive patients without undermining incentives to drive provider efficiency. Although framing a robust formula may be technically difficult (see Sheldon *et al.*, 1994; Majeed, 1998), a move towards widening the use of capitation funding has lately been given strong official policy emphasis (see NHS Executive, 1996a; 1997a). There are plans for such funding methodologies to be used for setting the budgets of all purchasers of public health care services in the future.

Yet concentrating on the monetary rationale that fund-holding might have given to such actions could have distracted attention away from a more likely reason why GPs, and not just those in the scheme, may have carried out risk selection. This was to avoid heavy workloads by rejecting high demand patients from their practice lists, like those who regularly request night visits or surgery appointments for marginal reasons. Moreover, such patients need not necessarily be expensive in the context of receiving services from community and hospital providers. Consequently if finance is not the only or even the strongest motivation to avoid certain patients, perhaps the fund-holding scheme was a 'red herring' for research into such behaviour by GPs. Hence studies into discrimination against patients, in so far as the analysis currently stands, may not yet be complete.

A two-tier health service

The other recent development over the equity debate concerns the possibility that a two-tier service evolved where patients of GP fund-holders received preferential services at NHS hospitals to those who were registered with practices remaining outside the scheme. While past disclosures about this were based on anecdotal evidence (see Dixon, 1994), they have been quite plentiful (for example, see Samuel, 1992; Dobson, 1993; Fisher, A. 1993; Fisher, P. 1993; Luxton, 1993; McAvoy, 1993; McCullough, 1993; Wright, 1993). Most commonly the controversy centred upon the speed of access to services and suspicions that the waiting times for hospital admissions of non fund-holding and fund-holding patients were inequitable can be seen as a root cause of the Labour Party's antagonism towards the scheme (see Bevan, 1998). It also explains why the new government ruled that NHS hospitals should admit patients solely on the basis of medical need from April 1998 (see Murray, 1997; NHS Executive, 1997b).

With regards to this issue, at the heart of the debate lie contrasting ideas about the effects of markets. Le Grand (1991a) wrote that a common criticism of conventional markets is based upon their potential to compromise social justice by fostering and maintaining inequalities, and intimated that suspicions could exist about quasi-markets having similar effects. Alternatively, Glennerster *et al.* (1994a) proposed that market systems tend to resist arbitrary behaviour, which complies with Barry's (1987) assertion that they have egalitarian repercussions because competition is a persistent equalising force.

As to whether a degree of inequity did exist between fund-holding and non fund-holding patients, arguments had been made which supported both angles of the debate. Such contradictory disclosures were even made in pieces published around the same time. For example, Ham (1996b) claimed that fund-holding did reduce the waiting times for hospital appointments of patients registered with general practices participating in the scheme. But another work published that same year took a different line. The Audit Commission (1996a, p. 21) suggested that waiting times for fund-holder and health authority patients, the latter being those of non fund-holding GPs, were 'usually similar overall, although their seasonal patterns may differ'.

In truth, there was a conspicuous lack of demonstrable evidence to corroborate either argument. This verdict is compatible with an earlier observation, cited previously, that allegations concerning the existence of a two-tier service were largely based upon anecdotal evidence (Dixon, 1994). It is this controversy, where judgements previously had closer ties with conjecture than certainty (Robinson, 1996), that provides a key theme for this study.

As such, this book concerns one aspect of the changes to the NHS introduced in 1991, the parity of hospital waits. However, it is necessary to fill in the broader rationale behind the reforms to place the more detailed study that follows into its proper context and illustrate why an investigation into waiting times is both relevant and important. For this reason, detailed below is a sketch of the background to and expectations of the quasi-market reforms.

HISTORICAL BACKGROUND

In the UK a period of almost continuous growth in state welfare following the second world war was halted in the mid-1970s (Le Grand, 1990) as the inflation fuelling oil crisis of that decade stimulated attempts to control public expenditure (Ham, 1992). For a decade or more the consequence of this for the NHS was a phase of 'belt-tightening' rather than particularly radical reform (Glennerster *et al.*, 1994a). Nevertheless, certain steps had been taken that can be seen as opening the way for the more significant changes which occurred later.

For example, the government experimented with ideas like the resource management initiative to try and influence clinicians to control costs (see Ham and Hunter, 1988; Packwood *et al.*, 1991). Attempts were also made through the introduction of general management to instil features of private sector management into the service (Allsop, 1995), which may have meant that some managers more committed to the traditional format of the NHS were less likely to be retained (Thompson, 1993). This complies with some commentators considering the move towards general management to be an important step in laying the foundations for the later quasi-market reforms (see Saltman and von Otter, 1992; Butler, 1993; 1994).

Yet the previously mentioned 'belt-tightening' may concur with the fact identified by Barr *et al.* (1988) that Britain was spending less on medical care as a proportion of gross domestic product than most other OECD (Organisation for Economic Co-operation and Development) countries. But despite this, they also made the point that it did not seem to cause a genuine crisis in public health. This was because nothing indicated that the health of the population was suffering because of the relatively low spending (they also claimed that there is no obvious relationship between a state's expenditure on medical care and the health of its population). Moreover, Britain continued to appear at least as healthy as most other developed countries. Indeed, with regard to the achievements of health service agencies, Loveridge (1992, p. 216) described the performance of NHS providers before the reforms were implemented as 'world class'.

Nevertheless, despite such commentaries the health service was not an arena in which the government escaped condemnation. A burden was generated as the decreased growth in NHS funding coincided with a continuing acceleration in the demand for its services. In part this reflected the additional services required by an ageing population, plus the rise in people's expectations of the health service as medical technology has advanced (Ham, 1992). During the mid-1980s this tension was magnified by a number of factors which attracted extensive media coverage and criticism of government health policy. These included such things as ward closures (Butler, 1994), scandals about the failure to treat particular patients (Maynard, 1993a), severe shortages in nursing staff (Ham *et al.*, 1990), plus a lack of medical equipment (Butler, 1992). Another commonly cited source of criticism was an increasing public discontent with the length of NHS waiting lists (for example, see Bartlett, 1991a; Butler, 1992; Glennerster and Matsaganis, 1994).

The initial response of the government was to announce in December 1987 an addition of around £100 million for the NHS to ease the problems. Yet this had little immediate effect in relieving pressure on the Conservative administration (Ham *et al.*, 1990). In short, they were embarrassed to be faced with a widespread perception that under their control the health service was in a state of financial crisis. Margaret Thatcher reacted to the predicament by announcing a formal review of the NHS (Klein, 1995). The decision was revealed during an interview on a BBC (British Broadcasting Corporation) current affairs television programme, *Panorama*, in January 1988 (Ham *et al.*, 1990; Maynard, 1993a), and allegedly came as a surprise to some of her ministerial colleagues in the cabinet (Maynard, 1993b). This course of events led to claims that the review was 'an explicitly political response to the intense concern that had arisen about the supposedly low level at which the NHS was funded' (Butler, 1993, p. 59).

The NHS review

The initial priority in the review was to find alternative ways to finance the health service (Ham *et al.*, 1990). However, ideas related to the financing question such as a social insurance scheme that would include the right for people with private insurance to opt out of the national scheme were, although considered, subsequently rejected. Despite the evidence that the Thatcher administrations were committed to a critique of state institutions (see Silverman, 1990), this was perhaps due to the government's realisation that the existing tax funded service with cash limits might be a rather better way of controlling overall expenditure (Butler, 1992; 1993; Klein, 1995). Financing issues thus gave way to a debate about methods for achieving a more efficient use of NHS resources (Butler, 1993; 1994; Hunter, 1993).

It is noteworthy that the timing of the review followed a visit to Britain by the American economist Alain Enthoven, who had written a paper suggesting the introduction of an internal market could have important benefits for the NHS (Enthoven, 1985). This work is seen as having much influence in driving the reform process (Wagstaff *et al.*, 1993), and the idea that hospitals should compete against each other for income in a quasi-market gained particular favour as the review developed (Ham, 1992). Following the review, the government outlined its plans for the health service in the White Paper entitled *Working for Patients* (Department of Health, 1989a). A separation of the purchaser and provider functions in the organisational structure of the service was the major proposal in this document.

Enthoven's (1985) proposition was to favour health authorities as having a purchasing role in an internal market. This was intended to address various criticisms he had made of the NHS which he saw as caught in a grip of forces that made change exceedingly difficult to bring about, a scenario he called a gridlock. Problems he identified included the difficulty in closing unwanted hospitals, the lack of incentives to run services more efficiently, and because resources did not follow patients, the consultants who treated more would not enjoy any extra reward or means to do the job. He saw an over-centralisation in pay settlements as making it harder to attract staff in some areas, and a shortage of local responsibility in paying for buildings which increased the chances that space would be wasted. He also perceived a lack of financial accountability in terms of knowing the costs of running services and in performance against budgets. Moreover, he felt patients were not considered as a central enough priority to be taken seriously.

Yet there was an alternative proposal as to who might undertake the purchasing function.   Maynard (1986) had argued GPs were sensible candidates for such a role, and put forward the thought that all GPs could purchase all services for their patients.   The notion that GPs should have a purchasing task was a late arrival as a serious option in the review discussions when Kenneth Clarke became the Secretary of State for Health, and he became the chief advocate for the initiative (Glennerster *et al.*, 1994a; Timmins, 1995).

As such, there were two competing ideas for purchasing the hospital and community health care services.   One has been called top-down funding through health authorities, the other bottom-up through GPs (Glennerster, 1997), and the government 'went for both at once' (Glennerster, 1992, p. 181).[4] However, restrictions on the range of services coming within the purchasing remit of GPs and minimum patient list size requirements for the practices volunteering to take on the role did make the scheme outlined in the White Paper less radical than Maynard's (1986) initial idea.

A cautious start

The quasi-market was formally launched in April 1991 following the passage through parliament of the NHS and Community Care Act 1990. Hence there was a relatively brief interval of not too much longer than a couple of years from the finish of the review at around the end of 1988 to the start date.   This was the case even though the service has not been considered by some as notably responsive to attempts to change it in the past (see Dennis, 1993a; Spurgeon, 1993a).   The speed of the implementation might thus be an example of March and Olsen's (1989) model whereby major structural change can be made to large organisations

---

4.   This dual-purchasing configuration can also be linked in some ways to the idea of Mullen (1990; 1993) that there are two main types of internal market. One is purchaser led, the other patient led. Mullen (1993) felt the NHS was in reality closer to the purchaser led model, though it had attributes of the patient led type as well. Nevertheless, patients were more likely to have greater influence on the purchasing decisions of fund-holders than health authorities (Glennerster *et al.*, 1998) and some referrals may even be made due to pressure applied on GPs by patients (Coulter, 1992a). When considering such points alongside Bryden's (1992) claim that fund-holders could have had greater freedom from the constraints on making extra contractual referrals that health authorities may have placed upon other GPs, it is plausible that fund-holding was somewhat more akin to a patient led system than health authority purchasing.

The 1991 Reforms: Questions, Background and Rationale 13

resistant to transformation through a process of radical shock (see Ferlie *et al.*, 1993; Tilley, 1993). It also complies with the suggestion of Williams (1990) that the medical establishment in the UK had resisted change for too long under the banners of ethics and clinical freedom, and the connotation that the more conservative elements of the profession needed to be shaken out of their complacency.

Nevertheless, the reform proposals had aroused intense debate and controversy on a number of fronts. An example that illustrates this was the row over the extent to which public providers acquiring trust status would sit outside the mainstream NHS, and whether this was a step on an agenda leading towards an enlarged private provision of health care (see Peck and Spurgeon, 1993a). By April 1991, and for the initial period after this date, such accusations were making the government play down the market element of the reforms (Baggott, 1994). This would appear to correlate with William Waldegrave replacing the rather more abrasive Kenneth Clarke as Secretary of State for Health in November 1990 (see Hunter, 1993).

With the government thus exhibiting an apparent desire to preserve its standing in the popularity stakes, or at least avoid its position becoming irreparably damaged, the quasi-market in its early days generated very little competition. The first year was even characterised by an approach that prohibited purchasers from making major changes to providers' established activity levels (Appleby *et al.*, 1993; 1994). This interval corresponds with what Ferlie *et al.* (1993) called a pseudo market, in which the changes are a symbolic reform bringing little substantive variation to the inherited pattern of relationships. In such a situation the reorganisation is primarily a re-labelling exercise. Such caution may have connections with Bartlett and Le Grand's (1993) point that the success of the reforms was more likely if uncertainties in the system were limited so as not to undermine long-term planning. March and Simon (1993), however, claimed that even conventional markets can often exhibit considerable stability and predictability.

Yet the formulation of this 'steady state', seen by Caines (1993) as the first cloud on the horizon for the idea of survival through performance, was probably driven by the impending 1992 general election. Its continuation was thus not a guaranteed feature for the longer-term, which relates to the way in which the Audit Commission (1993) thought the system should mature. Whilst agreeing that the immediate relationship between purchasers and providers at the start of the reforms should be collaborative, they felt that health authorities required the freedom to alter their purchasing patterns if they were to be fully effective. Moreover, once the election was over, and won by the Conservative Party despite the hostile political conflict over its health care strategy, market structures containing the capacity for fiercely competitive behaviour were still in place and signs began to appear that they would be used (Butler, 1993).

Nonetheless, this point is not supposed to exaggerate the free nature of the quasi-market introduced through the 1991 reforms. Although the fundamental principles of market theory are explained below in order to convey the key ideas that inspired the changes, the internal market was always regulated. And whilst Arvidsson (1995) claimed more information needed to be acquired about the topic of regulation, different types of quasi-market produce diverse regulatory regimes (Challis *et al.*, 1994). Ferlie *et al.* (1993) identified two types of regime as being likely in a managed health care market: control by government or self-regulation by professionals. It is likely that there were elements of both in the post-reform NHS, maybe the former in particular. It is thus probably appropriate to think of that system as a form of 'managed competition', a phrase used by Klein *et al.* (1996). Indeed, this term also seems to correspond with other commentators use of the term 'planned markets' (see Saltman and von Otter, 1995; Saltman, 1996).

PURPOSES OF THE REFORMS

In line with the change in the priorities of the NHS review (away from finding fresh means of funding the service), none of the traits of the quasi-market appeared to contradict a crucial feature of the established system. The state still retained control of financing the NHS. But regardless of this continuity, the notion that any reform to a public service must surely be undertaken because the government involved wants to accomplish something through the change has an obvious and extremely compelling logic. The organisational split between purchasers and providers was clearly meant to change the behaviour of these key agents in some way (Drummond, 1993). But that remark is not a precise observation. The introduction of a quasi-market into the NHS therefore raises the query as to what it was actually supposed to achieve. In addressing that question, this section will also examine what the former Conservative Government of the time may have found so attractive in the idea of public sector market systems.

The theoretical nature of markets

A market is a network where buyers (purchasers) and sellers (providers) interact to exchange payment for goods and services. Certain constraints will exist to the exchange relationship. For instance, this can include the effect of income and price in terms of the resources that are available to buyers for paying the price at which an item is being sold, and the access of purchasers to a market for the produce they might wish to buy. Prices can also be seen as a communicator of information (for example, see Steele, 1993), and in textbook economics prices play a central role in bringing supply and demand into balance. If supply exceeds demand the price would fall, and if demand exceeds supply the price should rise. Prices can therefore give signals to suppliers as to whether they should expand or contract supply (for example, see Williams, 1987) and indicate the measurement of value to purchasers plus the extent of costs to providers (see Maynard, 1987).

A market can be competitive if purchasers have a choice between alternative providers competing for their business. Perfect competition requires numerous purchasers and providers interacting in the market attempting to win orders or buy at the best possible price. Hence providers would have an incentive to increase efficiency in order to reduce the costs of production so that they can lower their prices and become the preferred supplier chosen by a purchaser. In reality price may not be the only consideration for purchasers and other factors could be the quality of the produce or service plus the speed of its delivery, though this should not be taken as an exhaustive list. The notion that greater efficiency comes from a multitude of sellers competing for the business of a large number of buyers equates with the principles of the neo-classical market (Ferlie *et al.*, 1993).

Although this is a very brief interpretation of the nature of markets, and possibly rather a one-dimensional view as well, it seems to highlight quite successfully the prevailing view of the Thatcher regime as to how markets were perceived to work and also the basic principles behind the NHS reforms. The crux of these was surely the proposition that competitive pressures induced by markets provide a spur to efficiency (Taylor-Gooby and Lawson, 1993; Flynn and Williams, 1997). A further temptation might conceivably have related to the potential for prices to communicate information, even though Culyer *et al.* (1990) had reservations about instinctively accepting prices as effective signals to health care purchasers. Hence the basis for the reforms appear rather different to Gray's (1992) ethical support for market systems as a way of enabling personal well being through individual autonomy.

Public choice, government failure and market failure

In many ways the reforms have their origins in public choice theory. This places the market in a central position to enable rational agents operating within it to supposedly advance prosperity for society in general (Self, 1993), whilst also adopting a theme that promotes small as responsive in the context of institutional design (Bobrow and Dryzek, 1987). Indeed, this latter point connects to Mintzberg's (1979) work on organisation theory. He argued that benefits from the decentralisation of hierarchical structures include a greater stimulus for motivation, quicker responsiveness to local conditions, and decisions made from a better understanding of local conditions. Moreover, Cox (1992) saw the changes as symbolic of the Conservative Government's distaste for the kind of communal action incorporated in the original design of the NHS, while Bloor and Maynard (1997) described the 1991 reforms as an ideological experiment.

In short, the reform proposals might have been indicative of an ideological commitment that monopolies should be broken up and systems deregulated to allow competition. Limits exist to the effectiveness of bureaucracy (Starkey and Hodges, 1993) and quasi-markets were pictured as the means to enhance the efficiency of the public sector (Gray and Jenkins, 1993; Taylor-Gooby and Lawson, 1993). The validity of this understanding of that government's doctrinal sympathies appears to be emphasised by their introduction of quasi-market reforms into other areas of the public sector. For example, Ball *et al.* (1994), Glatter and Woods (1994), Johnes and Cave (1994), plus Levacic (1994) have all discussed such policies in the field of education. Meanwhile, Knapp *et al.* (1994), Means *et al.* (1994), Taylor and Hoggett (1994), Mannion and Smith (1995), plus Means and Langan (1996) addressed the use of quasi-markets in community care.

The expectation that introducing a quasi-market would enhance efficiency in the NHS may well have been driven on a theoretical level by some of the problems identified by Le Grand (1991d) in his discussion of the theory of government failure. Namely, that government provision could be inefficient because public providers are usually, though not always, monopolies that are protected to a large extent against actual and even threatened competition from profit maximising organisations, as well as bankruptcy and take-over. This reduces the incentives to keep costs to a minimum and will induce what is known as X-inefficiency, the production of a commodity at more than the minimum possible cost. The pressures applied on public sector managers by their political masters to improve the efficiency of their organisations are routinely seen by market protagonists as less effective than market competition and contestability.

Furthermore, government failure suggests the state cannot gather all the information it requires to manage the economy effectively, and that there are too many limits to a government's ability to set objectives centrally (Thompson, 1990). Such a perspective also figured in the arguments of

Osborne and Gaebler (1992). They put forward their case for extending the use of markets and entrepreneurial spirit in the public sector by arguing that hierarchical and centralised bureaucracies designed in a past era do not function well in modern societies. This sentiment also conforms with the view of Leibenstein (1987) that the nature of hierarchies can be a source of inefficiency. Paton (1992) referred to the market or hierarchy debate as representing competitive efficiency versus the planned meeting of needs, although Pitelis (1991) proposed that aspects of market relationships are themselves hierarchical and so the choice is really between market hierarchies and non-market hierarchies.

Yet if markets can motivate organisations to at least make an attempt to produce a commodity at the minimum possible cost, a circumstance known as X-efficiency, this and allocative inefficiency[5] are not mutually exclusive concepts (see Le Grand, 1991d). They can coexist alongside each other. For instance, the UK public health system may in the pre-reform period have delivered a better outcome in terms of life expectancy and other health indicators such as infant mortality at a lower cost than the US private system. Even if the US system was more X-efficient through the effect of markets, and that has yet to be firmly established, it could still be highly inefficient in an allocative sense. This is because health care may not be distributed in a way that coincides with the needs for services of different sections of the population (see Le Grand, 1991d).

Spurgeon (1993b) pursued the tension between markets and allocative efficiency by claiming that it is only in conditions of virtually perfect competition where the market will be efficient in an allocative sense. Barr (1993) also argued that unrestricted markets are highly inefficient, though the NHS quasi-market was not actually an unrestricted market (see Dennis, 1993b). That competitive markets can result in an allocation of a commodity that is socially inefficient is the principal rationale for the theory of market failure, and is paradoxical to the theory of government failure that prompted the NHS reforms. Along with the pursuit of greater social equality (see Le Grand, 1982), the prospect of market failure is likely to have been one of the most important historical arguments for state intervention (Cowen, 1988). Indeed, Eckel and Steinberg (1993) saw market failure as a factor behind the existence of many non-profit organisations.

---

5. Outside the concept known as X-efficiency, Glennerster (1992) discussed two other types of efficiency. Allocative efficiency is to distribute resources in such a way that produces the closest possible match between what can be produced and what consumers want. Productive efficiency is associated with goods and services being produced in the most efficient manner.

Yet aside from any dispute over the merits or drawbacks of government intervention and markets, the belief of the Thatcher regime in the virtues of markets (see Appleby *et al.*, 1994; Dixon, 1998) made their views accord more with the theory of government failure. Moreover, the introduction of a quasi-market into the NHS probably embodied a dual belief (or hope). Whilst conventional markets can fail on the basis of allocative efficiency and public monopolies might not facilitate X-efficiency, quasi-markets could achieve both. Equal access may be preserved by keeping services financed by the state while also introducing an element of competition (see Glennerster, 1998).

Choice, responsiveness and efficiency

A basic principle of the quasi-market was that money should follow the patient (Ebrahim, 1993). Hence the former Conservative Government doubtless anticipated that a system where NHS service providers competed with each other, and with those from the private sector, for revenue from purchasers would have the potential to overcome many of the perceived defects of the bureaucratic model of the welfare state. This observation is upheld by a remark made in official governmental literature. It was stated that providers would 'produce a better quality service and encourage other hospitals to do even better in order to compete' (Department of Health, 1989b, p. 3). The importance attached to improving 'quality' in the service was emphasised by Gregory and Walsh (1993) as well.

It has also commonly been asserted that the new system was expected to give providers incentives to expand efficiency, choice and responsiveness (Bartlett and Le Grand, 1993; Propper *et al.*, 1994; Le Grand, 1994a; Bartlett, 1995; NHS Executive, 1995a). Such propositions appear to comply closely with the passage in *Working for Patients* that reads:

> NHS Hospital Trusts will earn revenue from the services they provide. They will therefore have an incentive to attract patients, so they will make sure that the service they offer is what their patients want. And in turn they will stimulate other NHS hospitals to respond to what people want locally. (Department of Health, 1989a, p. 4)

The theory was that in order to sustain long-term viability, providers would need to respond to and satisfy the demands of well informed purchasers who act in the interests of their client population (see Harrison and Nutley, 1993; Haycox, 1993; Kind *et al.*, 1993). This should enhance the efficiency of the system. The question is what type of efficiency was the dominant aim? It has been alleged that the Conservative Governments since 1979 gave priority to controlling public expenditure by granting a higher status to economic objectives than social policy goals (see Allsop, 1989; 1995; Hart, 1994), and Brazier *et al.* (1990) defined cost-effectiveness as an aim of the reforms. Therefore, X-efficiency could well have been an intended objective of the quasi-market, at least to some extent.

Yet if the government had been seeking to reduce public expenditure by introducing a quasi-market they would have been disappointed by the outcomes (Glennerster and Le Grand, 1995). This does not necessarily contradict the possibility that more productivity could be obtained from the resources than might otherwise have been the case. But to change from a hierarchical to a market system may often raise the administrative costs of the structure (see Williamson, 1975; 1986; Bevan *et al.*, 1989). For instance the expense of separate purchasers and providers negotiating contracts with each other, known as *ex ante* costs, plus what are called the *ex post* costs of monitoring the outcomes of the exchange, are likely to increase the transaction costs of the system.

Further, it is often accepted that this did happen in the NHS quasi-market (for example, see Bartlett and Harrison, 1993; Cook, 1993; Wall, 1993; Robinson and Le Grand, 1995), even if some health service staff may disagree with such a conclusion (see Walsh, 1995). Even so, there need not necessarily be just a negative side to any such increase. For instance, a prime justification for transaction costs is the attainment of information (Holstrom and Tirole, 1989). If raised transaction costs has made the NHS more rich in information, in theory this could easily have had positive spin-offs for patient care (Glennerster *et al.*, 1994a).

From this, although it is hard to imagine the former government could have been totally oblivious to the prospect that the quasi-market might be administratively expensive, they still went ahead with their plans. Consequently, in view of the apparent willingness to tolerate or at least risk the danger of higher transaction costs, it does not appear either sensible or adequate to accept an extension of X-efficiency as the sole or even major objective of the reforms.

Doubts must thus exist over the extent to which the Thatcher administration was concerned with X-efficiency when trying to raise efficiency, choice and responsiveness. Any hope that some level of cost reduction would be achieved through competition may well have been just one goal that initially existed alongside other perhaps even more important priorities. It therefore seems a broader definition of efficiency should be adopted to identify the goals that drove the government's plans for the NHS, beyond a simplistic reduction in public expenditure.

Hospital efficiency: shorter waits via competition

Sources have already been cited which proposed that an area where there was a great deal of political and consumer concern about the performance of the NHS was hospital waiting lists. While levels of demand (the patients coming forward with an illness and being referred by GPs to hospital) will affect the equilibrium between waiting times and waiting lists, it seems logical to assume that the length of waiting lists would normally correlate directly with the length of the waiting times. This point was strongly emphasised by Yates (1987). He asserted that there is a clear and indisputable association between the length of waiting lists and the waiting times for surgical procedures. Long waiting times will lead to long waiting lists, while shorter waiting times will mean there are shorter waiting lists.

Moreover, waiting times may also have a large impact on the day to day experiences of many consumers of health services, the patients. Long waits for operations could mean they suffer some sort of inconvenience like, for example, pain, continuing illness, or time off work. In assessing the impact of the reforms on patients, waiting times thus look a legitimate comparator for measuring the relative merits of GPs and health authorities as commissioners.

From this, it seems reasonable to suggest that one aspect of the efficiency goals of the 1991 reforms was to lower waiting times and encourage higher patient throughput at hospitals by making them responsive to purchasers. This idea also falls into place with the concept of choice, as a competitive market may give opportunities to customers to express their interests in ways not often available in a monopolistic public service (Glennerster, 1992). By discussing of the concepts of exit, voice and loyalty, Hirschman (1970) explained why this might be so. Purchasers should have more potential to influence a provider through discussion or negotiation if they hold an opportunity to move their custom elsewhere. To extend the responsiveness of suppliers, the influence of voice is increased when the option of exit is available to the buyer, and the option of exit derives from a choice between alternative providers.

A further bridge between the efficiency goals of the reforms and a reduction in waiting times was provided by an observation of Frankel (1993). He argued that while health care rationing had been orchestrated by making patients wait for elective surgery, this was consistent with the NHS selecting for relative neglect those conditions where treatments are unequivocally effective and markedly desired by the population. This interpretation is linked to the reforms by the claim of radical economists that the extension of market forces is the only way to forge a strong link between that demanded and that produced (see Loveridge and Schofield,

1993). Moreover, this falls into place with the view of Spurgeon (1993b) that the quasi-market was expected to enable purchasers to target specific categories of patients on waiting lists.

As such, the publicity given to the waiting list problem for elective surgery by the media, making it a political crisis for the government, looks a significant factor in provoking the most radical restructuring of the NHS to date. Hence a better control over waiting times can be implied as a serious aim of the reforms, with the changes 'intended to redirect activity towards those areas which may better reflect health needs, as these are perceived by the population' (Frankel, 1993, pp. 1-2). To an extent the reorganisation may thus have had its origins in a fairly limited part of the service, elective surgery. This view is supported by the continuing weight attached to the reduction of waiting times by the last government, as shown by the production of guidelines for health service professionals, managers and clinicians, on how to meet this aim (see NHS Executive, 1996b).

On balance, it seems that the extension of hospital efficiency through making them more responsive to the choices open to purchasers must lie very near the heart of the reforms. The demand side factor where patients were placed on the waiting list was linked to the supply side factor where patients were removed from the list on the receipt of their operations. It seems rational to accept that the period between these events, the time on the waiting list, was likely to have been driven by how promptly purchasers made hospitals admit patients. From this, the increased throughput of patients at hospitals, as implied by shorter waiting times, is thus the form of productive efficiency used here as the basic measure of the effectiveness of the alternative purchasers within the internal market. To apply, or perhaps adapt, Glennerster's (1992) definition of productive efficiency (cited earlier), shorter waits are taken as indicative of hospital services being produced in a more efficient manner.

CONCLUSION

This book has relevance to policy. The early indications after the 1997 general election were that the new Labour Government looked to be assessing its options regarding the structural format of the NHS, which appeared to involve exploring different models for the commissioning of services (see Fletcher, 1997; NHS Executive, 1997c). Attitudes which can fittingly be recounted as resembling open hostility to fund-holding in the early years of the scheme (see Labour Party, 1993) had been reported as softening a little over time (Barrowcliffe, 1996).

Reports in the GP press even stated there were no immediate plans to abolish fund-holding in the first two years of the new government's term of office (Brown, 1997). That impression seemed to be upheld by the tone of governmental publications (see NHS Executive, 1997b), and complied with the view of Gosden *et al.* (1997) that not enough was known about fund-holding to make a firm decision about its future. Yet such a life expectancy was unlikely to be seen as adequate by Bosanquet (1996), who felt the weightiest gains from the scheme could have taken at least ten years to accrue.

But the new Labour Government's White Paper on the future of the NHS (Department of Health, 1997), whilst described as marking evolutionary rather than revolutionary change (Dixon and Mays, 1997), clearly signalled the direction in which the service would move. The internal market and fund-holding has now been formally abolished even though the former system's central characteristic, a separation between the commissioning and provision of services, has remained. New primary care groups have incorporated all GPs since April 1999, and these groups will eventually take over the commissioning function of health authorities. While this may reflect Coulter's (1995a) view that other models of GP involvement in purchasing might have been as effective as fund-holding, it could also be that primary care groups might be more of an extension to the fund-holding scheme than its replacement.

Yet even with the plans for both health authority and single practice purchasing to become a feature of the past, the intricacies of the reform proposals could mean there is still room in the foreseeable future for many uncertainties to develop. For example, there are to be four different levels of primary care groups. The first level actually resembles health authority commissioning during the internal market, with some GPs just having more chances to give them advice. At the other extreme, the third and fourth levels at which primary care groups will formally become primary care trusts, GPs should have much independence from the health authority to make their own purchasing decisions.[6] Although the White Paper states that such groups will be expected to move towards the higher levels, it is difficult to estimate how long such a process might take, especially if a health authority is obstructive to groups wishing to do this.

As such, the true nature of the development of primary care groups may well be in some doubt, making it necessary to use lessons from the fund-holding era to assess whether primary care groups will be more effectively run by GPs or health authorities. Moreover, Ham (1997b)

---

6.   Though the labels 'primary care group' and 'primary care trust' will sometimes appear together in the text of this book, they are used without distinction.

stated that any one purchasing configuration is unlikely to be appropriate in all circumstances. This brings a continuing need to evaluate the commissioning process and although Maynard (1996) suggested there is often a lag between research and the use of what it discovers, this book advances the attainment of evidence concerning the purchasing function. While focusing upon one type of outcome, the speed of access to elective surgery, it indicates which of the internal market's two main commissioners achieved more or less than the other for that particular service.

This leads directly on to a second and connected theme in the discussion of waiting times, which is equity. If it were clear at the outset which of the two main purchasing options, health authorities or GPs, was to be the better commissioner, there would be little case for experiment. However, if one purchaser achieved shorter waits for their population than the other, was this fair? If waiting times were not equal, was this because practices within the fund-holding scheme were over funded, or might they simply have been better purchasers of elective surgery than health authorities? This book will address these queries.

In doing this, the book breaks new ground in the existing literature. For instance, the Audit Commission (1996a) claimed some studies of fund-holding (namely, Glennerster *et al.*, 1994a; National Audit Office, 1994)[7] have tended to consider the achievements or not of the scheme on the basis of fund-holders' own views. Nevertheless, it still became the most studied aspect of the 1991 reforms (Dixon and Glennerster, 1995). Yet the same cannot be said about health authorities, despite the fact that they were the internal market's largest purchasers. Little work has been performed, let alone completed, that evaluates their effectiveness as commissioners. Both of these points, an alleged over-reliance on fund-holders' opinions of themselves and the relative neglect of health authorities by the research community, has made it difficult to get firm evidence about the comparative effectiveness of each purchaser type.

There is also a further endorsement for that suggestion. The lop-sided nature of the research whereby health authorities were relatively neglected may have removed the use of tangible control comparators from some studies of fund-holding. This could arguably have led to any results of the scheme being compared against what might either be an unrealistic image of perfection, or an overoptimistic vision of what should have been accomplished. For example, *What the Doctor Ordered* (Audit

---

7. Readers intending to search for these two works from details provided by the Audit Commission (1996a) should guard against being misled by their referencing. Glennerster was misspelled 'Glennester' whenever this author was cited in the paper, and the National Audit Office document was mistakenly dated 1995, rather than 1994.

Commission, 1996a) was probably greeted by many critics of fund-holding as a faultfinding piece of research into the scheme. Yet a framework used in this study for testing success was whether practices were 'turning the world upside down' (Audit Commission, 1996a, p. 89). As this seems such a very formidable yardstick can the conclusion reached, that not enough were doing this, really be too much of a surprise?

In line with that reservation, might it not have been more useful to look at whether fund-holders were bringing greater benefits and doing better than health authorities, or vice versa? Perhaps a chief weakness of the Audit Commission's (1996a) study was that it left the impression fund-holders were generally underachieving, but quite simply the judgement may not be either fair or balanced. Against such a challenging standard as turning the world upside down how many health authorities had managed to fulfil this target? After all, whilst the project had not dealt with the proficiency of such bodies as commissioners, an off-the-cuff remark was made that 'in some areas, the new health authorities will have their work cut out to establish their own credibility as purchasers *vis-a-vis* the GPs' (Audit Commission, 1996a, p. 98).

As such, measuring the success or otherwise of fund-holders against some image of what would be 'nice' if they achieved it, whilst ignoring the performance of health authorities in the same field of care, says little about the relative strengths and weaknesses of the internal market's predominant purchaser types. Idealistic expectations might not always be the best mechanism for comparing the effectiveness of separate agencies. Hence it is feasible that whilst fund-holding may not have been perfect, it could have been an improvement on the alternatives, with the reverse also being plausible. But with little comparative work having been performed the style of the research to date fails to show which of these possibilities was true, an inference implied by Ham and Shapiro (1995). Overcoming that deficiency in the existing literature is an important objective of this book.

Plan of the book

Having discussed in this chapter the background plus goals of the reforms and identified the questions to be addressed, the remainder of the book is arranged as follows. The primary objective of the second chapter is to discuss the reasons why the waiting times of fund-holding and non fund-holding patients might have differed. These are the hypotheses that were investigated during this study. The third chapter will explain the format of the NHS in the area where the research was conducted, and clarify the methodologies used for the investigation. The fourth chapter provides a comparison of the waiting times of fund-holding and other patients for the elective surgery covered by the fund-holding scheme. This is therefore a central part of the book that demonstrates whether there were differences in the waits of these groups, and goes on to consider if any contrasts can be attributed to fund-holding practices participating in the scheme.

The next three chapters all address the hypotheses that might explain contrasts in waiting times. The fifth chapter considers whether fund-holding practices were systematically over funded in the area where the research took place and the sixth compares the surgical case mix of fund-holding and non fund-holding practices. The seventh chapter deals with the impact of contracts on waiting times, the effect of the information and incentives applicable to each purchaser, the relationships between providers and different commissioners, and the impact of purchasers moving work away from hospitals. Finally, the eighth chapter addresses the policy implications of the study in the context of the present government's intentions. This discussion will cover the concepts of purchasing leverage, hospital behaviour, equity and efficiency.

2 The Quasi-market and Waiting Times: The Hypotheses

The format of the NHS internal market has been described elsewhere in varying detail by numerous authors (for example, see Culyer, 1993b; Paton, 1994), and was briefly outlined near the beginning of the previous chapter. The first purpose of this chapter is to cover the structure of the quasi-market and explain the main characteristics of the key actors within its constitution. This leads to a discussion of the factors that potentially could offer realistic explanations why the waiting times of fund-holding and other patients may have differed. In essence, that part of the chapter identifies the hypotheses that were investigated during the course of this study.

PROVIDERS

During the lifetime of the internal market, some publicly financed health services were actually supplied to patients by private providers. This happened when either a GP fund-holder or health authority commissioned care for NHS patients from non-public hospitals or a wide range of independent private contractors that can include, for example, mental health counsellors and physiotherapists. This option was used more frequently by fund-holders than health authorities (Bartlett, 1995; Paton, 1996), albeit probably to quite a limited extent as it is likely that NHS patients would always have mostly received their care through public institutions.

Prior to achieving trust status, public providers came under the organisational umbrella of what is often called their responsible or host health authority. They were the agencies known as 'directly managed units', a term referring to the hierarchical command that health authorities held over them. So that these providers could be both organisationally distinct and managerially independent from the direct control of the health authorities that were likely to be their main customers, they were given an opportunity to attain 'trust' status. This meant gaining formal autonomy from the health authority by breaking away from it, although there is some debate about how far the severance was actually achieved and what the nature of the split should be.

For instance, Graham (1993) stressed the need for trusts to build on the pre-existing continuity of their relationships with health authorities in order to avoid instability, while Hargadon (1993) argued that for the quasi-market to be allowed to work, trusts which fail should not be bailed out.[8] Either way, directly managed units were encouraged to acquire trust status. Moreover, in line with Hill's (1993, p. 138) comment a few years ago that the growth in their number was becoming a 'stampede', Hamblin (1998) confirmed that it took six years from the start of the quasi-market for all NHS providers to become trusts.

Types of NHS trusts

Although what follows represents a guide rather than a definitive list and it might well be possible to find exceptions, there are four main sorts of trust. One is the type providing ambulance services. The commissioning of ambulance services, which generally relates to the response to emergency call-outs and the time it takes to get such patients to hospital, did not fall within the standard fund-holding scheme. It was thus commonplace in the quasi-market system for ambulance services to be purchased for patients by health authorities. The exceptions to this rule occurred when a 'total purchasing project' took on the task. These were either a single or more usually a group of general practices that acted as a sub-committee of their health authority to commission services outside the standard fund-holding scheme (see NHS Executive, 1996c).

Another form of trust is the hospitals providing a range of acute services. Many have accident and emergency departments, admissions to which can be made via concerned GPs, acquaintances of patients, or by self-referrals. Such services were excluded from the standard fund-holding scheme and, again with the exception of any total purchasing projects, were purchased by health authorities. Hospitals also perform diagnostic services like pathology and x-rays, as well as other procedures for patients referred by GPs such as physiotherapy plus outpatient and maternity services, with the latter also having been outside the fund-holding scheme. Outpatient investigations can lead to a wide range of other treatments at the same or different provider, embracing such things as oncology services and elective surgery, the latter being operations performed on patients who have been

---

8.   On the basis of interviews with health authority staff, Glennerster *et al.* (1994a) implied that such organisations had in some areas (outside London) bailed out public providers for long periods. The contractual deals between these bodies had initially represented a concern to stabilise the market and protect NHS hospitals.

called in from a waiting list. This covers clinically urgent cases as they are also placed on a waiting list, usually just for a shorter period of time than are routine status patients.

An alternative kind of trust are those which provide a range of what are called community services, rather than the kind of acute episodes summarised above. Such trusts usually employ the district nurses and health visitors attached to GP surgeries, whose services were purchased by fund-holders, as well as having responsibility for supplying more specialised nursing care in the community. Generally they also provide treatments required by people with learning disabilities, plus a range of outpatient and inpatient mental health services, the latter involving sites used for institutional care which were not covered by standard fund-holding. Such trusts may also supply some other services, chiropody for example, in a community setting like a health clinic rather than an acute hospital. Indeed, some could even rent a site in an acute hospital for this sort of activity.

The final type of trust includes those where the task of supplying acute and community services has not been divided between separate bodies, but one organisation provides them both. When acute and community providers were severed from the direct control of health authorities to become trusts, the decision as to whether they would split into distinct or combined organisations was based upon local circumstances. For example, the acute and community provider arm of a health authority could have been ready to acquire trust status in different years, and if each took the earliest opportunity to do this they will obviously have been separated.

Did competition between providers exist?

If a major objective behind the 1991 reforms was an improvement in the efficiency of providers, the performance of trusts, which Peck and Spurgeon (1993b) saw as tending to lead the quasi-market, was surely one of the crucial bench-marks against which the success of the changes should be measured. Smee (1995) felt their establishment offered two distinct advantages over the hierarchical command and control system: that of operational independence for health care providers and market type incentives. The ways in which trusts responded to the demands of competition are thus most relevant to the success or otherwise of the quasi-market experiment. However, concerning this point, certain conditions may have to be met. Purchasers would need a degree of choice between different service providers (Culyer and Posnett, 1990; Bartlett and Le Grand, 1993), and be willing and able to exploit the alternatives (see Glennerster *et al.*, 1994a).

Regarding the question of whether commissioners really had enough choice between alternative providers, the balance of opinion in the literature seems to give a degree of weight to the premise that they did. Despite the early doubts of some observers that enough genuine options existed to make the system adequately competitive (see Bartlett and Harrison, 1993; Freudenstein, 1993), a number of other commentators came to a rather different conclusion (see Appleby *et al.*, 1994; Bartlett and Le Grand, 1994a; Glennerster *et al.*, 1994a). The view that effective competition may exist, at least to an extent at the margins, seems backed in part by the evidence of Mahon *et al.* (1994) that some people are willing to travel to hospitals other than their local one, especially to where there are shorter waiting times. Nevertheless, this tendency was by no means reported as being uniform amongst all patients.

As such, perhaps the quasi-market should not be seen as ultra-competitive? After all, the substantial size of most trusts makes the provider side of the system quite concentrated (Challis *et al.*, 1994), and competition would be increased by a higher number of smaller hospitals (Bartlett and Le Grand, 1994b; Le Grand, 1994b). The sheer size of NHS providers could thus give the system a monopolistic character, leading to speculation that part of its competitiveness may be reliant on hospitals being motivated to increase their efficiency to ward off the threat of new units entering the market. Yet in reality the high set-up costs for new providers appear very problematic in making the internal market contestable in this way (see Robinson and Le Grand, 1995; Ferlie *et al.*, 1993). In view of this, the competitiveness of the system might be more dependent on both the capacity and the willingness of commissioners to move some patients between providers. It is therefore necessary to consider the characteristics of the purchasers.

PURCHASERS

To some extent the range of purchasers operating within the internal market altered over time (Mulligan, 1998a). For example, various forms of commissioning groups evolved around the country in which GPs were meant to acquire greater input into and links with the purchasing policies of local health authorities (for example, see Black *et al.*, 1994; Graffy and Williams, 1994; Balogh, 1996; Ham, 1997c; Mays and Mulligan, 1998). The genuine progress made by these sorts of group is not absolutely clear, although Glennerster *et al.* (1998) concluded that those achieving the greatest success were the ones most closely resembling fund-holding.

Another kind of commissioning agency were the aforementioned GP total purchasers who were delegated a budget to buy a wider range of services than those covered by the standard fund-holding scheme. In reality, there were often some treatments not taken on board by these groups, so arrangements may have fallen short of genuinely making them 'total' purchasers (Mays *et al.*, 1997). But despite such developments, health authorities and fund-holders dominated the history of purchasing in the NHS quasi-market. This dual-purchasing configuration meant that the commissioning of health care services on behalf of patients was undertaken by agencies with very different attributes, characteristics and even incentives. The major features of health authorities and GPs as purchasers are discussed below.

Health authorities

Since the 1991 reforms there has been a noticeable process of amalgamation between health authorities (Robinson, 1994). At first this occurred through some district health authorities combining, but the trend continued when district health authorities and family health services authorities were merged in April 1996 following the Health Authorities Act 1995 (Paton, 1996). These events halved the number of health authorities in England and Wales to about 100 (Willis, 1996). Although family health services authorities did not have a true commissioning role, the general amalgamation process has tended to concentrate health authority purchasing power into a decreasing number of such organisations.

This trend could well have signalled an attempt to curtail the chances for providers to manipulate small purchasers (see Paton, 1992), although the potential for reducing administrative costs by combining smaller districts was possibly an even greater motive behind the changes. As more providers became trusts, the loss of direct managerial control by districts over the hospitals they were coincidental with had probably removed the need for so many smaller scale health authorities.

A primary function of health authorities was to assess, interpret and analyse the health care needs of its resident population (Williams *et al.*, 1993) and set contracts with providers to satisfy those needs to the maximum possible extent that was consistent with its cash limit (Tennison, 1992). It was anticipated that this process, by which health authorities should successfully secure measurable improvements in the health of their resident populations, could become more sophisticated over time (Akehurst and Ferguson, 1993). The role of health authorities as the internal market's main commissioner was evident by the range of their responsibilities. In short, they purchased all hospital and community services for patients of non fund-holding GPs, plus those services not covered by the fund-holding scheme at any point in time for patients registered with GP fund-holders.

Research on the performance of health authorities as commissioners has been quite sparse (Mulligan, 1998b), although Opit (1993) did claim that their job was made more difficult because they could have had their purchasing strategies subverted by fund-holders.[9] This idea may connect with the claim of Challis *et al.* (1994) that purchasing power was diluted by the growth in the number of practices joining the fund-holding scheme (even though health authorities have always remained the major commissioner in the internal market). Beyond this, Mulligan (1998b) reviewed the evidence that existed on health authority purchasing, and that survey suggests the true impact of such organisations remains unclear. For example (although there are others), the contribution of health authorities in driving an increase in NHS activity since 1991 is unknown, as was their impact on switching expenditure between providers. On balance, the research on health authority commissioning looks inadequate.

Moreover, the structure of the purchasing configuration in the internal market appears to reflect two competing theories. First, the perceived efficacy of health authorities is coincidental with a need for the power of large providers (NHS trusts) to be countered by substantially sized commissioners. The second focuses on the strength of small purchasers that might be less inhibited and more flexible because of their limited size. It is this notion that provides a rationale for the fund-holding scheme, which is discussed in the following section.

Fund-holders

During the initial period of the quasi-market fund-holders purchased a limited range of acute hospital services, although they also had budgets for practice staff and prescribing drugs. But in 1993 their purchasing remit was extended when a range of community based services were also brought into the scheme (see Glennerster *et al.*, 1994a). In fact prior to the new government postponing the eighth wave of the scheme, practices with a list size of only 3,000 patients could take on the purchasing function for the

---

9. Opit (1993) endorsed this claim by using an OPCS (Office of Population Censuses and Surveys) publication from 1989, a couple of years prior to the start of the 1991 reforms, to allege that many health authorities had restricted funding termination of pregnancies. The point was also made that where this had happened fund-holding practices 'in the same district can decide to finance all or none' of these abortions in their own client population (Opit, 1993, p. 84). However, termination of pregnancy operations were not even covered by the standard fund-holding scheme until April 1996 (see NHS Executive, 1995b), some three years after Opit's (1993) paper was published.

community services, including district nursing and health visiting, plus diagnostic tests (see NHS Executive, 1994b). Beyond this, over the years the scope of the acute services covered by fund-holding grew. For elective surgery, the standard scheme was extended significantly in April 1996 (see NHS Executive, 1995b). From that date it was generally the major or very costly procedures, including such things as organ transplants and brain surgery, which were still excluded (see NHS Executive, 1995c).

Participation in the fund-holding scheme was always voluntary (Audit Commission, 1996a). For practices wishing to enter it on an individual basis there were list size requirements that had been relaxed over the years. The original proposal in *Working for Patients* (Department of Health, 1989a) had been for practices to have at least 11,000 patients, although this was reduced to 9,000 by the time fund-holding actually started. The minimum in England eventually fell to 5,000 (Audit Commission, 1996a) for the standard scheme, although smaller practices could group together to satisfy this condition. Some fund-holding practices pooled a proportion of their managerial resources to become what were known as multi-funds, though wide variations in the take-up of this option in different areas were reported (see Audit Commission, 1996a).

A number of objectives were identified for the fund-holding scheme. One was to give GPs the opportunity to enhance the quality of services on offer to patients, another to improve the balance of care between the primary, community plus hospital settings and reduce duplication between these sectors (National Audit Office, 1994). Other goals were to stimulate providers to be more responsive to GPs and patients by improving the quality of the services they offer (Department of Health, 1989c). Fund-holding was also seen as a way of increasing the sensitivity of purchasing to local needs (Willis, 1993), promoting value for money, and improving consumer choice (Dixon and Glennerster, 1995). Lerner and Claxton (1994) described such targets as ambitious.

In enabling purchasing decisions to be taken at a level nearer the patient, a rationale for fund-holding seemed to be an expectation that by enabling consumer preferences to inform and determine priorities in secondary care services, efficiency should be advanced. This accords with reports of some fund-holders extending the services provided at their own surgeries, thus altering the site of service provision (see Dixon and Glennerster, 1995). This trend was often represented by the development of 'outreach clinics' (Bailey *et al.*, 1994; Lapsley *et al.*, 1997), when outpatient clinics were held at practice premises. Yet any benefits from this restricting the 'did not attend' syndrome by extending convenience for patients might also have been balanced by some disadvantages. Harris (1994) argued that outreach clinics could involve consultants too much in direct services to patients rather than training and professional development. Moreover, Coulter (1996) proposed that there was little evidence to support a shift of care to general practice anyway.

Various authors have seen GPs as having a gate-keeping role in which, through their referrals, they filter patients into the more specialist sector of health care provision (for example, see Coulter, 1992b; 1998; Oswald, 1992; Fleming, 1992; Harvey, 1993; Dixon *et al.*, 1998). They therefore possess at least a theoretical ability to determine the adequacy of the provision of expensive hospital services. This links to the economy objectives of the scheme as it may thus have been a recognition of the importance of this gate-keeping function of general practice, and was conceivably an attempt to make GPs more responsible for their own control of it (Bryden, 1992). Davis (1993), however, saw the attempts to do this as contradicting the opportunities for user-choice.

Alongside the intention to make GPs more responsible for their referral habits, the same pressure was placed on prescribing (Hoey, 1995). By having a budget for drugs, against which savings could be retained by practices, an incentive was placed in the system to control prescribing costs. However, Petchey (1995) was sceptical over the efficiency of fund-holders in prescribing, and there were suggestions that mechanisms other than fund-holding could have been used to restrain drug expenditure (see Paris *et al.*, 1994). Nevertheless, there is evidence that the scheme curtailed the growth in drug costs in two ways, despite the contrary claims of Keeley (1994; 1997a). This was by increasing the rate of generic prescribing and cutting the average cost per item (Bradlow and Coulter, 1993; Maxwell *et al.*, 1993; Dowell *et al.*, 1995; Harris and Scrivener, 1996).

Suggestions were made that the early containment of prescribing costs by fund-holders was not sustained (for example, see Stewart-Brown *et al.*, 1995). That finding coincides with a study in Northern Ireland where disincentives in the budget setting system, with savings being deducted from the following year's allocation for drugs, made the curbing of costs a temporary trend (Rafferty *et al.*, 1997). This would appear to complement the judgement of Goodwin (1994) who, although not referring specifically to drugs, stressed the importance of incentives within the internal market.

On reflection, Dixon and Glennerster (1995) have already admirably reviewed much of the research into the fund-holding scheme, and there seems little point in rewriting that article here. However, what is most important for the purposes of this research was that they noted the absence of any evidence from systematic study (at that point) to demonstrate whether or not a two-tier service was actually occurring. Not surprisingly, therefore, so is proof concerning the relative influence of factors that may possibly have made it happen. These issues are addressed in the following sections.

DEBATES AND HYPOTHESES: AN OVERVIEW

At a general level this book examines two contesting theories about commissioning in a public sector quasi-market: the financial power of large purchasers against the potential flexibility of smaller commissioners. Waiting times are a good test for the strength of each theory. There are various reasons why waits might differ, which can be categorised into two general groupings. Contrasts could be caused by one commissioner being a more effective purchaser than is the other. At a more detailed level, factors that can contribute to purchasing effectiveness cover contractual matters, incentives, information, relationships, and market flexibility. Yet even if differences in waits were established, they might not be related to purchasing effectiveness. Perhaps the surgical case mix of each population was radically different (although this could be caused by purchasers' decisions, it might also result from chance or demography), or financial resources were not distributed fairly between the commissioners.

These possibilities will all be discussed. In effect, each of the sections that follow relates to the hypotheses that were investigated for this study. The first main hypothesis, and the sub-hypotheses that comprise it, deals with the generosity of fund-holders' budgets.

WERE FUND-HOLDERS BUDGETED OVER GENEROUSLY?

Numerous reports exist about the benefits of fund-holding (for example, see Bain, 1992; 1994; Coulter, 1992c; Glennerster *et al.*, 1992; Leese and Drummond, 1993; Newton *et al.*, 1993; Wisely, 1993; Glennerster *et al.*, 1994a; Smee, 1995). Yet claims had been made that achievements were tempered by unfair advantages given to practices in the scheme. For example, Dixon (1994, p. 775) remarked that positive accounts of fund-holders' successes were marred by accusations of overgenerous funding, and health authorities used their alleged under funding as a 'convenient smokescreen to hide local inefficiencies'. In brief, critics of the scheme suggested that a systematic over funding of the practices in it laid at the root of benefits enjoyed by their patients, including alleged shorter waiting times. Because fund-holders' budgets were subtracted from health authorities' cash limits, this would have consequences for non fund-holding patients:

Overgenerous funding of fundholders means fewer resources available for the patients of non-fundholders, the consequences of which are likely to be most acute in areas with high numbers of fundholders...elective surgery is the area where inequities are most apparent. (Dixon, 1994, p. 772)

However, popular usage of this hypothesis does not guarantee its accuracy, and the comment of Robinson *et al.* (1993) that there was little empirical evidence to support such views still holds true. Indeed, in a more recent piece Dixon and Glennerster (1995) made the point that while mounting anecdotal evidence suggested a two-tier service may have developed, this could have been for a number of possible reasons. Although one of these was the over funding of practices in the scheme, the true impact of this is unknown. This is not a major surprise considering the relative scantiness of research in this field.

Frostick and Wallace (1993) did address this issue and suggested that alleged variations between the treatment levels of fund-holding and other patients implied GPs in the scheme had received an overgenerous level of funding. However, any such variations could be caused by a number of other factors, including differences in referral rates or contrasts in the genuine health care needs of each population. Alternatively, Opit (1993) claimed a simple test of the fairness of fund-holders' budgets could have been made by assuming every practice was in the scheme, grossing up the allotment for the services they purchased and seeing what remained of the health authority allocation. Without giving any indication of where or if this had been performed, the approach was taken as indicating that fund-holders' budgets were excessive. This non-evidence based assertion was supposedly validated by citing an anonymous report in an edition of *The Health Service Journal* (24 October 1991), published just a few months into the scheme's first year, about the under spends of some practices in it.

Dixon *et al.* (1994) performed a more evidence-based study in the North West Thames region, and claimed that fund-holding patients were budgeted more generously than non fund-holders were. They reached this judgement by estimating the totals spent on specific hospital treatments by health authorities in 1993/94 and the amounts allocated to fund-holding practices for the same services. There were, however, problems with this study. Bowie and Spurgeon (1994) expressed reservations about it because some important inferences were only based upon rudimentary data, with one set of assumptions used for non fund-holders and another for fund-holders.

A different line was taken by Glennerster *et al.* (1994b) who maintained there was more to suggest that first wave fund-holders were generally under rather than over funded. This was carried forward by Glennerster *et al.* (1994a) claiming that there was little to support accusations that fund-holders were consistently budgeted over generously. National average costs showed fund-holders on an aggregate basis were getting 15 per cent less in their budgets than would have been expected, with a more detailed study in the Oxford region indicating a 9 per cent shortfall for such practices. This view received earlier support from Brogan (1993), yet it contrasted with another study that suggested fund-holders were over funded by about 15 per cent (see Glennerster *et al.*, 1994a).

Similar to contrary assertions concerning waiting time differences, the literature thus incorporates opposing viewpoints regarding the budgetary position of fund-holding practices. This could imply that budget setting for fund-holders was something of a lottery, with both gainers and losers at practice level. Substantial variations in the size of budgets received by fund-holders to purchase hospital services (see Day and Klein, 1991) may support this view.

Consequently, in any waiting time comparison it is crucial to test the fairness of the level of resources apportioned to fund-holders in the relevant area. If their patients did benefit from shorter waits than non fund-holders, was this because they received inequitable budgets? The investigation into the funding hypothesis therefore represents an important element of this study, and the possible ways in which inequitable funding may have come about is discussed next.

Different funding methodologies: an overview

Dixon (1994) argued that financial inequity between health authorities and GP fund-holders had been made inevitable because of the different methodologies used to fund them. Whilst the cash limits of health authorities were set on a weighted capitation basis (see NHS Executive, 1994c), fund-holders traditionally received most of the hospital services element of their budgets according to past activity levels (see NHS Management Executive, 1991). Practices' allocations had routinely been set according to the value of their activity in part of their final year outside the scheme. This was not the original intention of the government (Glennerster *et al.*, 1994a), but the delay in framing a robust method of formula funding for general practices led to the immediate plans for setting fund-holding budgets through a capitation methodology being abandoned.

With the different methodologies used to fund health authorities and practices, there were various factors that could feasibly result in inconsistencies between their budgets, and each will be discussed in some detail. But it is worth mentioning one area in which this problem should not arise. Mohan (1995) claimed fund-holders with substantial numbers of patients with private health care insurance might have been over funded because such patients were less likely to be a call on the practices' budgets for NHS services. Yet practices with a 'well-off' list of patients might have made less use of public services in the period used for measuring their historic NHS activity. So they would not receive funds for the private services received by their patients. It also seems unlikely that practices would be able to persuade such patients to use the NHS in a relevant year. People have private insurance in part to buy shorter waits (Calnan *et al.*, 1993), and such patients of non fund-holding GPs may have been unwilling to endure longer waits for the sake of the practices' future budget.

The effect of provider price changes

Perhaps a more likely reason why different funding methodologies could have resulted in inequitable budgets was the possible existence of a policy stipulating that the resources of fund-holding practices should be increased in line with their local NHS provider's price changes. The suspicion was that this could have given incentives to providers to hike the prices they charged for services to fund-holding patients beyond the percentage increase the health authority received to its cash limit for inflation. If they did and the budgets of such practices were raised by an equivalent percentage, because the value of fund-holders' budgets had been subtracted from their health authority's cash limit, the funds retained by the health authority for its own purchasing function would have been reduced. For services covered by the fund-holding scheme, this would have disadvantaged non fund-holding patients.[10]

Dixon *et al.* (1994) investigated this issue and found no evidence that fund-holders were consistently charged higher prices than health authorities in the North West Thames region. Their limited analysis indicated that eight out of twelve hospitals actually charged fund-holders lower average prices than the health authorities. Therefore, if such practices were over funded (and it was reported earlier that they had claimed this was the case), it seems providers charging them higher prices than the health authority was not the reason. But this fails to guarantee that the same thing happened

---

10. The prospect that the prices charged to one purchaser would affect the amount left over for the other might undermine Dawson's (1994) view that both NHS policy makers and academics overestimated the importance of open information on prices. When markets are characterised by contestability, she felt that open information on prices (which tend to be unique and secret to each purchaser) is not a requirement for a dynamic and competitive system.

in other areas. The prices charged to different purchasers thus deserve consideration in this study.

Recording activity

A further concern over the historic data budget setting methodology is an aspect that was at the very heart of the system, the recording of the activity of practices preparing for fund-holding status. Dixon (1994) raised the prospect that when surgeries and hospitals each monitored the activity of practices over a period of their last year outside the scheme, the two sets of data were often difficult to match. It was claimed that the level of activity recorded by practices was consistently higher than providers' records. Reasons given for this were that the discharge information produced by hospitals might be poor, episodes of care could mistakenly be recorded more than once, and treatments outside the fund-holding scheme, including emergency services, may have been counted towards the budget. The argument was reinforced by an accusation that if a practice recorded more activity, it secured a higher budget and as more entered the scheme, non fund-holders' resources would 'be squeezed further' (Dixon, 1994, p. 775).

Such arguments reflect a widespread belief among critics of the fund-holding experiment. To genuinely be the case, however, a number of conditions have to hold. First, the records of practices would have to be an overestimate of their true activity pertinent to the fund-holding scheme. Yet this might not be as likely an occurrence as implied by Dixon (1994). It was in the interests of health authorities to check and challenge the data, and the accuracy of the capture of information improved rapidly since the internal market began. And where a hospital's discharge information was poor, this could result in practices being under funded. For instance, notification that an episode of care had taken place may not be sent to the GP surgery and because practices mostly rely on hospitals for the specifics of their patients' treatments, they would have no formal record of the activity. Hence relevant activity that should have been recorded towards the budgets of practices could easily be missed, rather than counted twice.

Second, the errors in distinguishing between fund-holding and non fund-holding episodes (such as taking emergency as elective cases) would have to be skewed in one direction. Yet elective treatments might just as easily have been confused as emergency admissions and thus not counted when they should have been? But either way, the point made earlier about the rapid improvements in the accuracy of NHS data is important. It is important not to exaggerate the likelihood of errors in the data collection process. Third, Dixon's (1994) argument appears dependent on the records of practices, not providers, always being accepted in the final analysis as the true count used for the calculation of budgets. But in any district where the records of hospitals were finally used when there were discrepancies between the two sources of data, the point seems to lose its relevance.

From this, while the arguments of Dixon (1994) may well be useful in highlighting potential problems with the data collection exercise, some of the assumptions on which they were based appear rather one-sided. It seems quite feasible that the true activity of future fund-holders in the relevant period had as much chance of being understated as overstated. Considering this, the inaccurate recording of data might have a rather limited scope for making a material difference to the size of their budgets. Both sides of this argument, and the consequences, were summarised by the Audit Commission (1996a):

> If through errors in budget setting fundholders were given a larger proportion of a district's healthcare allocation than is justified on past patterns of referral, then less would be left to spend on the healthcare of non-fundholders' patients...But the opposite would be the case should fundholders' budgets be underestimated. (Audit Commission, 1996a, p. 106)

However, outside the accuracy of the data collection, there are other concerns over the historic data budget setting methodology. This relates to the standard period in which the historic activity of future fund-holding practices was used for budget calculation purposes (the first six months of their last year outside the scheme). For this might not be a fair indicator of each practice's normal level of activity pertinent to the scheme. Such suspicions are aroused due to two potential scenarios. One is that significantly more activity could have occurred in the first six months than in the second. If so, this would mean that new fund-holders could receive a greater share of health authority resources than might actually be fair. This prospect is discussed next. The other worry over the data collection period concerns the possibility that prospective fund-holders may try to inflate their patients' usage of NHS services (this will be discussed later).

Non fund-holding work: the six-month balance

Of the two possible grounds why the data collection period could be untypical of the normal activity of practices preparing for fund-holding status, one would not be their fault, or would have no links to the conscious actions of the GPs concerned. The other could indicate almost deceitful behaviour by the practices. It is the first that is dealt with in this section. It relates to a point made by Glennerster *et al.* (1994a) in order to explain why health authorities may have tended to run out of money more quickly than fund-holders, rather than automatically putting it down to such practices being over funded:

> Hospitals had an incentive to get through as much work for their district as their capacity permitted them to do as fast as they could. When they finished their contracted total of procedures they would then hope to persuade the district to give them some more money to continue to treat patients. (Glennerster *et al.*, 1994a, p. 173)

The inference was that by contrast, fund-holders running out of money early were not likely to attract the same publicity and political pressure to find additional resources for the provider, but were more prone to give the impression locally that the practice could not manage its affairs properly. This point can be taken further by hypothesising that in such circumstances the health authority would probably not have had the funds in reserve to afford precisely the same level of activity at the hospital as occurred in the early part of the year. Rather, it would perhaps have maintained a steady admission of patients, albeit at a slower rate than the one at which the provider started the year for non fund-holders.

The idea that more non fund-holding activity might have taken place earlier rather than later in the year may be reinforced for another reason. It seems feasible that even if a district did not find extra funds for a provider later in the year, there might still have been advantages for hospitals in meeting its health authority contract prematurely. This could have enabled the provider to cover most of its fixed operating costs early, so relieving managers and clinicians of later pressure while offering an opportunity to maximise income by fast-tracking fund-holding work free from any demands to meet the health authority's targets. Such manoeuvring may also uphold the assertions of the Audit Commission (1996a) about the existence of seasonal variations in the waits of fund-holding and other patients, even though it was not stated which group had longer or shorter waits in what period of the year.

If the scenario that providers tried to meet their main obligations under the health authority contract as quickly as possible is correct, the following proposition can be made. With new fund-holders ordinarily having their budgets calculated in line with the value of their activity in the first six months of their last year outside the scheme, they will be funded on the basis of the half year in which most of their activity took place. Whether this happens because providers attempt to get more money from health authorities or so that they can then concentrate on maximising their income from fund-holders is immaterial, the outcome will be the same. If so, a compelling argument can be made that on joining the scheme, new fund-holders' budgets would have been overgenerous. Further, if that first year budget is carried forward in an ongoing process as the baseline or nucleus of practices' allocations in future years, allegations that the resources left over for the care of non fund-holding patients would have been unfairly diminished begin to look quite persuasive.

Practices inflating activity

There are suspicions that practices in their last year outside the scheme may have accelerated the usage of hospital services during that period to surreptitiously increase their budget (see Keeley, 1994). This idea was also promoted by Bartlett (1995, p. 18) who wrote that such practices 'boost their rates of patient referral in the year prior to becoming fund-holders'. Yet this is far from being a straightforward matter, which is shown by the apparent complexity of the rate of GP referrals as a topic of study.

For example, although Riis (1982) claimed the intricacy of medical practice can be exaggerated, various factors affect the decisions made by clinicians (Gambrill, 1990) and their referral patterns (Wilkin and Roland, 1993). That may conform to the lack of a consensus on what a desirable rate of referral may be (see Coulter, 1992d; Russell and Grimshaw, 1992). This seems reflected by reports of wide variations in the referral rates of different GPs (see Coulter *et al.*, 1990; Haines and Armstrong, 1992; Jones, 1992; Wilkin, 1992), the reasons for which remain obscure (Roland, 1992a). Nevertheless, the contrasts are not adequately explained by conventional measures of need (Sanders *et al.*, 1989; Wilkin and Smith, 1987). Indeed, there is not even a known relationship between high and low referral rates and quality of care (Roland *et al.*, 1990; Roland, 1992b; 1992c) although in gross terms, large fluctuations in the numbers of referrals have not generally been observed (Farrow and Jewell, 1993).

At first glance, the subject therefore looks something of a 'minefield', and could perhaps offer some camouflage from audit to any GPs who hiked referrals to try and increase their budget offer. Yet new fund-holders were customarily budgeted according to the actual treatments and episodes of care given to their patients, not the number of referrals they make and raising referral rates is, on its own, unlikely to have had a parallel effect on activity levels. Hence if a practice referred twice the number of patients as usual, this would not necessarily have doubled their activity. For instance, extra referrals by GPs in a preparatory year could well clog hospital services up by increasing demand without a corresponding expansion in the capacity of providers. This could result in extended waiting lists for all patients using a hospital. That may slow any growth in the treatments given to those from practices in their final year outside the fund-holding scheme to a level much less than the increase in such GPs' referral rates.

Moreover, most referrals are made for outpatient appointments, though episodes of care like pathology, physiotherapy, and x-rays can also be provided as a direct consequence of an action by a GP. Yet elective surgery, by far the most expensive service that was covered by the standard fund-holding scheme, is not supplied until a hospital doctor has seen and investigated the patient through an outpatient clinic and decided surgery is justified. As such, GPs cannot just send people off for an operation to increase their activity in the data collection period. A patient actually has to need one in the opinion of a hospital clinician.

Nonetheless, if GPs preparing for fund-holding status were going to try and increase activity, as elective surgery was so much more expensive than the other services in the fund-holding scheme, this may well be the area they would have concentrated on to make a material difference to their budget. There could be borderline, clinically non-urgent cases where a GP can choose whether, and at what point in time, to refer or not. In such circumstances it seems reasonable to presume GPs might have a degree of choice over the timing of a referral for a patient who may need an operation. They may have an opportunity to decide whether to do this immediately or to wait and see how a condition develops so as to ascertain if it improves without surgery. A tangible chance to inflate surgical activity could thus exist.

But for services that are received by patients as a direct consequence of referral by a GP, which therefore look the most direct way in which a practice can manipulate its activity levels, there are difficulties in doing the same. For example, these episodes of care are amongst the least expensive that were covered by the standard fund-holding scheme. Also, for services like pathology, physiotherapy and x-rays, in some areas the budgets of fund-holders were not even set on the basis of the past activity levels of individual practices (see Glennerster *et al.*, 1994a). If a simple capitation system had been utilised instead, the financial advantages for individual future fund-holding practices in, for example, requesting many more blood tests, was significantly diluted as the costs of their additional activity is spread out among many practices.

In addition, rational behaviour need not just be concerned with maximising budget size. For example, increasing activity for pathology means GPs would need to explain to more patients why they were having their blood, or whatever else, tested. Such a burdensome task may have undermined any financial temptation for doing this, particularly if practices had to pay overtime to practice nurses for working extra sessions to accommodate a large increase in the samples taken. Similarly, raising outpatient activity would mean GPs dictating more referral letters, which not only becomes a repetitive and time consuming job for them but may incur additional costs within the surgery if typists had to work more hours. Such events may reduce practice profits and avoiding that could have been far more important to GPs than increasing their fund-holding budget.

In view of this, the finding of Coulter and Bradlow (1993) that fund-holders had not altered their referral patterns since joining the scheme might not be too surprising, which strengthens the idea that practices preparing for fund-holding status may not have acted surreptitiously. Also, if practices had artificially increased their referrals in the year prior to attaining fund-holding status, they might be expected to have lowered them again after joining the scheme in order to create savings. Coulter and Bradlow (1993) found no evidence of this happening in the Oxford region. Yet work in the same area detected a growth in the referral rates of some control practices outside the scheme who were preparing for fund-holding status, though the rise continued after they had joined the scheme (see Surender *et al.*, 1995). Nevertheless, Howie *et al.* (1994) suggested referral rates did drop after entry into the scheme, but this was accompanied by an increased use of direct access services.

From this, the question of whether fund-holders accelerated activity prior to their entry into the scheme seems to warrant a revisit for at least two concrete reasons. One is the apparent contradiction between the work of Coulter and Bradlow (1993), Howie *et al.* (1994), and Surender *et al.* (1995). The other is the fact that most of the studies were conducted in the earlier days of the quasi-market.

Further, it seems likely that if practices were trying to expand their surgical activity to enhance their budget, there are uncertain time gaps that occur between the GP sending a referral letter and the admission of patients for an operation. This suggests their activity would increase over the whole of the year in question. For even if GPs were skilful enough to increase referrals in such a way that the number of patients joining the surgical waiting list was increased, it is most unlikely that the rise in activity would conveniently be concentrated into one half-year window. Common sense suggests many such patients would be admitted during the second half of a year. It just does not ring true that GPs could manage to condense any such rise in their patients' surgery into a single six month period, as the sense of timing required would be nothing short of miraculous.

The distribution of movements in funding

Another factor that could feasibly have caused an imbalance in funding between fund-holders and health authorities was the distribution of additional monies coming to the NHS in a district, or indeed the division of reduced allocations. Most obviously this relates to the funds that health authorities received for inflation, though the move from setting their cash limits through the RAWP methodology to a weighted capitation system also resulted in changes to the cash limits of some districts. For example, if a health authority was shown by the capitation formula to be under funded through RAWP, it probably received growth to its cash limit to move it closer to the capitation allocation. Alternatively, if a district's allocation under the RAWP system exceeded the amount that was implied as appropriate under capitation, it could have lost funds from its cash limit.

If this latter possibility had been the case and a health authority lost funds in this way, it would seem unfair if longer-term fund-holding practices were able to keep their existing budgets in full. For these allocations would have been set at a time when there was more funding for the NHS in the district. Alternatively, if a health authority gained money through the move from RAWP to capitation, it would seem inequitable if fund-holders received an excessive (or insufficient) proportion of the extra funding, pro rata to the sum acquired by the district. The same point can be made about an increase for inflation. In principle, whatever amount was received by a health authority, the total passed on to fund-holders should have correlated fairly with the district's addition.

Summary

There are a number of factors that might conceivably have resulted in an imbalance in funding between GP fund-holders and health authorities. However, there is no guarantee that any of them ensured fund-holders were budgeted over generously. In short, the important point that needs to be made here is that there is no clear evidence about fund-holders either being over or under funded. Though Dixon *et al.* (1994) made a valuable bid to investigate this issue on a scientific basis, they were faced with inherent difficulties due to the limited data available to them. There is consequently a need to examine the funding issue and the matters just discussed will be addressed later (see the fifth chapter).

CASE MIX

It has been claimed that differences in the waiting times of fund-holding and other patients might result from what is probably a more obscure (but no less tangible) factor than inequitable funding or purchasing effectiveness: differences in the surgical case mix of each population (see Black, 1998). Case mix has been defined by the National Case Mix Office of the NHS Executive as 'the mix of cases, types of patients and types of treatments' (see NHS Executive, 1997d, p. 1). In terms of surgery, the case mix is thus the assortment of operations performed on patients.

For the hypothesis to be valid that fund-holding patients' shorter waits resulted from case mix variations there would have to be very different average waiting times for particular types of operations. To give a simple and fictitious example, perhaps the average wait for cataract surgery at a hospital was far longer than for joint replacements. If this was the case, the validity of the hypothesis rests on the notion that proportionately more non fund-holding patients required cataract surgery than those of fund-holding GPs, whilst the incidence of joint replacements was far more common amongst fund-holders.

In reality, it is likely that this type of split between the operations given to each group of patients would have to be repeated amongst more than one sort of procedure to make a material difference to average waiting times. As such, there would have to be significant contrasts in the case mix of each population. The activity of fund-holding patients would generally be skewed towards those operations with shorter waits, with the reverse being the case for non fund-holders, and the effect of this on average waits would need to be significant. To investigate this hypothesis, comparisons will therefore need to be made of the case mix of surgical procedures received by fund-holding and non fund-holding patients, taking into account the waiting times for specific groups of operations. The case mix hypothesis was tested on this basis and a full discussion concerning the nature of the investigation, plus the results of it, are reported in the sixth chapter.

THE EFFECT OF CONTRACTS

The review of the potential reasons why waiting time contrasts might occur have so far centred on factors outside the theories concerning the relative effectiveness of GP fund-holders and health authorities as purchasers – inequitable funding and differences in case mix. Concerning the latter, however, the reasons why case mix contrasts may be down to demography, chance, or purchasers' decisions will be discussed in the sixth chapter. Yet it is also necessary to consider how contrasts in waits could be explained by the ways in which commissioners performed the purchasing role. It is from this point that the discussion focuses more heavily on hypotheses dealing with the relative merits of each commissioner in controlling waits, rather than unfair advantages or even accidental outcomes.

The contracting process was one of the key characteristics of the internal market. The intention had been for purchasers and providers to be linked by contracts rather than management hierarchy (Robinson and Le

Grand, 1995). Although Checkland (1997) claimed that the rhetoric of contracting had turned out to be stronger than the reality, it seems fair to suggest that on balance the true impact of the contracting process on many aspects of NHS services remains uncertain. For this reason the effect of contracts on the respective waiting times of patients registered with practices inside and outside the fund-holding scheme requires investigation.

Three types of agreements were used in the quasi-market: block contracts, cost-per-case contracts, plus cost and volume contracts (Figueras *et al.*, 1993; Paton, 1996). Health authorities had sometimes used straightforward non-attributable block arrangements that could install rather obscure links between activity and payments, to simplify the management of their large deals with local NHS trusts (Paton *et al.*, 1998). The purchaser agreed to pay the provider a pre-set annual fee, normally in twelve monthly instalments, for its services. A benefit may be that they were administratively simple to run, although this advantage might be balanced by a danger that the links between the income and activity of providers could have been weakened (Ellwood, 1993). Fund-holders, and indeed some health authorities, using block contracts commonly utilised a more sophisticated form of this arrangement (NHS Executive Trent, 1995).

Fund-holders often applied 'floors and ceilings' to their block contracts for many services (although less so for pathology and community nursing). The way these worked was that the twelve monthly payments were taken as the baseline value of the activity that would ideally be performed. Say the actual level performed fell between 98 per cent and 102 per cent of this figure, no rebates or additional payments may have been due from either side. If the value of the actual activity increased beyond the 102 per cent figure, the purchaser could be liable for extra payments to the provider, usually at marginal rates (meaning the extra activity is paid for at less than the full price of the treatments). There might have been a ceiling, say the 105 per cent figure, and any activity beyond that level was free to the purchaser. Otherwise, the provider may have been liable to reimburse any shortfall in the activity performed below the 98 per cent total to the commissioner. This type of arrangement should have motivated the provider to perform about the right level of activity.

Cost-per-case contracts were used more by GP fund-holders than health authorities (Glennerster *et al.*, 1994a; Robinson and Le Grand, 1995; Spurgeon *et al.*, 1997) and involved a payment for each relevant episode of treatment given to individual patients at a price that should have reflected the complexity of the procedure. Whilst probably the most information-rich of the agreements, they were also likely to be the most expensive to implement and use (Bartlett, 1991b). This suggests transaction costs for providers that contracted with a large number of fund-holders may have been high (Le Grand and Bartlett, 1993).

Cost and volume contracts were in effect a combination of the other two and whilst having different titles, conceptually they were very similar to block agreements with floors and ceilings. A pre-set annual fee was agreed for a certain quantity of activity, with additional cost-per-case payments made to a defined limit if it was exceeded by an agreed extent, or indeed reimbursed if less than the pre-set level of work was performed.

Glennerster *et al.* (1994a) developed a theory of contracting that linked cost-per-case contracts with flexibility for the purchaser. The prediction was that health authorities would run block contracts with local NHS providers, whilst fund-holders would have been more willing to use, and tolerate the costs, of cost-per-case arrangements in order to force change from hospitals. However, in doing this it is not just the practices that would have had to endure higher administrative costs. The transaction costs sustained by the hospitals were also likely to increase (Bartlett, 1991b).

This theory also links to the notion that GPs would have had greater capacity to move work away from hospitals as the flexibility offered by their choice of contracts made them less tied to a single provider. This in turn connects to the idea that they would have been able to exact shorter waiting times for their patients than health authorities could have done for people registered with non fund-holding practices. Beyond this, the question can also be raised as to whether fund-holders had specified shorter waiting times in their arrangements with providers than the health authority did, or perhaps practices with cost-per-case contracts had been able to warn hospitals by threatening to refer patients elsewhere.

In sum, for differences in waits to be driven by contracts, one of two conditions was required. Either fund-holders stipulated shorter waiting time targets in contracts which were met by hospitals. Or different sorts of contract could have provoked dissimilar responses from providers. Hospitals might have admitted patients of fund-holders utilising cost-per-case agreements more promptly than those called in under a health authority block contract. If so, patients admitted under cost and volume contracts may have shorter waits than those called in through block contracts, but longer waits than patients treated on a cost-per-case basis. This reasoning can be taken a stage further. If the form of contract did drive contrasts in waits, it would surely be expected that patients registered with GP fund-holders using block agreements would endure longer waits than their counterparts from other such practices admitted under cost-per-case arrangements. These queries will be addressed in the seventh chapter.

EXIT THEORY

A related explanation for waiting time differences has more to do with the power and willingness of commissioners to move patients than the precise form or content of the contracts between purchasers and providers. It relates intimately to the work of Hirschman (1970), cited in the first chapter. The basic set of premises behind this hypothesis is as follows. Fund-holders had the budgets to pay for the care received by their patients, or at least for those services covered by the scheme, and could refer them to specific providers. They had the option to move work and thus income away from a hospital. Hence they may no longer have been so reliant on a single provider that previously could have held a virtual monopoly over the provision of various services to their patients.

At first glance this hypothesis has links with the one concerning contract types. Both deal with fund-holders having had the flexibility to move work away from providers. But there is a subtle and important difference. The contract hypothesis relies on hospitals reacting differently to contract types by admitting patients covered by cost-per-case agreements more promptly than those under block contracts. Yet exit theory focuses on providers responding in dissimilar ways to the purchaser type, not the form of contract. As such, the idea rests on the principle that fund-holders using block agreements could have exerted as much leverage over hospitals as those utilising cost-per-case contracts by being able to reduce the scale of their commitment. In theory, practices that used block contracts should have exacted the same benefits for patients as those using cost-per-case contracts because providers will wish to safeguard income under 'floors and ceilings', and also their prospective earnings in future years.

From this, whatever type of contract practices use, in an environment where resources are scarce the exit option may have pressurised hospitals to do everything they could to safeguard their workload, and consequently income, by satisfying the demands of all fund-holder customers. Yet this proposition on its own does not explain the hypothesis fully. Whilst it complies with the inference of Frostick and Wallace (1993, p. 241) that many hospitals were forced to favour fund-holding patients because their GPs held a 'small but significant percentage of the funds', why should this group have been the main or only beneficiaries? After all, health authorities controlled a larger and more significant proportion of the resources used to commission services. Providers may therefore have been even more reliant on health authority business than on fund-holding work. For services covered by the fund-holding scheme, should this not have worked to the advantage of non fund-holding patients and if not, why not?

Monopsony versus a multitude of purchasers

The answer to this question may well lie in the gap that exists between the purchaser and patient in health authority commissioning. Every UK resident has a right to be registered with a GP and it seems highly probable that the huge majority will be. As such, for every service commissioned by a health authority, which constitutes the entire range of care obtainable through the NHS, GPs come between it and the population it represents. In the case of the elective surgery covered by the fund-holding scheme, these were the non fund-holding practices.

This may well complicate the purchasing function for health authorities. By quoting a comment made by a hospital finance director, Glennerster *et al.* (1994a) publicised the view that it is GPs, not health authorities, who send patients to providers. It is therefore GPs who drive the business of hospitals, not health authorities. The latter are perhaps relegated to the role of having to second-guess the demand of practices and their patients for various aspects of care by imposing their own arbitrary limits to a range of services. Consequently, health authority commissioning must surely be further removed from the eventual consumers of the service, the patients, than GP purchasing. Moreover, if this makes it difficult for populations to be genuinely absorbed into the decision making of health authorities beyond a symbolic level of involvement, the assertion of Stewart and Walsh (1992) that the internal market was not really patient-led looks to have a convincing logic.

The remoteness of health authorities from their client population also countered Schofield and Hatcher's (1993) desire to see local communities controlling and planning health care services to meet their own needs. For citizens were tied to the strategies of their local health authority as it is hard to imagine any would leave the area where they live simply to have their services purchased by an alternative health authority. This led Glennerster *et al.* (1998) to call them monopoly purchasers, giving the system a monopsonistic character. Of course, the quasi-market was not a pure monopsony. The existence of GP fund-holders in any health authority area meant that there was more than one purchaser. However, each part of the dual-purchasing configuration represented a tendency towards two competing systems: the principles of monopsony against a less concentrated order where a number of fund-holders, closer to patients, functioned.

The closeness of GPs to patients, alongside their referral role, meant they had much greater control than health authorities over when, if, and to whom a patient was sent for more specialised care at a hospital. This was an advantage that looks hard to transfer to health authorities, regardless of the range of contracts they might hold with providers. If health authorities are to hold some sway on activity levels themselves, they may have to persuade or coerce GPs to abide by set guidelines. These could be unpopular and incite uncooperative behaviour by some GPs, while others might have chosen to become fund-holders. Indeed, preserving referral freedom was reported by the Audit Commission (1996a) as the third most prevalent motive for practices to join the scheme.

Consequently, health authorities may well be restricted in the degree to which they can influence the GPs of the patients they purchase for, and enticing them to alter their referral patterns could be very difficult indeed. They might thus have had only a negligible opportunity, dependent on delicate negotiations, to persuade non fund-holding GPs of the virtue in changing their referral habits in order to find shorter waiting times, better quality services for patients, or cheaper prices. Hence it is feasible that trusts may have seen health authorities as 'captive' purchasers, a notion implied by Propper *et al.* (1998).

A sensible conclusion to reach from these viewpoints may be that health authorities were commissioning on behalf of a population with which it had little close contact, and over which they had little control. GPs would appear to hold a strong advantage in both these respects. They are the gatekeepers to most health care services delivered outside the general practice setting. Without pressure from a health authority, it is they who make the final decision as to where a patient is referred. Providers may be sensitive to the exit option if they need to retain business in order to maintain or even increase their workload and income. From this, it seems that the advantages derived from the exit option in the context of increasing the responsiveness of providers were likely to rest with fund-holders more than with health authorities.

Summary

Fund-holding practices may well have been able to agree at partnership level whether they would move referrals for a particular specialty from the local provider to a competitor. Exit theory suggests this closeness to patients could have given GP fund-holders greater bargaining power over hospitals than was available to health authorities. This leverage could have enabled such practices to acquire benefits for their own patients which were not open to people represented by a health authority. Devolving budgets to the level of general practice might thus have given GPs who were motivated to try and acquire shorter waiting times for their patients the opportunity to do just that. As money followed the fund-holding patient, if fund-holders made hospitals aware they were willing to move clients elsewhere, they could have found their negotiating position, with an analogy being Hirschman's (1970) concept of voice, strengthened. The exit hypothesis will also be addressed in the seventh chapter.

The idea that GP fund-holders had more control over the referral process and thus a greater capacity to move work between providers, which in turn enhanced their leverage, connects to another possible reason why the waiting times of patients represented by health authorities and fund-holding practices could have varied. Namely, the information each purchaser had to act as an effective commissioner plus the motivation they had to use it for the benefit of patients. The next section discusses the possible effect of these issues on the waiting times of patients.

INFORMATION AND INCENTIVES

If the outcomes of a quasi-market are measurable to some extent by its effect on the standards of services being provided, success is likely to be dependent at least in part on how well purchasers advocated the interests of their clients in negotiations with providers. This idea was surely the basis of Loveridge and Starkey's (1992) claim that fund-holding was making GPs the patient's champion once more. However, the Department of Health (1990) plus Ham and Spurgeon (1993) both suggested that the internal market gave health authorities the opportunity to fulfil the 'champions of the people' role. From this, the types of information and incentives possessed by the two main purchaser types in the NHS quasi-market could easily be an important factor in the priority they gave to shortening the waiting times of patients.

There are different kinds of information and incentives, and the level at which each is applicable to health authorities and GPs varies. This idea compliments the notion put forward by Glennerster *et al.* (1998) that the effective commissioning of different sorts of health care services may require dissimilar types of information and incentives. For instance, the types needed to be proficient in purchasing one kind of care, say elective surgery, might well be very different to those required, for example, to competently commission accident and emergency services. However, while it is possible that this could mean health authorities would be good, relatively speaking, at purchasing some things and GPs others, this is not necessarily the case. Either could have greater access to the kinds of incentives and information that facilitates better performance at commissioning most, or perhaps even all services.

However, the precise answer to what the most important types of information and incentives might be for commissioning what kinds of services is so far unresolved, being an area of study still in its infancy. Nevertheless, there now follows a discussion of the classes of information that may be available to health care purchasers.

Information

The form of information which is available to anyone is undoubtedly a crucial factor in enabling rational decisions, and is thus likely to have a strong influence in determining the effectiveness of health care purchasers in their role (see Bartlett and Le Grand, 1993). After all, contract monitoring requires a supply of good information (Spurgeon, 1993c). Beyond this, Glennerster *et al.* (1998) saw four types of information as likely to be necessary for purchasing health care services competently. One was the data on area wide health needs and disease trends, which is connected to epidemiological research and study. Considering the relatively small numbers of patients registered with individual general practices, this kind of information is obviously going to be more accessible at health authority rather than GP level. This was surely the rationale behind Roland's (1996) opinion that GPs may not be the best people to plan the health care of wide populations.

Another type of information derives from what Glennerster *et al.* (1998) called health technology assessment. This relates to things like researching the cost effectiveness of therapies to elicit evidence for the success of various treatment options. The evolution of this type of data is not well developed. In reality, work towards the attainment of such data seems more likely to be performed at a level above that of general practice, and quite probably higher than local health authorities. Whatever level this enterprise is progressed at, the eventual provision of such information should be valuable to and usable by any type of purchaser.

A further kind of information identified by Glennerster *et al.* (1998) as relevant to purchasing in the NHS is that on the organisational and clinical efficacy of providers. This has links with an appraisal of quality which, although not impossible to define in the context of health care (Koch, 1993), may often be difficult to measure (Kerrison, 1993).[11] Concerning this variety of information, when their roles are separated the purchaser is likely to have less information about the quality and outcomes of the service than is the provider (Propper, 1993a; 1993b). Yet such an asymmetry of information may have been a less severe problem for fund-

---

11. With regard to quality in health care, Koeck and Neugaard (1995) wrote of an experiment in Vienna where competition between hospitals was based upon the quality of services rather than the price of them. It was, however, too early to ascertain the success or otherwise of the project.

holders than health authorities because GPs do have a direct and daily contact with patients through their surgeries (Le Grand, 1994a).

From this, GPs may 'get a feel' for service quality as it affects specific people. Patients personally telling their GPs how they got on at hospital could well be a cheap way of giving an important, albeit anecdotal and small scale impression about the quality of various services and the attitudes of clinicians at a provider. While such opinions could also be unrepresentative, it might be better than having nothing. If a health authority was going to acquire such data, perhaps either through questionnaires to patients or by interviews with GPs, the task could be time consuming and expensive.

While it is important not to overestimate the likely level of data that could pass to GPs in this way, to whatever extent it does happen, personal contact with patients is a source of data from which health authorities are distanced. Information to health authorities on a provider's services could have more to do with impersonal quantities obtained from the hospital, albeit useful ones like bed occupancy statistics and the volume of treatment episodes. Such data can of course be supplied to GPs as well. Moreover, their closeness to patients may also give GPs a good source of data about waiting times – an impression of the waits at local hospitals. Patients may complain to GPs about the length of their wait, or perhaps attend for consultations in pain or discomfort because of it. This could even lead to the use of the exit option, with referral patterns being changed and patients sent elsewhere.

GPs are also likely to have greater access to a fourth sort of information – the views, preferences and concerns of patients (Glennerster *et al.*, 1998). Again, this has links to the closeness of the relationship between GPs and their patients. Some practices have formal participation groups in which a number of registered patients, although not necessarily a representative sample, have meetings with GPs and managers about a range of matters. Yet more than this the most obvious source of such feedback is probably again the 'day to day' consultations at surgeries. As mentioned previously, it is feasible that through this mechanism GPs could get strong impressions about the waiting times for particular types of surgery at local hospitals.

In sum, there are different sorts of information, some of which manifest more at the level of general practices than health authorities, with the reverse being true for others. As a general rule, information on smaller groups of people and indeed individual patients is likely to be more robust at practice level, whilst for larger populations health authorities seem to have a major advantage. Of course, there are channels through which data can pass between the two purchaser types. The GP contract introduced in 1990 required general practices to provide various data to health authorities in annual reports (see Department of Health and Welsh Office, 1989; Health Departments of Great Britain, 1989) that, when aggregated, contributes to knowledge on area wide health needs. Conversely, it is hard to think of a good reason why health authorities could not share public health data with GP purchasers. Perhaps the dilemma has more to do with the prediction of Glennerster *et al.* (1994a) that GPs might have only limited interest in it.

Incentives

Glennerster *et al.* (1998) cited four types of incentives that health care purchasers could possess. One was a desire to procure a sense of professional satisfaction that can result from doing a good job. This connects with Dunleavy's (1991) idea that self-interest may not be the only motivation for professional staff. Things like saving lives and improving the lot of patients brings its own reward (Glennerster *et al.*, 1994a). Their responsibility for the everyday care of patients makes it easy to picture the presence of this kind of motivation in GPs. For health authority staff, such incentives constitute what Le Grand (1997) called knightly behaviour and according to the public choice literature it might be naive, or at least over optimistic, to accept its existence to a particularly large degree (for example, see Niskanen, 1971; 1973). Nevertheless, to avoid cynicism it might be feasible that health authority staff could be motivated to some extent, even if less than GPs, by factors such as helping patients.

Yet some may not see this account of GP motivation as a very balanced view, and perhaps this doubt might have some validity. Does the possession of a medical degree automatically guarantee that doctors will be selfless servants to their patients' interests? The former politician Enoch Powell – quoted in Klein (1995), observed that one of the first things all health ministers discover at or near the outset of their term of office is that the only subject they are destined to discuss with the medical profession is money. This does not sound too compatible with knightly behaviour, though there might be some difference in their individual (more knightly) and collective (less knightly) behaviour. This is not to say that doctors will be unconcerned about the well being of patients. But in the context of rationality any motivation derived from improving the fate of patients, and despite Enoch Powell's comments it seems reasonable to accept that this probably happens to some extent, might be strengthened if other rewards arise as well.

This proposition falls conveniently into place with another form of incentive identified by Glennerster *et al.* (1998), that of minimising time costs and job complexity. For this can also be seen as being stronger the closer a commissioner is to patients. The logic of this conclusion is chiefly based upon the premise that if GPs can, for example, shorten their patients' waiting times, this may well reduce their workload as patients treated promptly at hospital could require less care in general practice. It is also possible that GPs will be inconvenienced less by patients asking them to expedite their admission date (linking to the previous discussion of their information on waiting times). Such benefits will not be accrued by health authority staff if they shorten the waits of patients. It is hard to imagine many people would badger such personnel to try and obtain an earlier admission. GPs are much nearer to patients and would surely spring to their minds before an anonymous bureaucrat at a health authority office.

A further sort of incentive discussed by Glennerster *et al.* (1998) was organisational survival, job security and promotion prospects. For health authority staff this might have been reinforced by fund-holding producing competition in purchasing, though there are other reasons why it could exist. In a climate where year on year efficiency savings must be found in administration costs and mergers between health authorities have been common, the tenure of NHS executives may not be as long-lived or safe as it once was (Flannery, 1996). This can put staff under pressure to discharge duties to high standards, and if good performance is measured against governmental directives like keeping waiting times down, sufficient incentives might have existed in respect of organisational survival and job security regardless of fund-holding. Promotion prospects may also be enhanced by high performance, and these incentives could be more explicit and powerful for health authority staff than for self-employed GPs in secure partnerships.

The other kind of incentive considered by Glennerster *et al.* (1998) was the maximising of personal monetary gain. Though it links to promotion prospects for higher paid jobs, this incentive could possibly offer motives to health authority employees to try and profit via illegitimate means, or through performance-related pay. Yet the modest impact of the latter as an incentive to NHS managers (see Dowling and Richardson, 1997) suggests this might have only a limited effect. Glennerster *et al.* (1998) also made the point that GPs could have a monetary incentive in attracting patients to keep their practice list buoyant. The remuneration of GPs is partly dependent on the list size of their practice, most notably through the capitation fees payable for all patients registered with their practice. From this, economic theory suggests GPs could try to compete for patients by performing well as purchasers. The validity of the theory thus relies upon the existence of competition for patients between GPs.

The notion that competition for patients could be an incentive may be endorsed by some fund-holders giving the protection of their list size as a reason for joining the scheme (see Audit Commission, 1996a). Nevertheless, the possibility remains that patients might be too apathetic, loyal to their existing GPs, or unaware of the performance of alternative commissioners, to switch practices and so make this a wholly convincing or credible theory. Moreover, such doubts appear supported by Thomas *et al.* (1995) failing to find evidence that patients move between practices in large numbers for any other reason than changing their address. This could suggest that the theory might have a weakness and if this scepticism were warranted, it would be unlikely to disappoint Crump and Griffiths (1993) who opposed the idea of purchasers competing against each other.[12]

In summary, similar to the forms of information which may, or might not, be available to distinct commissioners, there are also various types of incentives. It is feasible that alternative kinds of incentives could be more, or less, applicable to different purchasers. It is possible that any professional pride in improving the fortunes of patients, and the greater convenience this brings to daily work routines, could motivate GPs more than health authority staff. It may also be that the enhanced job security and promotion prospects that could derive from being recognised as an effective commissioner may be a stronger incentive for health authority staff than GPs in relatively secure partnerships. The promotion prospects of NHS managers are linked to their earnings potential, and it is thus possible to see how this might work as an incentive for good performance as a purchaser of health care services.

Who should purchase what?

With the mix of different types of both information and incentives that were applicable to purchasers in the NHS internal market, it seems that each may have contrasting relevance to the performance of health authority staff and GPs in a commissioning function. If information and the incentives to use it has consequences on the efficacy of a purchaser, that has an outcome on the kinds of services received by patients. In turn, disparities in the weightings given to the factors by alternative commissioners reduce the confidence that can be attached to any prediction. Good forecasts about the relative performance of different purchasers are thus difficult.

Nevertheless, Glennerster *et al.* (1998) did attempt to shed some theoretical light on the possible impact on each purchaser type of the different forms of information and incentives. The suggestion made was

---

12. Support for policies that sustain collaboration between purchasers was also emphasised by Moore and Dalziel (1993).

that health authorities might be most effective at roles which relate to the broad community, which falls into place with their wider needs assessment for quite large populations and their public health function. Meanwhile, GPs may be best at purchasing services where the gains are more private to themselves. Taking this notion forward, it seems to coincide with the idea that there were distinct advantages for fund-holders in, for example, lowering waiting times for elective surgery because this may stop patients moaning during consultations that occur in the meantime.

However, if this theoretical position is realistic, it provokes another line of thought. During the internal market, were the majority of NHS services being commissioned by the wrong purchaser, meaning the one that was least likely to do the best job? Every item of service received by patients has a potential impact on the workload and convenience of GPs. Say a practice nurse does not bother to give a patient with below par immunity their recommended flu jab and the individual subsequently develops influenza as a result, that person is likely to need an appointment with their GP to obtain treatment for their symptoms. The same principle holds for hospital services both inside and outside the standard fund-holding scheme. A sub-standard physiotherapy department could mean that more patients might go and see their GP because of aches and pains than would otherwise be the case. A poor oncology service implies more terminally ill patients requiring intensive care at the level of general practice.

A similar argument can be made for just about everything in the context of health care services. People not admitted quickly enough to hospitals, or being discharged from them in a poorer condition than need otherwise be the case, affects general practice in a negative way. When patients undergo health care, at the point at which a treatment is received it is an individual episode of care on a single person. If that service is shoddy, patients are more likely to turn to GPs for assistance. GPs thus have an incentive to shape hospital services for the benefit of patients, which does not exist at the health authority. If a patient requests a night visit following the receipt of second-rate care at a hospital, it is not an employee of the health authority who gets a telephone call in the middle of the night.

Therefore, might GPs be better purchasers of most health care services, including many of those that were outside the standard fund-holding scheme? So what does that thought say about the purchasing configuration in the quasi-market? Could the most profitable role for health authorities have been to aggregate area wide public health and epidemiological data for use by GP commissioners to purchase a range of services far beyond what was in the standard fund-holding scheme? Or was the prediction of Glennerster *et al.* (1994a) that GPs may have little interest in such matters right? It is uncertain what the correct answer to this question is, even though the present government's reforms to the NHS make it a crucial debate. But there is another hypothesis that may offer a practicable explanation why the waiting times of fund-holding and other patients could have differed – the relationships of key actors operating within the system. This possibility is discussed in the following section.

RELATIONSHIPS

The foundation for this hypothesis is that patients' waiting times could be determined by the relationships between individuals representing the purchasers and providers. As a starting point for a discussion of this idea, Ferlie (1994) considered the relationship issue on a general basis in three contexts. One was that the system could have what was called a relational nature because of the continuing relationship between the chief officers of trusts and health authorities. Another was that a high degree of continuity for senior staff at these bodies might make the system socially embedded. The other was that the internal market could have been institutionally embedded if managers were conscious of the need to meet the regulatory targets imposed by higher tiers.

It is noticeable that the slant of these ideas rests heavily on the alliance between health authority and trust managers, with an apparent assumption that the appointed chief officers at both may have a long-term relationship since a time before the provider achieved trust status. While an association between established suppliers and customers in conventional markets can often alter over time (see Langlois and Robertson, 1995), the impression is aroused that this might be a rather cosy relationship. However, the role of GPs as commissioners may well have made the connection between providers and at least some of the purchasers rather less comfortable, if suspicions that there is a degree of rivalry between the elements of the medical profession are correct. After all, Harrison *et al.* (1990) plus Strong and Robinson (1990) predicted fund-holding could cause cleavage between consultants and GPs. It would thus appear sensible to not restrict the inquiry into relationships to just those between non-clinical managers.

There is a history behind such forecasts of the impact of the fund-holding scheme on the relationships between hospital consultants and GPs. This is the clear division in the NHS between primary and secondary care (see Roland, 1992d; Boaden, 1997), alongside the firm and long-standing detachment of these two sections of the medical profession (see Honigsbaum, 1979). Traditionally hospital consultants have held the highest and most prestigious position in the profession's hierarchy (Levitt and Wall, 1984; Pollitt, 1984; Handysides, 1994a; 1994b) with decisions over which patients were called in from a waiting list, and in what order, having long been under their control (Frankel, 1993). This means that if consultants had retained their authority in this respect, and Chinegwundoh (1997) implied that to an extent they had, for any purchaser wishing to curb waits it would appear that they were the people most worth influencing.

This proposition complies with both the claim of Light (1997) that surgeons control the waiting lists, plus Hamilton's (1997) argument that the onus to reduce waiting times lies with purchasers. From this, who influenced such hospital clinicians the most, GP fund-holders or health authority staff and out of the two purchasers which wanted to influence them the most? In sum, does a relationship between two sets of clinicians, consultants and GPs, have a different effect to the involvement of health authority staff in the commissioning process?

Relationships inspired by the fund-holding scheme

One cornerstone of the engagement of GPs in purchasing was the idea that fund-holding halted a trend in which they lost power and status in their relationship with consultants (see Roland, 1991; Wisely, 1991; Corney, 1994; Glennerster *et al.*, 1994a; Glennerster, 1995; Mant and Towse, 1996). If money followed fund-holding patients to the providers where they were referred, exit theory suggests this would increase the weight of GPs' voice. This may have given them greater influence over providers than that enjoyed by health authorities, whose purchasing might perhaps be more akin to patients following the contract or second-guessing the demand of GPs. From this, Baeza *et al.* (1993) claimed the reforms had much to do with enhancing the power of GPs to sway hospital policy, a judgement that ties in with Stott (1993), a hospital doctor, having considerable doubts that GPs should be commissioners. Yet despite such judgements there is another prospect concerning the relationships of consultants and GPs.

Rather than having a relationship based on antagonism, could consultants and GPs find dealing with each other preferable to negotiating with non-clinical managers? Of course, such doctors do work alongside managerial staff at both hospitals and general practices. But the contracting process between fund-holders and hospitals was more likely to bring together clinicians than the relationship between providers and health authorities. After all, a health authority may have had a director of public health plus a medical advisor dealing with prescribing issues, but as far as the employment of doctors is concerned, that might have been it (although there could always be differences at distinct health authorities). Moreover, directors of public health were unlikely to negotiate contracts with hospital doctors. However, whilst consultants may not personally have settled agreements with practices in the scheme, their on-going contact with GPs through the referral process could have made clinical interaction in the commissioning procedure more common when fund-holders dealt with providers than when the health authority did.

So far the theory concerning relationships is that fund-holders could have had more influence in persuading hospital doctors to admit patients promptly than health authority staff for the following reasons. To adopt Hirschman's (1970) terminology, holding budgets may have expanded the weight of GP's voice to give them a greater opportunity to negotiate shorter waits for their patients. This outcome might flow from either a relationship based upon animosity or otherwise a spirit of tolerance if consultants feel trading with professional colleagues is favourable to dealing with managers. Perhaps the association could even be symbolised by goodwill. However, things might not be that straightforward.

The complication is founded on the question of whether the admission of patients was still down to the decision of consultants? After all, there is a prospect that hospital clinicians might over recent times have been incorporated more into the financial, and indeed other priorities of their providers (see Harrison and Pollitt, 1994). Could this mean they adopted new criteria for choosing whom to admit when? Or had decisions pertaining to the admission of patients been passed to non-clinical management? Such areas require investigation and in-depth interviews were thus conducted with both consultants and trust managers to explore their views over relationships with purchasers.

The other form of social relationship that may have arisen (as a result of fund-holding) is that membership of the scheme could have made the GPs concerned more visible to hospital consultants. It is feasible that trusts held open days for fund-holding GPs where they were shown around clinical departments at the hospital, and hosted meetings whereby fund-holders as a group or individually met consultants and managers to discuss service issues? If this was so and non fund-holders were excluded, could the greater exposure for GPs within the scheme have made a difference to the speed of admission for their patients? Moreover, if it did the effect could again go two ways. The hospital clinician and fund-holders might have developed warm relationships, or they could have antagonised each other. These topics shall be addressed in the seventh chapter.

Relationships not inspired by the fund-holding scheme

Another reason why fund-holding patients might have had shorter waiting times was that their GPs could generally have had a different form of social relationship with hospital consultants than those outside the scheme, but this was not caused by fund-holding status. Perhaps fund-holding may have tended to attract GPs that differed from those who chose not to enter the scheme, a viewpoint that was advanced by the Audit Commission (1996a) plus Baines and Whynes (1996).

From this, did fund-holding GPs have the types of personalities that enabled them to influence consultants to admit their own patients more quickly than patients of a similar clinical urgency registered with other practices? If this was the case, then it was not the scheme *per se* that would have enabled fund-holding patients to enjoy shorter waits but the personalities of their GPs and the relationship they had with hospital doctors because of it. If so, it would surely be the case that patients of these GPs would be admitted sooner whether or not the practice was fund-holding. However, the prospect that this was a real cause of disparities in waits may have lessened as large numbers of GPs with presumably many different character types and working habits joined the scheme.

It may also be fair to note the possibility that some GPs could have obtained shorter waits for their own patients for reasons that go beyond the relationship hypothesis. Perhaps it had something to do with the way they practice, instead of their relationship with consultants. Or their patients might have been of a social class or had such attitudes that they took it upon themselves to pressurise hospital doctors to admit them quickly for their operations, rather than the GP doing this.

Whatever the case, the point still remains that prior to acquiring fund-holding status, patients of such practices would be expected to have had shorter waits than people registered with other practices. If this happened, it would not be fund-holding that shortened waiting times. Shorter waits after a practice joined the scheme would be a continuation of a trend for patients that existed prior to fund-holding status. Therefore, whether shorter waits were due to the relationships between GPs and consultants or something else is less important than actually showing whether or not this trend was evident prior to fund-holding status. This query will be addressed in the fourth chapter.

Summary

The potential impact of relationships on waiting times has a number of traits. Who chose which patients were admitted when, and if it was consultants did they take such decisions in line with policy set down by non-clinical staff? Did any equalisation in the status of GPs and consultants enable the fund-holders to persuade or even coerce hospitals to hasten the admission of their patients? Or might the waits of fund-holding patients have been reduced by a harmonious professional link between GPs and consultants? If so, was such a clinical interface more beneficial to patients in the purchasing process than a doctor to non-clinical manager association? Moreover, did fund-holding increase the prominence of GPs in the scheme beyond the level enjoyed by other family doctors and if it had, did this have any relevance?

Otherwise, did GPs within the fund-holding scheme tend to have different characteristics to those outside it by always having tried, and succeeded, to persuade consultants to admit their patients promptly? If this were the case, fund-holding would not have made any difference. Such GPs would surely have been shortening the waits of their patients whether or not the practice participated in the scheme. After all, GPs do retire and resign but the fairly infrequent incidence of this means that partnerships were very largely made up of the same people prior to and during fund-holding status. Neither does it seem likely that the essence of GPs' personalities changed when they became fund-holders. Because of this it looks safe to accept that if waiting times were cut after practices joined the scheme, it must have had something to do with fund-holding status, not the personalities of GPs.

CONCLUSION

The hypotheses that could feasibly explain why the waiting times of fund-holding patients might have been shorter than those endured by other patients have been covered in some depth. The framework for a study into this issue must necessarily cover a number of theoretical positions. These range from questioning if fund-holders had been budgeted over generously, or whether differences in the case mix of fund-holding and non fund-holding activity provide the answer. If the first of these was true the system gave fund-holders an unfair advantage, while the second would indicate that if their patients enjoyed shorter waits, this might have had more to do with chance (or luck) than the effectiveness of GPs in a commissioning role. Yet it will also be discussed in the sixth chapter how case mix differences could be created by the conscious decisions of purchasers, and by demographic characteristics.

Other possible reasons relate to variations in the way purchasers operated. This includes the impact of contracts, the information and incentives relevant to each commissioner, the effect of the exit option, and the relationships between key agents within the system. If any of these factors explain why fund-holding patients may have had shorter waits, then this could well suggest that elective surgery might be best commissioned at the level of general practice, rather than by health authorities. Unless, of course, any relationships between hospital consultants and fund-holders that facilitated shorter waits for patients were not driven by GPs' membership of the scheme. In sum, all of the areas discussed in this chapter were addressed. An explanation of the ways in which they were examined is a fundamental objective of the next chapter.

3 The Study: Geography and Methodology

This chapter has two primary functions. The first is to identify the location of the research project and outline the configuration of the NHS in the area. Much of the data for this task was taken from a health authority document named *West Sussex Health: Reference Atlas 1994/95*, although some use was made of other material, most notably the business plans of local NHS trusts. The second purpose is to clarify the research methodology.

WEST SUSSEX: GEOGRAPHY, DEMOGRAPHY AND DESIGN OF THE NHS

The research was a case study that centred on a large county in the south of England, West Sussex, which covers just over 1,988 square kilometres. The county is divided into 155 wards, as defined by the 1991 census data, and has 116 postcode sectors. It comprises 7 local district councils, those of Adur, Arun, Chichester, Crawley, Horsham, Mid Sussex and Worthing.

According to the OPCS statistics that are used to calculate health authority cash limits, West Sussex has a population approaching 750,000. Compared to some areas of major conurbation, it is relatively stable with far less movement between the lists of general practices than is often the case. As is usual, the population registered with general practices in the county is a little higher than the OPCS figure, in October 1996 totalling 760,484. However, the OPCS total has not been attributed to the level of individual general practices. This has prompted the health authority to base its analyses at practice level, including its current moves toward capitation funding for primary care groups, upon patient numbers according to its own population register. Hence whenever population numbers are discussed in the book, such as the percentages given in table 3.1, the totals will relate to the slightly inflated figures recorded by the health authority as registered with GPs.

This creates no inconsistency with the health authority receiving its cash limit on a capitation basis according to its OPCS population. For there is no reason to imagine that the patient numbers on the health authority register for one set of practices, fund-holding or not, would be any more or less inflated compared to the OPCS population than the other. Also, it is considered that the number of people living within West Sussex but registered with practices outside it are evenly balanced by those who reside in other health authority areas but are on the lists of GPs inside the county.

West Sussex itself has quite diverse characteristics. Much of the county is rural, but there are also a number of heavily populated urban neighbourhoods. Within this environment there are various sites which can only be described as extremely affluent, although it does have some very deprived localities as well. Jarman scores are measures of deprivation that were developed to connect GP remuneration with the socio-economic indicators of the practice list. The indicators are weighted against eight variables to assess whether a practice is eligible to receive deprivation payments, as an attempt to match pay to workload. On the basis of Jarman scores calculated for the 1991 census, much of West Sussex is quite prosperous, while the most deprived wards are found in Crawley, which also has the most people from ethnic minority groups, Worthing, Bognor Regis, Littlehampton, and Lancing. There is also a single deprived ward in Chichester.

The population density is highest in Crawley and Worthing, the characteristics of which are very dissimilar in the context of age bands. While the county altogether has a lower proportion of young children than the average for England and Wales, Crawley is the main exception to this and has a considerably higher level. In contrast, the proportion of elderly people in Worthing far exceeds the national average.

Health authority configuration

Prior to the 1991 reforms, and indeed for a time after the changes, the county of West Sussex was split into three separate district health authority areas, each named after the general vicinities they covered, Chichester, Mid Downs and Worthing. The trend towards health authority amalgamation has already been described. These three districts formally became an example of that tendency when they merged to become the West Sussex Health Authority in April 1995, although in reality they had been acting as a unitary body for at least a year before that. The West Sussex Family Health Services Authority also formally combined with the main health authority in April 1996.

Public providers

All of the public providers in the county have become self-governing trusts. There is an assortment of hospital, community, or combined hospital and community NHS trusts as well as the local ambulance service. The last of these became a trust in April 1995 when it merged with the parallel service in East Sussex to form the Sussex Ambulance Service NHS Trust. Hence there are examples of each of the four types of trust highlighted in the previous chapter. The public acute and community providers were arranged as follows.

The Crawley Horsham Health Services NHS Trust used to be part of the provider unit of the Mid Downs District Health Authority before it gained trust status in April 1993. It was a combined hospital and community provider, with acute services primarily centred at Crawley Hospital, although some occurred at Horsham Hospital. As the name suggests, the towns of Crawley and Horsham were the main centres of population in its catchment area. In April 1998, some two years after the time span of this research, the acute sector of the trust merged with the nearby (though external to West Sussex) East Surrey Healthcare NHS Trust in Redhill to become the Surrey and Sussex Healthcare NHS Trust. At the same time, the community sector of the trust was annexed to the equivalent provider in Chichester.

The Mid Sussex NHS Trust is another combined acute and community provider. Acute services are provided from the Princess Royal Hospital in Haywards Heath. Before trust status in April 1994 it was the other arm of the Mid Downs District Health Authority's provider function. The main towns in its locality are Haywards Heath and Burgess Hill.

The Royal West Sussex NHS Trust is an acute provider, the St Richard's Hospital in Chichester. Before becoming a trust in April 1994 it was the acute provider for the Chichester District Health Authority. The community provider in the locality was the Chichester Priority Care Services NHS Trust, which also achieved trust status in April 1994. The largest centres of population served by them were in the city of Chichester and the town of Bognor Regis. Subsequent to the Chichester Priority Care Services NHS Trust incorporating the community arm of the Crawley Horsham provider in April 1998 (as mentioned above), it changed its name to the Sussex Weald and Downs NHS Trust in January 1999.

The Worthing and Southlands Hospitals NHS Trust is, as the name suggests, an acute provider comprising two hospitals, Worthing Hospital and Southlands Hospital in Shoreham-by-Sea. It became a trust in April 1994 and the hospitals were previously the acute provider arm of the Worthing District Health Authority. The principal community service provider in the locality is the Worthing Priority Care NHS Trust, which achieved trust status in April 1993. The chief towns served by the providers are Worthing, Shoreham-by-Sea and Littlehampton.

The other West Sussex public provider is the Queen Victoria Hospital NHS Trust at East Grinstead, in the far north east of the county. However, there is something of an anomaly over this provider. Although the hospital is just within the boundaries of West Sussex, prior to becoming a trust in April 1994 it was part of the acute provider arm of the Tunbridge Wells District Health Authority. With the merging of districts, Tunbridge Wells now comes under the West Kent Health Authority and a manager from the Queen Victoria Hospital confirmed that West Kent remains the host health authority for the trust, rather than West Sussex. The geographic location of the acute NHS providers is shown in figure 3.1, which also gives the boundaries of the old district health authorities. The southern boundary of the county is part of the coastline of the English Channel.

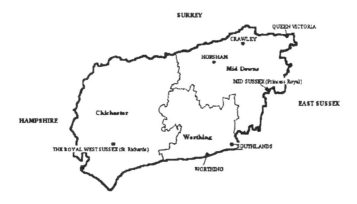

Figure 3.1   Map of West Sussex showing the boundaries of the former district health authorities and the position of acute hospitals that comprise NHS trusts

Each distinct NHS provider in West Sussex that supplies acute services offered the same range of operations covered by the fund-holding scheme to all patients, regardless of the status of their practice. This does not mean they all provide the same services. For example, one might not have an ophthalmology department while another does. But the one that does will have offered the same range of eye operations to all patients, whether fund-holding or not. Also, when individual providers are named throughout the book, to achieve consistency they will be called by the basic name of the trust, whatever their status at that point in time. For instance, if something to do with St Richard's Hospital in 1993 were to be discussed, it would still be called the Royal West Sussex provider, even though the trust of this name was not formally conceived until April 1994.

The growth of fund-holding

In the context of the number of practices participating in the scheme and the proportion of patients covered, fund-holding grew considerably in West Sussex during the first seven years of the internal market, reflecting a wider national picture identified earlier by the Audit Commission (1995). In fact the ratio of the population covered by fund-holding GPs in the county during the first five years of the scheme exceeded the quota given by the NHS Executive (1995d) for the whole of England. Four first wave practices had almost 8 per cent of the population on their lists. The next year close to 17 per cent of patients were registered with fund-holding GPs, rising to nearly 29 per cent in the 1993/94 financial year. This increased to over 41 per cent from April 1994 and more than 47 per cent for the 1995/96 financial year.

Although this study covers the four years to March 1996, the scheme continued to grow after this date. The population coverage was nearly 63 per cent in 1996/97. The following year, four existing fund-holding practices in East Grinstead went live with a 'total purchasing' project to commission a range of the services outside the standard scheme, as well as continuing to purchase those inside it. When five practices became seventh wave standard fund-holders at the same time, the standard scheme and GP total purchasers covered nearly 69 per cent of patients. This figure would have increased still further from April 1998 if the eighth wave had been allowed to go ahead.

Another three practices, covering a little more than 1 per cent of patients, have been acting as community fund-holders since April 1996 (an option mentioned in the previous chapter). As such, for the last three years of the internal market, over 70 per cent of the people registered with West Sussex practices were covered by GP purchasers in some way, with the very large majority under the standard fund-holding scheme.

The development of GP purchasing in the county, giving more precise percentages of the patients covered, is provided in table 3.1. The number of practices involved in directly commissioning health care services can be compared to a total in the county that hovers around the century mark, although the precise figure does not remain constant. Patients of retiring single-handed GPs have occasionally been subsumed within the lists of other existing practices, and though rare it is not unknown for some partnerships to split. Between 1994 and 1996 the number of practices fell from 101 to 97.

Table 3.1   Growth in the coverage of fund-holding in West Sussex during the first seven years of the internal market

Wave and year	Standard scheme		Total purchasers		Community scheme		Aggregate	
	No of practices	% of patients	No of practices	% of patients	No of practices	% of patients	No of practices	% of patients
1. 1991-2	4	7.9	0	-	0	-	4	7.9
2. 1992-3	10	16.5	0	-	0	-	10	16.5
3. 1993-4	18	28.9	0	-	0	-	18	28.9
4. 1994-5	29	41.1	0	-	0	-	29	41.1
5. 1995-6	34	47.4	0	-	0	-	34	47.4
6. 1996-7	52	62.8	0	-	3	1.3	55	64.1
7. 1997-8	53	63.6	4	5.3	3	1.3	60	70.3

For the period covered by this research project, 1992/93 to 1995/96, standard fund-holders and health authorities were the only two types of purchaser that functioned in the West Sussex internal market. Neither the East Grinstead total purchasers nor the community fund-holders, which along with standard fund-holders were formally superseded by primary care groups, had enacted such a role during the relevant four years. There were no operative commissioning groups at the time, either.

RESEARCH METHODOLOGY: AN OVERVIEW

The research had two main goals. First, to demonstrate whether patients registered with GP fund-holders had shorter waiting times for elective surgery, relative to the patients from non fund-holding practices. Quantitative research techniques were used to address this aim. Second, to establish the reasons for any such differences. Qualitative research methods were utilised to test many of the hypotheses covered in the last chapter which may explain any contrasts in the waits of the two groups of patients, although some inquiries required the further use of quantitative techniques.

The database

The West Sussex Health Authority, via its patient information database (PID), supplied data for every patient admitted from the waiting list who underwent an elective surgical procedure covered by the fund-holding scheme during the 1992/93, 1993/94, 1994/95 and 1995/96 financial years. The operations occurred at the four public providers of acute services for which it acted as the host health authority, the Crawley Horsham, Mid Sussex, Royal West Sussex, plus Worthing and Southlands providers. As was previously mentioned, two of them supplied a range of community services as well. Although details were also given for the private patients that had operations at the hospitals covered by these providers, the research obviously concentrated on those whose treatments were financed by NHS purchasers. The database contained no information about NHS funded patients, financed either by a health authority or more probably a fund-holding practice, who received treatments at private hospitals.

The initial twelve months of the quasi-market from April 1991 to March 1992 was not included in the database for a number of reasons. Firstly, there were only four first wave fund-holding practices in the county that financial year, and two of those came from East Grinstead and thus primarily used the Queen Victoria provider. Secondly, the PID data was considered by the health authority to be more reliable from the second year onwards. The third justification was that the 'steady state' in 1991/92 might well have made it an untypical period.

For each provider in every year the database gave the date patients were placed on the waiting list following the outpatient attendance plus associated clinical investigations, the date of their admission for an operation, and the number of days between these events (net of any period of deferral). The latter represents the length of stay for each patient on the waiting list, although for a relatively small number this was not recorded. The database also gave each patient's GP practice, the health authority or fund-holder that purchased the operation, and for people on the list of GPs outside the scheme who later joined it, the future fund-holding identity code for that particular practice. Other details included were the consultant responsible for the care, the clinical specialty, the procedure date, the discharge date, the operation performed, the half year in which the episode occurred, each patient's waiting list classification plus diagnosis, and whether the admission was made as an inpatient or day case.

Limited personal details, namely the patient's gender and date of birth, were also given. These details enabled a random check of the accuracy of the PID data, initially against the contents of the medical records for patients at a large fourth wave fund-holding practice. The data from these two sources were compared for forty patients who had operations relevant to different specialties both before and after this practice entered the scheme. Following a comment by Black (1998), this checking procedure was later repeated at another three practices, this time auditing a dozen patients at each who were still alive and registered with them, and whose episodes were spread over the four years. Each one of these practices came from the catchment areas of different hospitals, and not the same locality as the original practice participating in this process. This was the only check on randomness in choosing these three further practices. In this way, data relating to all the providers that are central to this research were covered.

In no cases did serious discrepancies come to light, suggesting much confidence can be attached to the accuracy of the database. Although in some instances the information on dates was not too precise it was still possible, at the very least, to establish from the medical records that a particular patient did undergo a certain operation and had been placed on the waiting list at an approximate point in time. This backs the forceful claim of a health authority manager that their own tests show that for operations after the first year of the internal market, the PID data is very accurate.

QUANTITATIVE RESEARCH

The waiting times of fund-holding and non fund-holding patients were compared on a year on year basis at each provider separately. This was because different providers could have distinct priorities and characteristics that might become hidden if they were all compared as an amalgam. Circumstances at a single provider may also change as years pass by, and if so this should also become more visible with separate comparisons per provider for each year. Such benefits seem to outweigh any disadvantage resulting from a relatively small number of operations being performed on fund-holding patients, perhaps because few practices from a provider's catchment area was in the scheme at a specific point in time. In fact the only time this looks to have conceivably undermined the comparison was for the Royal West Sussex in 1992/93 when only a single fund-holding practice used the provider.

Measuring waiting time differences: were they fact or fiction?

Differences in the waiting times of fund-holding and non fund-holding patients were measured at the 95 per cent confidence level through single factor (one-way) analysis of variance (ANOVA) computations. This hypothesis test uses the specific waiting time of every patient relevant to each population, and both the mean and median waits are shown in the tables to give a more comprehensive picture of their relative positions. For instance, the mean could feasibly be skewed (much increased) by a relatively few patients having very long waits.   Exhibiting the median should indicate if this was likely to have been the case.   If the distributions are not greatly skewed the mean and median will be similar.   Also the use of ANOVA (a parametric test) for comparing the large populations relevant to this study is validated by the central limit theorem.   For this shows parametric tests (reliant on normal distribution assumptions) as suitable even for groups with very skewed distributions if the sample size is comfortably over 100 (see Jordan *et al.*, 1998).[13]

Table 3.2   **Operations per specialty covered by the fund-holding scheme performed on NHS patients from the elective waiting list at four West Sussex providers over four financial years**

Specialty	1992-93 No	1993-94 No	1994-95 No	1995-96 No	Total	% of total
General surgery	3831	3988	3862	3575	15256	25.5
Gynaecology	2977	2611	2734	2414	10736	17.9
Orthopaedics	2102	2277	2896	3391	10666	17.8
Urology	1070	1416	2002	2182	6670	11.1
Ear nose and throat	1644	1514	1627	1675	6460	10.8
Ophthalmology	1599	1511	1468	1332	5910	9.9
General medicine	692	34	727	1294	3447	5.8
Geriatric medicine	1	43	141	148	333	0.6
Neurosurgery	46	35	44	83	208	0.3
Oral surgery	91	13	17	21	142	0.2
Paediatrics	0	0	43	0	43	0.1
Pain relief	0	0	7	33	40	0.1
TOTAL	14053	14142	15568	16148	59911	100.0

Comparisons were made on an overall basis and at an individual major department level.   The definition of major in this context was applied if a specialty had been responsible for some 10 per cent of all the operations on elective waiting list patients, on an aggregate basis at all the providers over the four years (see table 3.2).   As such, general surgery, gynaecology, ear nose and throat, orthopaedics, urology, plus ophthalmology were all considered as major.   Although ophthalmology fell just short of the 10 per cent mark, nearly all the activity for this specialty occurred at the Worthing and Southlands provider, where it is a very substantial department.

---

13.   As well as ANOVA, the student's *t*-test would also have been applicable for comparing the waiting times of two populations (non fund-holding and fund-holding patients). But the final results of the analysis would not be changed whichever was used (Kirkwood, 1988).   Comparisons performed through ANOVA and the *t*-test produced the same P-value (the *t*-test was also used to check the variances of the sub-samples, and the statistically significant results remained intact).

However, even if patients of GP fund-holders did have shorter waits than their non fund-holding counterparts, the doubts as to whether it was membership of the scheme that brought this about were highlighted in the previous chapter. Certain GPs may simply have been more persistent in trying to obtain shorter waits for their patients from consultants, whether or not they were in the scheme, and perhaps it was these types who eventually became fund-holders. If the shorter waits for such patients were not a consequence of their GPs acquiring fund-holding status they would surely have been admitted sooner whether or not the practice was fund-holding, and therefor prior to entering the scheme. This was tested by performing a 'before and after' fund-holding status exercise in the following way.

The database enabled any changes that occurred to the waits of practices' patients as they joined the fund-holding scheme to be observed. For practices which became fund-holders in April 1993, 1994 or 1995, the waiting times of their patients during the last year outside the scheme was compared, again through single factor ANOVA, to those of the other non fund-holding practices using the same provider. Like all the significance tests throughout the book, differences were taken as significant at the 5 per cent level or less (95 per cent confidence level). It will then be apparent whether prospective fund-holders had managed to get their patients admitted sooner than other non fund-holding practices, whilst they themselves were still non fund-holders.

A similar exercise was repeated for the same practices in the following year, once they had joined the scheme. The waits of patients from first year fund-holders were compared with the waiting times of those registered with the continuing non fund-holding practices in that year. From this, it will be possible to detect whether the waiting times for patients of new fund-holders change once they join the scheme, relative to those from practices which have remained outside it.

The funding balance

An important hypothesis that might offer a valid explanation as to why fund-holding patients may have enjoyed shorter waits is the conjecture that practices in the scheme had been systematically over funded. This is a difficult issue to address, simply because of the doubts over what a fair division of funds between a health authority and practices would actually have looked like. The methodology that was used revolves around three main lines of inquiry (discussed below), though other matters that relate to the way in which additional funds were distributed plus the impact of provider price changes are also considered, some of these on a more theoretical level.

First, what was the actual effect of GP fund-holders receiving their budgets for elective surgery on the basis of historic activity? The database shows what the outcome is of practices having been funded according to their activity in the first half of their last year outside the scheme. This entails comparing the activity of such practices in each of the two halves of what was called their preparatory year, the final twelve months outside the scheme. Second, monitoring the activity of future fund-holders in their last two years outside the scheme will show whether preparatory year practices had a higher level of activity than would be expected from the previous year, relative to the continuing non fund-holding practices. This will indicate if there is anything to suggest that practices inflated their activity in their final year outside the scheme.

Third, what do comparisons between the resources received by fund-holders and the level that would be appropriate according to a capitation formula tend to suggest? The West Sussex Health Authority claims to have been involved in the development of a formula for use at a general practice level. They were therefore able to compare the allocations for practices in and outside the scheme using the methodology explained in NHS Executive (1997a) prior to its publication. This part of the book will draw heavily on their work. In essence it is the evidence from all of the considered factors that will be used to judge if fund-holders were budgeted over generously and whether this hypothesis can thus be accepted as an explanation why their patients may have had shorter waits.

The case mix effect

Another hypothesis identified in the last chapter relates to the idea that differences in the waiting times between fund-holder and health authority patients could have been a consequence of large variations in the case mix of surgery provided to the two groups. The logic behind this idea rests on the principle that non fund-holding patients could have received far more operations for which there was typically a very long wait, whereas fund-holding activity might have been skewed towards those procedures which usually had much shorter waits. The database details the code and name of every surgical procedure given to each patient, which enables this hypothesis to be either confirmed or disproved.

The grouped case mix of fund-holding and health authority activity can be listed in a bivariate table, for which the significance of any differences between the expected and actual activity of the two groups can be calculated by way of chi square computations. Where statistically significant variations are found, the investigation will be taken further to ascertain if the following circumstances occurred. Was health authority activity skewed towards a preponderance of those procedures for which patients routinely had very long waiting times, with the reverse being the case for fund-holding patients? If so, did this have a material effect on average waiting times?

The relevance of contract types

A further possible explanation why the waiting times of fund-holder and health authority patients may have varied is the different forms of contract each purchaser commonly used. It is expected that health authorities would have predominantly utilised block contracts with local providers, with fund-holders mainly using cost-per-case agreements. If the various kinds of contract generated different behaviour patterns from providers, and overall fund-holder patients did enjoy shorter waits, this might lend support to the hypothesis that it was something to do with cost-per-case contracts that shortened waiting times.

However, the use of cost-per-case contracts by GP fund-holders was unlikely to have been a universal phenomenon. Moreover, if waiting time variances between fund-holding and health authority patients were genuinely caused by the common application of different sorts of agreement by the purchaser types, the following could be expected. Patients from fund-holding practices using block contracts would have had significantly longer waits than fund-holders admitted under cost-per-case arrangements.

The potential of contract types in causing waiting time differences between health authority and fund-holder patients is therefore approached by comparing the waits of fund-holders covered by different forms of contract, once again through single factor ANOVA. If differences between fund-holding patients covered by block, cost-per-case, plus cost and volume agreements are not shown to be significant, it is hard to see how alternative contract types can alone be accepted as an adequate explanation for any contrasts between the waits of fund-holder and health authority patients. In short, the hypothesis would no longer appear sustainable.

QUALITATIVE RESEARCH

Interviews were conducted with representatives from the providers, health authority and fund-holding general practices. The choice of what sorts of personnel were seen at these organisation types was based on the desire to make contact with the most key decision-makers at each, at least in the context of the topic being researched. Regarding the providers, this led to the primary interviews being held with a mix of senior clinicians and managers, namely consultants and the chief executives, though some managers of clinical departments and contract managers were also seen. Obtaining such a cross-section of views was important due to both the claim of Smith (1973) that single organisations are for the most part made up by groups of staff, plus Pollitt's (1993) suggestion that any complex body displays a number of contrasting and sometimes even competing sub-cultures.

Restricting the primary interviews to these groups also complies with judgements over the potential influence of other people at hospitals who could be considered relevant, most noticeably the non-executive membership of trust boards. Indeed, Ashburner (1993) claimed a couple of years after the quasi-market began that the true role of NHS trust boards had not even been established. The choice to interview the provider chief executives is backed further by their alleged heavy influence in determining the non-executive membership of trust boards (see Peck, 1993a). This may endorse a claim by the same author in another work that such board members were likely to experience major problems in having a significant impact on trusts (see Peck, 1993b). There is little hard evidence of these judgements being incorrect, or that the situation has since altered. It thus seems credible that consultants and chief executives would be far more relevant interviewees than would the non-executive board members of NHS trusts.

Moreover, the interviews with consultants also relate to the issue of how much their decisions conform to non-clinical policies. On this topic, Tremblay (1993) welcomed an extended role of doctors in management due to their purported ability to bridge a gulf between public understanding and the setting of priorities in an environment of scarce resources. Yet Harrison (1995) claimed the autonomy of clinicians had been reduced by the managerial drive towards tighter financial control over expenditure on services. This complies with Hutton's (1993) assertion that the desire of hospital doctors to provide the best quality service was tempered by a need to check costs in order to win business in a competitive environment. Additionally, Starkey (1992) wrote of the stronger managerial imperatives of financial stringency and control being placed on the medical profession. The interviews should thus widen knowledge regarding the extent to which consultants were incorporated or acquiesce with managerial priorities.

The surgical specialties that functioned at all of the four providers are general surgery, gynaecology and orthopaedics. A single consultant from each of these three departments was seen at all four providers. The individuals concerned were given assurances that their identities would not be publicised in the book. The interviews occurred from mid-January to late-April 1997. Of the dozen consultants, half were the clinical directors for their departments and the other six were not. For the sake of clarity, the division between clinical directors and other consultants is given in table 3.3. Because it is quite easy to trace the identity of a clinical director in a hospital's surgical specialty at a particular point in time, the providers' names have been withheld to protect the anonymity of those seen.

Table 3.3 **Division between clinical directors and other consultants interviewed from three surgical specialties at four providers**

Unit	General surgery	Gynaecology	Orthopaedics
Provider 1	Other consultant	Clinical director	Other consultant
Provider 2	Clinical director	Other consultant	Other consultant
Provider 3	Clinical director	Other consultant	Clinical director
Provider 4	Other consultant	Clinical director	Clinical director

The mix shown in table 3.3 was applied to try and obtain a decent cross-section of consultant opinion. For example, although clinical directors might be more aware of hospital-wide issues and thus represent a fruitful source of information, their holding of the post might result from particular characteristics or attitudes that may be reasonably common to them all. It was intended that the three interviewed at each single provider would not all be either clinical directors or other consultants, so ensuring a combination at every trust. The aim of interviewing a cross-section of subjects was also advanced by seeing two clinical directors and a couple of other consultants from each specialty. There were no other constraints on randomness in choosing the consultants to be seen.

Regarding the hospital managers, the selection process for the chief executives was obviously more straightforward because there is just one at each. All four of them were interviewed in May 1997. Six managers of the same three clinical departments as the consultant interviewees were also seen during November 1996. These sessions were primarily used to learn at an early stage who it was that tended to have responsibility at the hospitals for deciding which patients were called in when. The limited goals for the interviews somewhat lessened the importance of them, and hence only half of the twelve departments were covered.

For the interviews with GP fund-holders, those from East Grinstead were excluded because their local hospital was not a feature of the research. Apart from this exception, all other practices from waves one to five were divided into four geographical groups according to which of the featured acute providers' catchment areas they come within. Emphasis was given to practices from the first five waves because they participated in the scheme during the time-span of the research, up to the end of the 1995/96 financial year. Three practices were chosen from each group with no other consideration taken into account. The individual GPs seen were those named by each practice as having the lead responsibility for its involvement in the scheme during the research period. These doctors represented two first wave fund-holders, four practices from the second wave, one practice that joined in the third wave, three fourth wave fund-holders, and two fifth wave practices. The interviews took place during April and May 1997.

In addition to seeing GPs, informal discussions also took place with the fund-holding manager at four of the practices. These individuals were selected completely at random. The conversations cannot be described as formal interviews, but were largely used to ascertain their retrospective opinions on how they felt the budget setting process was conducted and its likely effects.

The primary interviews with representatives of the health authority were held with the chief executive and the director of public health. The purpose of this selection was to ascertain the health authority viewpoint from both a senior managerial and clinical perspective, similar to that of the providers. Of the two interviews, one was carried out in June 1997, the other in July 1997. Also held were some less formal discussions with various senior managers from the finance and contracting departments. A couple of these were to confirm the historic methodology that had been utilised to set the hospital services budgets of GP fund-holders. Each of these conversations covered the arrangements for different services.

For each group of subjects the interviews were conducted in a semi-structured manner. Pilot interviews were arranged for the sessions with consultants and GP fund-holders because there was a sufficient number of them to enable this. To do the same for other categories of interviewee, like the chief executives of trusts and the health authority plus the director of public health, was far more problematic because of the solitary nature of their positions within the organisations. When the offices of some such post-holders in other areas were contacted, there was a certain reluctance to devote time for what was seen as only being a rehearsal for research elsewhere. Hence pilot interviews were not conducted in these cases.

In short, the interviews were used to investigate a number of the hypotheses outlined in the previous chapter, although other topics were also covered. Amongst the subjects investigated were the impact of contractual demands, the effect of relationships between purchasers and providers, the incentives applicable to purchasers, plus the relevance of any threat or danger to hospitals in losing work. A guiding principle of the interviews was to word questions about the same issues to representatives from either purchasers or providers in the same way. Questions to fund-holders and health authority managers covering the same topic were identical, as were those to consultants and the chief executives of trusts. This does not mean exactly the same set of questions were asked of, for example, both sets of purchasers. Some of the questions to health authority managers may not have been appropriate for the GPs. But for the issues covered with both, the questions put to each group of interviewee were worded identically.

RELEVANCE TO THE WIDER PICTURE

In order to establish whether there were significant differences in the waiting times of patients who had their operations commissioned by either a fund-holding practice or health authority, the research process used a unique database covering four financial years, put together from the data held by a co-operative health authority. This offered an opportunity to demonstrate whether or not it is legitimate to deem that a two-tier service for elective surgery existed at four NHS providers operating within the internal market in West Sussex. It also provided a springboard to verify why the system worked in the way it did.

The extensiveness of the case study, covering four providers over four years, means its findings should be valuable in a wider context. None of the featured providers are major teaching institutions, they all seemed to encompass relatively standard district general hospitals, and although two of them as trusts were responsible for the provision of both acute and community services, this in itself is reasonably common.

Likewise, there is little reason to suspect GP fund-holders in West Sussex were out of the ordinary compared to those in many other areas, as well as being subjected to a frequently used budget setting methodology. The same can be said about the health authority. It went through the same structural convergence of smaller district health authorities and subsequently the local family health services authority as similar bodies elsewhere. As such, there is very little reason to question why West Sussex would not have been representative of a wider picture of the NHS quasi-market.

CONCLUSION

Perhaps the most important gain from the methodology adopted for this study is that it actually enabled a comparison of the performance of the two main purchaser types, albeit in just one important context, that of waiting times for elective surgery. The Audit Commission (1996a) warned that direct contrasts may be unsafe because fund-holders and health authorities operated under different rules, plus dissimilarities between practices inside and outside the scheme might not have been due to their status (fund-holding or not). However, it seems feeble to hide behind these obstacles and do nothing. Both purchaser types commissioned the elective surgery covered by the fund-holding scheme, and after the steady state in 1991/92, it is difficult to see how they performed this function under formal rules which gave one an advantage over the other.

For example, there was not a regulation that stopped one purchaser from being allowed to move work between hospitals whilst another could, even if there were circumstances that could have this effect. Similarly, distinct purchasers may have worked or done various things in alternative ways, such as the types of contract they ran, and indeed had contrasting relationships with other agents. But this is not the same as operating under different rules. In addition, it is possible to demonstrate if contrasts in waiting times between fund-holding and other patients were a continuation of an existing trend, or whether they originated when practices joined the scheme. As such, a satisfactory comparison between health authorities and fund-holders was possible. What is more, while the fund-holding scheme has been the subject of much attention by the research community (see Dixon and Glennerster, 1995), the lack of research into the effectiveness of health authorities as commissioners makes such a comparison of the purchasers important.

To close, various commentators discussed how research into the 1991 reforms and fund-holding could have been progressed (for example, Iliffe and Freudenstein, 1994; Coulter, 1995b; Dixon and Glennerster, 1995; Ham *et al.*, 1995). Regarding this matter, the logic of comparing the performance of the different purchaser types together looks compelling, particularly in the context of such a sensitive issue as waiting times. This may also address the perspective offered by Ham (1994) that important questions about the balance of health authority and fund-holding commissioning remained unanswered, a remark that still holds true. In short, the methodology adopted for this study used the waiting times for elective surgery to redress the lack of comparative studies into the relative effectiveness of health authorities and GP fund-holders as purchasers.

4 Differences in Waiting Times: Myth or Reality?

Whilst commencing with a review of the central issues that are both germane to and prevalent in the literature about waiting for treatment in the NHS, this chapter has two chief concerns. First, to demonstrate whether patients registered with fund-holding GPs had shorter waiting times, relative to non fund-holders. Second, to establish whether any such benefits that existed for fund-holding patients can legitimately be attributed to the participation of their practices in the fund-holding scheme. Preliminary findings relating to these questions were presented in the *British Medical Journal* (see Dowling, 1997). In the light of correspondence and comments provoked by this paper (see Black, 1998), the analysis was refined and possible objections to the findings explored. Whilst a brief initial response to these comments was published elsewhere (see Dowling, 1998), it is the revised results that are reported in detail here (with further matters also considered in other chapters).

WAITING IN THE NHS

Just about everybody requires health services at some point in their lives. Indeed, if someone actually avoided the receipt of any form of such care and was not neglected by service providers, their eventual death would presumably be a sudden and unforeseen event without a preceding period of illness. Whilst a few people may receive services solely from private suppliers, the limited scope of private health insurance – especially for the elderly, suggests the overwhelming majority of the UK population use the NHS at some time. Moreover, all NHS patients requiring elective care will inevitably experience a wait for their treatment because only those admitted for events like childbirth plus accident and emergency services do not endure any formal waiting period.

There are different events that mark the beginning of the waiting period for alternative services. Some, such as outpatient appointments, start with the referral by a GP and finish when the patient is seen at the hospital. In fact this is the case for all services provided as a direct result of a patient being referred by a family doctor. For elective surgery, the waiting time is the period between a patient's placement on the waiting list by a hospital doctor following an outpatient consultation and associated investigations to the point of their admission for the operation. The wait may occasionally be deferred or suspended for part of this time, for various possible reasons. For example, they could have an ill relative that necessarily delays the surgery, they might first need to lose weight before they undergo an operation, they may decline offers of admission, they could need other prior treatment, or be pregnant (see NHS Executive, 1996b).

The debate over waiting times for NHS services has traditionally focused heavily on elective surgery, even though the waits for other non-emergency services can sometimes be very long indeed. Moreover, Frankel and Robbins (1993) made particular reference to outpatient consultations in this respect. But historically it is only the waiting lists for elective surgery – the numbers of people awaiting an elective surgical procedure at a hospital at a given point in time, that have even been counted in the NHS (Yates, 1987). And the provision of elective surgery in the NHS has often been characterised by long waiting times for the service. A variety of reasons have been put forward to explain this, and over the years a number of solutions to the problem have been advanced.

Causes of long waiting lists

Various reasons might explain the persistence of long waiting lists in the NHS. One put forward some years ago was that over time the increased supply of beds could itself raise demand (see Culyer and Cullis, 1976). Harvey (1993) also offered several potential causes, such as the inclusion of people in the list who should not be on it. For instance, patients who died whilst on the list might in the past have remained on it for quite some time after their death, although the priority given to upgrading information systems since the reforms (see Malek *et al.*, 1993) should have made this type of incident far less likely. Another possibility suggested by Harvey (1993) was the deliberate maintenance of long NHS waiting lists by surgeons in order to oblige patients to have their operation on a private basis. Indeed, when the fund-holding GPs interviewed for this research were asked what they thought had been the causes of long waits in the NHS, one-third (four out of twelve) felt such manipulative behaviour by consultants was an important factor.

Harvey (1993) also mentioned the effect of hospital doctors giving priority to treating life-threatening conditions that hold only a small chance of a successful outcome. In theory it may be more rational to devote greater resources to less clinically interesting but curable ailments, which are the conditions most commonly found in waiting list patients. Nevertheless, if implemented this could feasibly compromise the advancement of medical knowledge. Some conditions might be curable now because resources were formerly devoted to treatments for them before there was much chance of a successful therapeutic outcome for the patients concerned. The other potential explanation for long waits that Harvey (1993) cited was an inadequate funding of the service, though little or no firm evidence exists to substantiate this (or any of the other possible reasons). For example, variations in the spending levels of the NHS in discrete areas of the country do not correlate with differences in the sizes of waiting lists in those districts (Yates, 1987).

Furthermore, the debate over inadequate resources relates to Smith's (1998) point that waiting lists are a mechanism for rationing non-urgent health care services in the NHS. While Frankel and West (1993) claim waiting lists will be misunderstood if they are seen in just this context, they made a number of almost positive points about them. First, leaving some patients on a waiting list was a way of rationing the responses to trivial conditions. It formally offered treatment even when there was little chance of it being performed. Second, waiting lists can be used as a political weapon to demonstrate a need for additional resources. Third, they minimise the time when staff may be idle by allowing a consistent throughput of patients. This also complements a point made by Yates (1987) that if waiting lists do enable a rational scheduling of patients through operating theatres, they may help to avoid the costs of excess hospital capacity.

Nevertheless, despite such points the existence of waiting lists is a long-term politically sensitive issue that has exacerbated public criticism for various governments, and the Thatcher administration was not exempt from these difficulties. Moreover, it seems that alarm over waiting times contribute to some people taking out private insurance (see Calnan *et al.*, 1993; Besley *et al.*, 1996). Despite the possibility that this could slow the growth in NHS costs and to some extent might thus be welcomed by those concerned with restricting state expenditure, over the years such concerns have induced a range of initiatives aimed at reducing waiting times (Edwards and Barlow, 1994). These were often short-term campaigns marked by temporary additional funding to increase surgical activity (Paton and Bach, 1990). Yet the problem has never permanently disappeared and assorted approaches have been put forward as to how the waiting list dilemma should be addressed.

Ideas to combat long waits

There have been various proposals for reducing the length of waiting lists. Examples include raising the amount of short stay and day case surgery to increase throughput, plus booking patients with an admittance date at the time of the outpatient assessment (see Frankel and West, 1993). To an extent both of these approaches are already applied in the NHS. Policy emphasis has been given to setting targets to increase the level of elective surgery performed on a day case basis (see NHS Executive, 1992), and some patients are given an admission date for the procedure at the time the decision to operate was made (see NHS Executive, 1994d). Other ideas include restricting the degree to which the private practice of consultants is allowed to limit their NHS commitments, plus publicising information on waiting lists with 'bottlenecks' or 'black-spots' identified and investigated (see Yates, 1987; Frankel and West, 1993).

Yates (1987) also promoted the idea that patients who have had long waits could receive compensation, as well as suggesting that the study of good practice in the management of waiting lists should be encouraged and when found disseminated to other hospitals. Yet despite the abundance of such options, the Thatcher government still chose to introduce a quasi-market in an attempt to resolve its problems over the NHS, including the public discontent with long waiting lists. Indeed, it seems that the fund-holding element of the 1991 reforms was particularly focused upon that part of the service. The initial list of procedures covered by the scheme included those where the problems of long waiting lists were most acute. Hence the Thatcher government's favourable view of the ways in which markets function seemed to coincide with the belief that at one level of economic analysis the continuation of waiting lists demonstrate the inefficiency of non-market forms of resource allocation (Cullis, 1993).

THE FORMAT OF NHS WAITING LISTS

NHS hospitals operate what West (1993) has called a multi-degree scale of urgency for running waiting lists. Patients awaiting elective surgery should generally be admitted for the procedure in a time-span that accords with their clinical urgency and in particular the necessity that they receive quick treatment in order to maximise the likelihood of a successful therapeutic outcome. For instance, patients requiring surgery for an operable form of cancer are likely to be admitted far more promptly relative to men on the waiting list for vasectomy procedures. That hypothetical example is not meant to minimise the importance of sterilisation services, just to indicate the differences that normally exist between the waits of the seriously ill and patients whose condition is not life threatening.

Even so, waiting times for people with similar conditions are not the same countrywide. They can differ considerably, even at different hospitals in the same area, especially for patients with a non-urgent clinical status. Moreover, because the seriously ill tend to receive relatively swift treatment, it is the long waiting lists and times for non-urgent patients that has been the focus of the political pressure applied on governments. But even when a patient's medical condition is not clinically life threatening, the duration of their wait is still important. Long waits for treatment can severely reduce people's energy, quality and enjoyment of life, a capacity to care for children or elderly relatives, plus prospects for work. In this context elective surgery is desired by the population, unequivocally effective, and deliverable at a comparatively low cost (Frankel, 1993).

Yet beyond these points, what is much less appreciated is the fact that there are three separate categories of the waiting list. These are the elective waiting, elective planned, and elective booked lists (see NHS Executive, 1994d; 1996b). Patients are placed into them according to their medical condition, though it will be shown that the policies of alternative providers in this context are not entirely uniform. Table 4.1 gives the precise breakdown of NHS patients from each category who received operations covered by the fund-holding scheme at the providers featured in this study.

The elective waiting, planned and booked lists

Elective waiting list patients, about 61 per cent of the NHS patients who received fund-holding operations at the four providers over the four years, are placed on the list by a hospital doctor without having their admission planned or booked for a specific time in the future. These are predominantly the patients given a routine clinical urgency.

Elective planned patients, over 9 per cent of the total, are given a date or at least an approximate time of admission for an investigative procedure as a planned sequence of clinical care. They may be called in at regular intervals for a diagnostic episode on some part of the body. For example, people with a family history of rectal or colon cancer might be admitted for a colonoscopy to check that area of their anatomy. Another common operation for such patients is a cystoscopy, an examination of the bladder. This procedure is often performed on a cyclical basis for patients who are in a period of remission or recovering from a malignant disorder of that organ to try and detect at an early stage any recurrence of the disease.

Table 4.1   Operations covered by the fund-holding scheme performed on NHS patients at four providers over four financial years

Provider and year		Elective waiting		Elective booked		Elective planned		Overall list	
		Wait given	Wait not given	Wait given	Wait not given	Wait given	Wait not given	Wait given	Wait not given
Crawley Horsham									
1992-93	No	3207	31	167	6	1	1127	3375	1164
	%	70.7	0.7	3.7	0.1	0.0	24.8	74.4	25.6
1993-94	No	3094	6	124	11	14	1100	3232	1117
	%	71.1	0.1	2.9	0.3	0.3	25.3	74.3	25.7
1994-95	No	3412	13	541	119	1	1000	3954	1132
	%	67.1	0.3	10.6	2.3	0.0	21.6	77.7	22.3
1995-96	No	3278	110	1613	233	43	433	4934	776
	%	57.4	1.9	28.2	4.1	0.8	7.6	86.4	13.6
Total	No	12991	160	2445	369	59	3660	15495	4189
	%	66.0	0.8	12.4	1.9	0.3	18.6	78.7	21.3
Mid Sussex									
1992-93	No	2383	3	645	31	178	0	3206	34
	%	73.5	0.1	19.9	1.0	5.5	-	99.0	1.0
1993-94	No	2088	1	495	25	128	0	2711	26
	%	76.3	<0.1	18.1	0.9	4.7	-	99.1	0.9
1994-95	No	2779	1	419	18	146	0	3344	19
	%	82.6	<0.1	12.5	0.5	4.3	-	99.4	0.6
1995-96	No	2838	2	589	16	168	0	3595	18
	%	78.5	0.1	16.3	0.4	4.6	-	99.5	0.5
Total	No	10088	7	2148	90	620	0	12856	97
	%	77.9	0.1	16.6	0.7	4.8	-	99.3	0.7
Royal West Sussex									
1992-93	No	1247	40	2632	546	174	18	4053	604
	%	26.8	0.9	56.5	11.7	3.7	0.4	87.0	13.0
1993-94	No	1384	169	3539	892	127	30	5050	1091
	%	22.5	2.8	57.6	14.5	2.1	0.5	82.2	17.8
1994-95	No	1839	30	5010	206	124	98	6973	334
	%	25.2	0.4	68.6	2.8	1.7	1.3	95.4	4.6
1995-96	No	3096	11	4209	150	570	178	7875	339
	%	37.7	0.1	51.2	1.8	6.9	2.2	95.9	4.1
Total	No	7566	250	15390	1794	995	324	23951	2368
	%	28.7	0.9	58.5	6.8	3.8	1.2	91.0	9.0
Worthing and Southlands									
1992-93	No	7216	125	1440	40	475	109	9131	274
	%	76.7	1.3	15.3	0.4	5.1	1.2	97.1	2.9
1993-94	No	7576	327	1570	60	672	141	9818	528
	%	73.2	3.2	15.2	0.6	6.5	1.4	94.9	5.1
1994-95	No	7538	329	1852	127	1089	94	10479	550
	%	68.3	3.0	16.8	1.2	9.9	0.9	95.0	5.0
1995-96	No	6936	165	2228	260	1174	126	10338	551
	%	63.7	1.5	20.5	2.4	10.8	1.2	94.9	5.1
Total	No	29266	946	7090	487	3410	470	39766	1903
	%	70.2	2.3	17.0	1.2	8.2	1.1	95.4	4.6
Aggregate		59911	1363	27073	2740	5084	4454	92068	8557
	%	59.5	1.4	26.9	2.7	5.1	4.4	91.5	8.5

Elective booked patients, close to 30 per cent, were given an admission date for the procedure at the time the decision to admit was made. These are commonly the patients given an urgent clinical status and have relatively short waiting times, for which the reason is often confirmed by the diagnoses. The striking observation, particularly at three of the providers, is how commonly one or more of the words malignant, carcinoma or neoplasm appear in the description, even though the category was by no means solely devoted to cancer patients and various other types of diagnoses are found as well.

Table 4.1 shows nearly 98 per cent of the elective waiting list, almost 91 per cent of booked patients, and close to 47 per cent of the planned list at the four providers over the four years had their waits recorded. The lower percentage for the planned list is explained by the apparent policy of the Crawley Horsham provider not to record the waiting times for this category, although there were a few exceptions.

Table 4.1 also implies that whatever policies or behaviour governs the placement of patients into certain categories of the waiting list, such decisions were not absolutely consistent over all four providers. The Royal West Sussex provider placed an unusually high proportion of their patients in the elective booked category with, over the four years, more than 65 per cent of waiting list patients given such a classification. This can be compared to just over 14 per cent at Crawley Horsham, and a little less than 19 per cent at both the Mid Sussex plus the Worthing and Southlands providers. Indeed, whilst cancer patients were routinely placed in the elective booked category at the Royal West Sussex provider, more without such a diagnosis were also placed in this list than at the others. As such, it appears people were classified as elective booked patients at the Royal West Sussex who would not have been at the others.

This tendency is shown even more clearly in figure 4.1. It is unmistakably the Royal West Sussex that stands out as unusual in the context of placing patients into the various categories of the waiting list. It can also be seen that the Mid Sussex plus Worthing and Southlands providers behave almost identically in this respect. The Crawley Horsham provider is not too dissimilar either, although they used the elective planned list more than the others did, even though the waiting times of patients in this category are rarely recorded. Additionally, it can be seen from table 4.1 that Crawley Horsham appeared to alter their policy for 1995/96 regarding the mix of patients they place in both the booked and planned lists. Overall, hospitals seem to reserve a reasonable degree of freedom in deciding which categories of the list to use for certain patients, although the principles outlined earlier certainly did still hold in general. In brief, whilst the elective waiting list primarily contains clinically routine patients, some may be more routine than other cases.

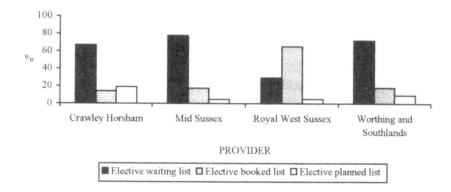

Figure 4.1   **Division of patients per category of the waiting list that received operations covered by the fund-holding scheme at four providers over four financial years from April 1992 to March 1996**

In view of this, a comparison of the waiting times for separate patient groupings may be more valid if it concentrated on those whose waits were most likely to be affected by the type of purchaser representing them. Policy directives stated that admissions for urgent cases must be made on the basis of medical priority alone (see NHS Executive, 1994c; 1996d). The identity of the purchaser should thus have had no relevance in the admission of patients to hospital who were either clinically urgent or required regular investigations. As such, waits for people on the planned and booked lists might not have been driven by whether the surgery was commissioned by a fund-holder or health authority, perhaps unlike the elective waiting list patients. This would still be the general rule regardless of any inconsistencies in the way hospitals divide patients between the three categories. Therefore, a study into the capabilities of alternative purchaser types to shorten waiting times could well be more fruitful when the analysis focuses on patients from the elective waiting list.

For even if there are some differences in the way separate providers categorise patients, patients with a routine clinical status are still liable to be mostly placed in the elective waiting list. In fact it seems logical to conclude that because the Royal West Sussex positioned a greater proportion of its patients in the booked list, out of those who were placed in the elective list there were likely to be proportionally more ultra-routine cases than at the other providers.

Nevertheless, it is still necessary to investigate whether it is correct that the waits of routine status patients were most likely to be dependent on which purchaser represents them. The forthcoming analysis thus covers not only the waiting times of patients from the elective waiting list, but also those on the other categories (plus the overall list).

From this, however, there is a further issue to be addressed regarding the division of patients between the waiting list categories. Black (1998) inferred that waiting time contrasts between fund-holding and other patients could have arisen if the proportion of each population placed in the elective waiting list differed. In response to this, table 4.2 gives the numbers and percentages of all fund-holding and non fund-holding patients from each category of the waiting list who received operations covered by the scheme at the four providers from 1992/93 to 1995/96. The aggregate percentages placed in the elective waiting list from each population were very similar, 61 per cent of non fund-holders and 60.5 per cent of fund-holders. On an individual basis, a larger proportion of non fund-holders than fund-holding patients tended to be placed in this category at Crawley Horsham, and to a lesser extent at Worthing and Southlands. The opposite trend is evident at both the Royal West Sussex provider and to a smaller degree at Mid Sussex.

There are different ways of looking at the possible outcome of placing more patients from one group of practices, fund-holding or not, in the elective waiting list. Firstly, because more routine status patients were placed in it, this might suggest one population might have had a higher proportion of non-urgent cases. This could skew their waits upwards.

The second alternative is that if any randomness between the ratio of urgent and routine cases was not a material factor, more patients of greater clinical urgency from one of the populations could be deliberately placed in the elective waiting list? If so, with the directive that standard waiting times should operate at distinct hospitals for urgent patients (see NHS Executive, 1994e; 1996d), as long as this obligation was met the average waits for the group with more of its number in the elective waiting list could feasibly be lowered. To an extent these suppositions are the antithesis of each other.

Although table 4.2 does not compare the waiting times of fund-holders and non fund-holders, it shall be used later to test the potential impact of differences in the proportion of each population placed in the elective waiting list on the waits of each group.

Table 4.2   **Operations covered by the fund-holding scheme on non fund-holding and fund-holding patients from each category of the NHS waiting list at four providers over four financial years**

Provider and year	Non fund-holding patients						Fund-holding patients					
	Waiting		Booked		Planned		Waiting		Booked		Planned	
	No	%	No	%	No	%	No	%	No	%	No	%
Crawley Horsham												
1992-93	2677	73.1	120	3.3	866	23.6	561	64.0	53	6.1	262	29.9
1993-94	2071	71.7	82	2.8	735	25.5	1029	70.4	53	3.6	379	25.9
1994-95	1873	68.5	346	12.7	515	18.8	1552	66.0	314	12.4	486	19.2
1995-96	1953	61.7	937	29.6	277	8.7	1435	56.4	909	35.7	199	7.8
Total	8574	68.9	1485	11.9	2393	19.2	4577	63.3	1329	18.4	1326	18.3
Mid Sussex												
1992-93	1791	72.9	537	21.9	129	5.3	595	76.0	139	17.8	49	6.3
1993-94	1474	78.7	319	17.0	81	4.3	615	71.3	201	23.3	47	5.4
1994-95	1667	81.2	305	14.9	80	3.9	1113	84.9	132	10.1	66	5.0
1995-96	1739	78.7	375	17.0	97	4.4	1101	78.5	230	16.4	71	5.1
Total	6671	77.6	1536	17.9	387	4.5	3424	78.6	702	16.1	233	5.3
Royal West Sussex												
1992-93	1215	27.6	3005	68.2	184	4.2	72	28.5	173	68.4	8	3.2
1993-94	1184	24.3	3567	73.1	129	2.6	369	29.3	864	68.5	28	2.2
1994-95	1295	24.9	3747	71.9	166	3.2	574	27.3	1469	70.0	56	2.7
1995-96	1759	38.8	2366	52.2	405	8.9	1348	36.6	1993	54.1	343	9.3
Total	5453	28.7	12685	66.7	884	4.6	2363	32.4	4499	61.7	435	6.0
Worthing and Southlands												
1992-93	6675	78.1	1347	15.8	524	6.1	666	77.5	133	15.5	60	7.0
1993-94	6485	76.5	1333	15.7	660	7.8	1418	75.9	297	15.9	153	8.2
1994-95	5173	71.7	1276	17.7	765	10.6	2694	70.6	703	18.4	418	11.0
1995-96	4337	64.3	1570	23.3	835	12.4	2764	66.7	918	22.1	465	11.2
Total	22670	73.2	5526	17.8	2784	9.0	7542	70.6	2051	19.2	1096	10.3
Aggregate	43368	61.0	21232	29.9	6448	9.1	17906	60.5	8581	29.0	3090	10.4

The changing status of some patients

There is another unavoidable complication to the impending comparison. As the number of practices joining the fund-holding scheme grew over the years, some people will have started their wait as a patient of a non fund-holding practice but actually had the operation after it joined the scheme. Therefore, a comparison based on the status of patients' practices at the time of the operation may lead to those people on the waiting list for a very long period before their GP practice joined the scheme having their entire wait counted towards the average for fund-holding patients. A couple of authentic examples from the database, where the patients' waiting times far exceeded the averages for the providers (and for one the patient's charter target), are now given to show the potential effect of this and why the avoidance of such pitfalls looks important.

A patient from a non fund-holding practice joined the elective waiting list of one of the providers on 3 October 1991. The practice entered the scheme on 1 April 1993, and the patient was admitted for the operation on 2 April 1993, performed on a day case basis the same day. Out of a recorded waiting time of 547 days, this patient was on the list as a non fund-holding patient for 545 days (99.6 per cent) and as a fund-holder for 2 days (0.4 per cent). Another patient of a non fund-holding practice joined the elective waiting list on 18 October 1990. This practice joined the fund-holding scheme on 1 April 1993 and the patient was eventually admitted for the procedure on 13 August 1993. Hence for a wait totalling 1,030 days, 895 were spent as a non fund-holding patient and only 135 as a fund-holder. Some 87 per cent of the waiting time thus elapsed whilst a non fund-holding patient and 13 per cent as a fund-holder.

Obviously for the first example where the patient was called in on the practice's second day in the scheme and the admission would have been arranged prior to 1 April 1993, it could be that this was too quick for a new fund-holder to influence it themselves. It may equally be possible that because the practice was soon to join the scheme and would no longer be reliant on the health authority contract, they made the provider aware of their intention to move the patient elsewhere in order to encourage the hospital to act rapidly. Or perhaps the practice had not been in contact about the patient, but as the provider knew they were joining the scheme they effected the admission to avoid the patient being moved to a competitor without warning. Whatever happened in this or the other case, there are many other examples that would have had similar effects. The study might thus be enhanced by concentrating on those patients registered with practices that did not change their status during the course of the wait.

Table 4.3 provides data for NHS patients from the elective waiting list whose practice did change their status during the wait. It gives the number of days spent on the list as a non fund-holding patient (the period prior to their practice joining the scheme), and as a fund-holding patient (the time after the entry of their practices into the scheme). It can be seen that for nearly 2,500 such patients, close to 59 per cent of their total waiting time occurred before their practices became fund-holders and a little over 41 per cent after this event. The total for each provider over the four years is also represented by figure 4.2, in which every bar represents the percentages detailed in the rows labelled 'total' for each provider in table 4.3.

Table 4.3   Time on elective waiting list as a non fund-holder (before their practice joined the fund-holding scheme) and fund-holder (after their practice joined the fund-holding scheme) by NHS patients whose practices joined the scheme during the course of the wait

Provider and year	No	Wait as non fund-holder Days	%	Wait as fund-holder Days	%	Total days
Crawley Horsham						
1992-93	16	2337	29.0	5719	71.0	8056
1993-94	172	28038	65.2	14993	34.8	43031
1994-95	231	42752	56.9	32429	43.1	75181
1995-96	56	7543	33.1	15260	66.9	22803
Total	475	80670	54.1	68401	45.9	149071
Mid Sussex						
1992-93	123	15439	65.2	8243	34.8	23682
1993-94	41	5489	69.8	2378	30.2	7867
1994-95	133	20413	70.1	8723	29.9	29136
1995-96	26	3442	41.1	4930	58.9	8372
Total	323	44783	64.8	24274	35.2	69057
Royal West Sussex						
1992-93	44	11587	62.8	6863	37.2	18450
1993-94	154	36650	70.4	15439	29.6	52089
1994-95	94	16089	49.0	16768	51.0	32857
1995-96	296	62028	65.1	33212	34.9	95240
Total	588	126354	63.6	72282	36.4	198636
Worthing and Southlands						
1992-93	205	28807	64.0	16219	36.0	45026
1993-94	324	44102	55.9	34848	44.1	78950
1994-95	433	55742	57.8	40699	42.2	96441
1995-96	121	9803	34.4	18674	65.6	28477
Total	1083	138454	55.6	110440	44.4	248894
Aggregate	2469	390261	58.6	275397	41.4	665658

Both table 4.3 and figure 4.2 clearly indicate that patients generally spent more time on the elective waiting list before their practice acquired fund-holding status than after it. This statistic alone suggests fund-holding patients may well have tended to have shorter waits than non fund-holders did. It also means that any comparison between fund-holding and non fund-holding patients which is calculated according to the status of their general practices at the time of the operation could distort the analysis by falsely inflating the waiting times of fund-holders. So in the first instance, for the waiting time comparison that follows, patients whose practice changed their status (joined the fund-holding scheme) during the course of their wait are excluded from the analyses.

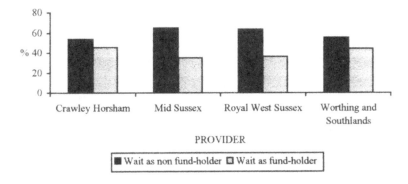

Figure 4.2   Split in the waits of NHS elective waiting list patients from April 1992 to March 1996 whose general practice acquired fund-holding status during the course of their wait

WAITING TIME COMPARISON

Table 4.4 shows the results of a comparison between the waiting times of patients on the elective waiting list from fund-holding and other practices after confining the analysis to those registered with GPs who did not alter their status during the wait. The ANOVA tests show fund-holders had significantly shorter waits in all sixteen cases. As mentioned in the third chapter, the table gives the mean and median waits of each group. Even though the distribution of waiting times tended to be skewed within the populations, the only case where the shorter mean of fund-holders did not match the relationship between the medians was for Worthing and Southlands in 1995/96. Here the mean wait of fund-holders was shorter than for the non fund-holders, but they had the same median (though it should still be noted that ANOVA tests use the waits of each individual patient).

It is also necessary to address Black's (1998) idea that the proportion of each population placed in the elective waiting list could determine any differences in their waits. For this to be the case (meaning either of the two options outlined earlier is feasible – that the preponderance of one population in the elective waiting list either lengthens or shortens their waiting times), one or other of the following circumstances would be expected. In cases where a greater proportion of non fund-holders had been placed in the elective waiting list than fund-holders, their waits relative to the fund-holders should consistently either be increased or decreased. If non fund-holders consistently had longer waits regardless of whether there was proportionately more or less of them in the elective waiting list than fund-holding patients, Black's (1998) hypothesis would no longer appear sustainable.

Table 4.4   Waiting times of non fund-holding and fund-holding patients on the NHS elective waiting list for operations covered by the fund-holding scheme at four providers over four financial years

Provider and year	Non fund-holding patients			Fund-holding patients			ANOVA
	Median	Mean	No	Median	Mean	No	P-value
Crawley Horsham							
1992-93	69.0	148.4	2655	62.0	111.8	536	<0.0001
1993-94	167.0	214.2	2067	65.0	129.2	855	<0.0001
1994-95	132.0	193.9	1865	58.0	119.1	1316	<0.0001
1995-96	168.0	194.6	1897	115.0	162.9	1325	<0.0001
Movement in mean	+46.2 days (+31.1%)			+51.4 days (+46.0%)			
Mid Sussex							
1992-93	54.0	94.6	1788	44.0	61.5	472	<0.0001
1993-94	62.0	112.9	1473	43.0	68.9	574	<0.0001
1994-95	62.0	118.3	1666	44.5	80.3	980	<0.0001
1995-96	59.0	125.8	1737	47.0	83.4	1075	<0.0001
Movement in mean	+31.2 days (+33.0%)			+21.9 days (+35.6%)			
Royal West Sussex							
1992-93	176.0	262.8	1179	61.0	92.9	24	0.0002
1993-94	245.0	270.4	1037	105.0	153.3	193	<0.0001
1994-95	284.0	282.0	1279	126.0	170.7	466	<0.0001
1995-96	153.0	205.8	1751	65.0	108.7	1049	<0.0001
Movement in mean	-57.0 days (-21.7%)			+15.8 days (+17.0%)			
Worthing and Southlands							
1992-93	74.0	129.1	6555	48.0	70.0	456	<0.0001
1993-94	83.0	134.4	6221	59.0	96.6	1031	<0.0001
1994-95	80.0	129.6	4942	62.0	103.7	2163	<0.0001
1995-96	83.0	136.1	4228	83.0	127.7	2587	0.0075
Movement in mean	+7.0 days (+5.4%)			+57.7 days (+82.4%)			

When the results from tables 4.2 and 4.4 are considered together, a trend substantiating either of the two possibilities just outlined is not revealed.   In cases where a greater share of fund-holders or non fund-holders was placed in the elective waiting list, either way it was the latter group that had the longer waits.   For example, proportionately more non fund-holding patients than fund-holders were in the elective waiting list at Crawley Horsham in 1992/93.   Non fund-holding patients at this provider that year had longer waits relative to the fund-holders.   At the Royal West Sussex provider in 1993/94, a higher percentage of fund-holders were admitted from the elective waiting list than was the case with non fund-holding patients. Yet the fund-holders again enjoyed shorter average waiting times.

Although just two contradictory cases have been itemised here, there are others that could have been used. This might indicate, beyond the basic understanding that more routine status patients are placed in the elective waiting list, the division of patients at the margins into separate categories had at most a somewhat peripheral impact on average waits. There may consequently be far more important factors that determined the waits of fund-holders and non fund-holders. In sum, the lack of any consistent link between the relative length of waiting times with the proportion of a population placed in the elective waiting list suggests that Black's (1998) suspicion was something of a 'red herring'.

Table 4.4 also shows that relatively nearby hospitals can have dissimilar waiting times. For example, waits are shorter at Mid Sussex than at the Royal West Sussex, although if patients in the elective waiting list at the latter are generally more routine than usual this may explain the discrepancy. Also, where non fund-holders' waits increased over the four years this was not associated with falling waits for fund-holders during the period. This may say something about another issue, the impact of the scheme on services for patients of non fund-holding practices. The search for evidence with regards to the fund-holding scheme having either a negative or positive effect on the waiting times of non fund-holding patients is discussed in the next section.

The zero-sum effect: trends in waiting times

Suggestions have been made that improvements in services to fund-holding patients acted as a catalyst for enhancing those received by non fund-holders in the same locality (see Leese and Drummond, 1993; NHS Executive, 1995e). Such commentators would see the shorter waiting times of fund-holding patients as a general efficiency improvement forced on hospitals by competitive pressures, and this was likely to 'drag down' the waits of non fund-holders also. With improvements filtering through to non fund-holders, this could have represented a 'no loser' situation as efficiency gains would be shared.

The opposing claim is that fund-holders may have secured better access to services at a direct cost to people registered with practices outside the scheme (see Fisher, A., 1993). The suspicion here is that non fund-holders would have waited longer than they might otherwise had done to accommodate the shorter waits of fund-holders. Also, there is a third possibility. The shorter waiting times of fund-holders could have had no influence on the waits of non fund-holders, either way. Perhaps it was excess hospital capacity being used. Whatever option is true, hard evidence on this question has not been available (Dixon and Glennerster, 1995). For that reason, this issue deserves consideration here.

Regarding the point of Fisher, A. (1993), cited above, that quicker access to services for fund-holders could have been at the expense of non fund-holding patients, what would be expected if fund-holders' shorter waits were directly linked to longer waiting times for other patients? Imagine the scenario where a fictitious hospital before the introduction of fund-holding operated on exactly 5,000 patients a year, a number representing its full capacity, each patient had the same clinical urgency, and these characteristics remained unchanged with the passing of time. During this twelve months consultants made no differentiation between clients for any other reason. Every single patient had a waiting time of 150 days. Together, patients receiving an operation that year therefore waited 750,000 days in total.

The next year another 5,000 patients had surgery but 500 of them, 10 per cent, were now registered with a fund-holding GP. Such practices managed to reduce the waiting times of their patients to 90 days, quite realistic considering some of the contrasts in table 4.4. Because the hospital has a constant capacity, the aggregate 750,000 days became spread unevenly between the two groups. The fund-holders waited a total of 45,000 days, but to accommodate this the 4,500 non fund-holders had their waiting times extended to nearly 157 days to make up the other 705,000 days. The next year practices covering a further 500 patients joined the scheme, and with the same number of first wavers they too had their waits lowered to 90 days. This led to the remaining 4,000 non fund-holders having their waits raised to 165 days, bringing the gross total to 750,000 days.

Precisely the same trend occurred in the following two years when a further 500 patients of the hospital's caseload were registered with fund-holders in each, and they also all had their waits reduced to 90 days. In year three, this meant the remaining 3,500 non fund-holders having their waiting times raised to almost 176 days to accommodate the fall for the additional fund-holders. In year four the continuing 3,000 non fund-holders had their waits increased to 190 days to oblige 2,000 fund-holders all having waits of 90 days. In every year for this hypothetical case, the 5,000 patients together waited 750,000 days.

This example produces the graph shown in figure 4.3. As each year goes by the waiting times of the remaining non fund-holding patients, whose number falls by 500 per year, rises to serve the increasing number (also 500 per year) of fund-holders enjoying shorter waits of 90 days each. Hence if shorter waits for fund-holders was part of a zero-sum effect where the waiting times of non fund-holders had to rise to accommodate this, graphs would show a widening gap between the lines representing the waits of the two populations as more practices enter the scheme. This gap would be even more obvious if fund-holders' waits fell as more practices join the scheme, rather than remain constant.

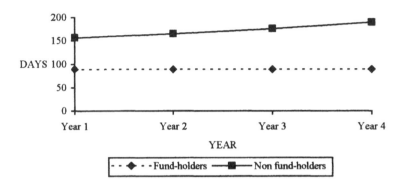

Figure 4.3   Trend in mean waits at a fictitious provider performing 5000 operations per year with an aggregate waiting time of 750000 days in each, if the number of fund-holders grew by 500 per year and all had a wait of 90 days

Figures 4.4 to 4.7, showing the genuine trends in waiting times at the four providers, indicate that reality bears little resemblance to the hypothetical example in figure 4.3. For instance, figure 4.4 shows that at Crawley Horsham the initial difference in the waits of the two populations widened then shrank. At Worthing and Southlands there was a gradual movement towards equality (figure 4.7). Moreover, figures 4.5 and 4.6 do not suggest the waits of the populations widened at Mid Sussex and the Royal West Sussex. In fact the trends for both sets of patients at each of these providers look fairly similar. At the Royal West Sussex (where the fund-holding sub-sample was shown by table 4.4 to be very small in 1992/93), the gap representing the waits of each group grew narrower then shifted downwards in 1995/96. Perhaps this could back the idea that efficiency improvements may have filtered through to non fund-holders?

Moreover, the correlation coefficient (Pearson's r) for the actual trends in waiting times for non fund-holding and fund-holding patients is also given in figures 4.4 to 4.7. The point to be taken into account for this statistic is that if the waits for the two populations were negatively correlated in such a way that non fund-holders' waiting times increased as the waits of fund-holding patients fell, the Pearson's *r* statistic would be a negative number. If the Pearson's *r* statistic is a positive number, the waits of the two groups are positively correlated (to some extent), and the trends in their waiting times move in a broadly similar direction.

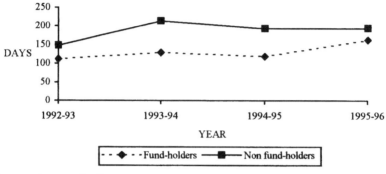

Pearson's r = +0.45

Figure 4.4   Trend in mean waiting times at the Crawley Horsham provider for patients on the elective waiting list whose practices' status (fund-holding or not) did not alter during the course of the wait

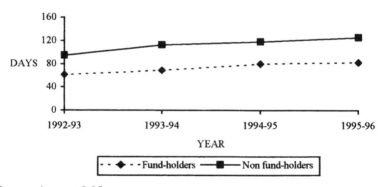

Pearson's r = +0.95

Figure 4.5   Trend in mean waiting time at the Mid Sussex provider for patients on the elective waiting list whose practices' status (fund-holding or not) did not alter during the course of the wait

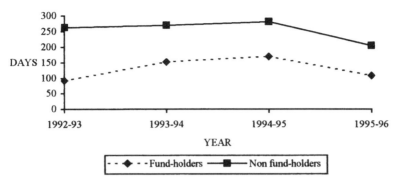

Pearson's r = +0.59

Figure 4.6 **Trend in mean waiting times at the Royal West Sussex provider for patients on the elective waiting list whose practices' status (fund-holding or not) did not alter during the course of the wait**

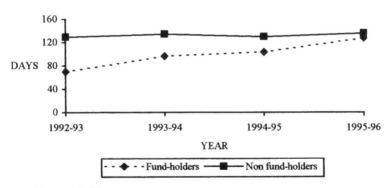

Pearson's r = +0.74

Figure 4.7 **Trend in mean waiting times at the Worthing and Southlands provider for patients on the elective waiting list whose practices' status (fund-holding or not) did not alter during the course of the wait**

Further, the nearer Pearson's *r* is to ±1.00, the more extreme is the correlation (either negative or positive) in the relationship between the two groups' waits (a value of 0.00 for Pearson's *r* would indicate that no linear relationship exists in their waiting times). From this, the fact that the actual Pearson's *r* statistic for all cases is a positive number (see figures 4.4 to

4.7) strongly indicates that the waits of both groups were positively, not negatively, correlated at each provider, and extremely so at Mid Sussex.

In sum, the trends in waiting times for each population, as shown in tables 4.4 to 4.7, do little to suggest that the shorter waits of fund-holders were achieved at the expense of other patients. The waiting times of non fund-holders do not seem to rise as those for fund-holders fall, or indeed vice versa. Nevertheless, it could still be over ambitious to claim the above evidence provides firm proof about the zero-sum effect. Any judgement that the apparent gradual narrowing of the gap in waits of each population at Crawley Horsham plus Worthing and Southlands shows efficiency improvements may be filtering through to non fund-holders should not be accepted without caution. But even with this qualification, the point that the trends do not match what would be expected if the waits of the two groups were negatively correlated does remain intact. In short, there is no clear evidence of a zero-sum effect.

Comparisons by specialty

However, to date the comparisons between the waits of fund-holders and other patients in table 4.4 have taken the elective waiting list as a single entity, thus failing to reveal the position at the level of individual major departments. Tables 4.5 to 4.8 now rectify this omission. Although a comparison is not made for the specific minor specialties, the data for those departments are included in the analyses for the overall elective waiting list at a provider for a year.

Table 4.5 shows that at Crawley Horsham there were significant differences between the waiting times of fund-holding and health authority patients for all four years in the general surgery department. Likewise, in three out of four years for gynaecology, and two out of four in the orthopaedic plus ear nose and throat departments. In fact for the 1993/94 financial year there was a significant difference within all four specialties. Yet the overall variance in 1993/94 was less than for the following year, even though the difference for orthopaedics in 1994/95 was not significant. It is also noticeable that for the minor specialties of general and geriatric medicine, waiting times were far shorter than in the bigger departments.

Table 4.6 confirms that at Mid Sussex the differences were significant for all four years in the general surgery, orthopaedic and gynaecology departments, in two out of four cases for urology, but only once in the ear nose and throat specialty. At Mid Sussex also there were consistently shorter waiting times for procedures within the general medicine department, relative to the major specialties. It is noticeable that Mid Sussex is the only provider in West Sussex that performed a service in the clinical field of neurosurgery. With the exception of 1995/96, waiting times in that department were also lower than for the major specialties.

Table 4.5 **Waiting times (in days) at the Crawley Horsham provider for operations covered by the fund-holding scheme on non fund-holding and fund-holding patients from the elective waiting list who spent the entire duration of the wait in one of these groups**

Year and specialty	Non fund-holding patients			Fund-holding patients			ANOVA
	Median	Mean	No	Median	Mean	No	P-value
1992-93							
General surgery	61.0	149.1	830	41.0	100.9	181	0.0004
Orthopaedics	238.5	264.1	356	104.0	158.2	50	0.0006
Ear nose and throat	101.0	158.1	735	96.0	137.2	190	0.0873
Oral surgery	84.0	81.1	15	97.0	97.7	3	-
General medicine	45.0	51.5	12	44.5	44.5	2	-
Geriatric medicine	4.0	4.0	1	-	-	0	-
Gynaecology	44.0	82.6	706	51.5	66.6	110	0.1323
TOTAL	69.0	148.4	2655	62.0	111.8	536	<0.0001
1993-94							
General surgery	149.5	210.3	706	62.0	118.3	320	<0.0001
Orthopaedics	403.0	333.6	287	169.5	197.9	68	<0.0001
Ear nose and throat	229.0	240.6	503	107.5	172.6	252	<0.0001
Oral surgery	175.0	175.0	1	-	-	0	-
General medicine	13.5	14.7	18	8.0	9.7	4	-
Geriatric medicine	8.0	18.4	28	8.0	11.9	14	-
Gynaecology	76.0	146.3	524	51.0	78.6	197	<0.0001
TOTAL	167.0	214.2	2067	65.0	129.2	855	<0.0001
1994-95							
General surgery	148.0	198.3	554	64.0	130.6	420	<0.0001
Orthopaedics	248.0	267.1	370	236.0	246.5	141	0.2756
Ear nose and throat	154.5	214.6	482	89.0	132.8	367	<0.0001
General medicine	15.0	17.1	51	15.0	20.3	46	-
Geriatric medicine	21.0	20.6	61	21.0	19.9	80	-
Gynaecology	72.0	136.7	347	43.0	60.6	262	<0.0001
TOTAL	132.0	193.9	1865	58.0	119.1	1316	<0.0001
1995-96							
General surgery	186.0	202.0	497	131.0	170.9	387	0.0010
Orthopaedics	229.5	223.0	400	190.0	217.8	225	0.6700
Ear nose and throat	160.0	192.1	530	142.0	187.6	453	0.6104
Oral surgery	119.0	119.0	2	-	-	0	-
General medicine	14.5	22.1	84	14.0	17.7	61	-
Geriatric medicine	15.0	17.9	83	22.0	21.8	65	-
Gynaecology	245.0	246.5	301	68.0	99.1	134	<0.0001
TOTAL	168.0	194.6	1897	115.0	162.9	1325	<0.0001

Table 4.6   Waiting times (in days) at the Mid Sussex provider for operations covered by the fund-holding scheme on non fund-holding and fund-holding patients from the elective waiting list who spent the entire duration of the wait in one of these groups

| Year and specialty | Non fund-holding patients | | | Fund-holding patients | | | ANOVA |
	Median	Mean	No	Median	Mean	No	P-value
1992-93							
General surgery	47.0	94.2	552	35.0	51.5	126	<0.0001
Urology	60.5	91.3	186	54.5	63.8	58	0.0129
Orthopaedics	104.5	178.0	214	76.5	103.4	48	0.0038
Ear nose and throat	171.0	154.6	124	146.0	142.6	25	0.4929
Oral surgery	56.0	56.0	1	-	-	0	-
Neurosurgery	18.0	29.3	41	21.0	24.4	5	-
General medicine	37.0	55.8	290	36.0	48.2	121	-
Gynaecology	49.0	67.0	380	39.0	48.8	89	0.0037
TOTAL	54.0	94.6	1788	44.0	61.5	472	<0.0001
1993-94							
General surgery	56.0	108.5	432	44.5	73.2	126	0.0035
Urology	42.0	71.9	85	49.0	61.6	39	0.4244
Orthopaedics	209.0	242.4	225	93.0	110.7	88	<0.0001
Ear nose and throat	224.0	226.6	78	169.0	173.2	33	0.0468
Neurosurgery	37.5	50.3	22	24.0	33.0	13	-
General medicine	29.0	44.0	347	24.5	34.3	148	-
Gynaecology	69.5	86.8	284	43.0	54.9	127	<0.0001
TOTAL	62.0	112.9	1473	43.0	68.9	574	<0.0001
1994-95							
General surgery	75.0	142.6	413	54.0	109.3	195	0.0087
Urology	55.0	90.3	160	32.0	55.6	97	0.0017
Orthopaedics	147.0	175.7	275	118.0	126.5	171	<0.0001
Ear nose and throat	110.5	179.4	90	90.0	157.4	39	0.4805
Oral surgery	140.0	140.0	2	-	-	0	-
Neurosurgery	52.5	88.9	28	72.5	71.6	16	-
Paediatric surgery	220.5	237.4	36	325.5	312.5	4	-
Pain relief	1.0	1.0	1	-	-	0	-
General medicine	30.5	40.0	358	25.5	30.2	258	-
Gynaecology	74.5	111.0	303	53.5	70.5	200	<0.0001
TOTAL	62.0	118.3	1666	44.5	80.3	980	<0.0001
1995-96							
General surgery	60.0	117.5	408	49.0	86.5	246	0.0011
Urology	39.0	69.5	137	38.0	64.6	86	0.6774
Orthopaedics	186.0	205.3	385	99.5	137.5	206	<0.0001
Ear nose and throat	196.0	226.2	137	112.5	187.4	50	0.1432
Oral surgery	56.0	56.0	1	-	-	0	-
Neurosurgery	109.0	168.6	41	66.0	118.2	30	-
Paediatric surgery	19.5	94.4	10	110.5	110.5	2	-
Pain relief	6.0	6.0	1	6.0	6.0	2	-
General medicine	24.0	33.4	346	24.0	31.9	267	-
Gynaecology	80.0	116.4	271	50.0	69.1	186	<0.0001
TOTAL	59.0	125.8	1737	47.0	83.4	1075	<0.0001

Table 4.7   Waiting times (in days) at the Royal West Sussex provider for operations covered by the fund-holding scheme on non fund-holding and fund-holding patients from the elective waiting list who spent the entire duration of the wait in one of these groups

Year and specialty	Non fund-holding patients Median	Mean	No	Fund-holding patients Median	Mean	No	ANOVA P-value
1992-93							
General surgery	199.0	270.5	324	140.0	152.6	5	0.2036
Urology	33.0	41.1	66	36.0	43.3	7	0.2160
Orthopaedics	291.0	337.3	456	53.5	70.8	4	0.6563
Ophthalmology	174.0	189.0	19	-	-	0	-
Oral surgery	78.0	142.8	6	-	-	0	-
Pain relief	70.0	113.4	7	-	-	0	-
General medicine	425.0	425.0	1	-	-	0	-
Gynaecology	118.0	200.1	300	85.0	110.1	8	0.1764
TOTAL	176.0	262.8	1179	61.0	92.9	24	0.0002
1993-94							
General surgery	306.0	291.5	301	108.0	162.2	44	<0.0001
Urology	53.0	85.6	181	63.0	68.4	51	0.2042
Orthopaedics	391.0	342.7	438	182.5	218.8	70	<0.0001
Oral surgery	111.0	146.8	5	-	-	0	-
Pain relief	125.0	125.0	1	-	-	0	-
Gynaecology	163.0	235.7	111	79.0	130.4	28	0.0052
TOTAL	245.0	270.4	1037	121.0	153.3	193	<0.0001
1994-95							
General surgery	306.0	287.2	364	164.0	211.9	92	0.0002
Urology	112.0	161.1	249	71.0	89.1	105	<0.0001
Orthopaedics	412.0	362.5	433	179.0	204.7	169	<0.0001
Oral surgery	297.0	273.1	8	132.5	192.0	4	-
Pain relief	139.0	119.0	5	132.5	132.5	2	-
Gynaecology	239.5	255.9	220	122.0	160.4	94	<0.0001
TOTAL	284.0	282.0	1279	126.0	170.7	466	<0.0001
1995-96							
General surgery	236.0	227.9	367	80.0	110.8	222	<0.0001
Urology	67.0	115.5	258	62.5	81.7	156	0.0007
Orthopaedics	335.0	307.8	569	153.0	195.4	242	<0.0001
Oral surgery	88.5	109.6	14	108.0	104.5	4	-
Pain relief	105.5	112.4	22	85.0	126.1	10	-
General medicine	44.5	58.6	278	35.0	39.7	247	-
Gynaecology	208.0	212.2	243	81.0	106.6	168	<0.0001
TOTAL	153.0	205.8	1751	65.0	108.7	1049	<0.0001

Table 4.7 shows differences were significant at the Royal West Sussex in three of four cases for general surgery, orthopaedics plus gynaecology, and in two for urology. Apart from a single patient who may have been categorised incorrectly in 1992/93, cases for general medicine were only covered by the elective waiting list in 1995/96. At this provider also,

general medicine patients had shorter waits than did those in the major specialties.

Table 4.8   Waiting times (in days) at the Worthing and Southlands provider for operations covered by the fund-holding scheme on non fund-holding and fund-holding patients from the elective waiting list who spent the entire duration of the wait in one of these groups

Year and specialty	Non fund-holding patients			Fund-holding patients			ANOVA
	Median	Mean	No	Median	Mean	No	P-value
1992-93							
General surgery	47.0	72.5	1601	31.5	52.0	130	0.0037
Urology	48.0	78.1	663	48.0	52.9	62	0.0767
Orthopaedics	161.0	235.4	849	63.0	76.4	37	<0.0001
Ear nose and throat	147.0	165.9	503	90.0	123.4	25	0.0827
Ophthalmology	126.0	148.1	1445	79.5	98.8	86	0.0001
Oral surgery	50.0	78.3	58	48.0	58.4	7	-
General medicine	17.0	20.8	212	20.0	20.9	30	-
Gynaecology	107.0	140.6	1224	52.0	81.7	79	<0.0001
TOTAL	74.0	129.1	6555	48.0	70.0	456	<0.0001
1993-94							
General surgery	76.0	119.8	1620	50.0	89.7	255	0.0001
Urology	56.0	107.7	846	49.0	74.4	175	0.0012
Orthopaedics	159.0	214.3	808	105.0	124.5	114	<0.0001
Ear nose and throat	220.0	213.8	509	101.0	153.7	48	0.0066
Ophthalmology	122.0	131.0	1193	91.5	111.1	238	0.0011
Oral surgery	59.0	80.0	5	78.0	78.0	1	-
General medicine	23.0	32.1	175	22.0	32.9	39	-
Gynaecology	73.0	100.2	1065	59.0	89.0	161	0.1036
TOTAL	83.0	134.4	6221	59.0	96.6	1031	<0.0001
1994-95							
General surgery	74.0	107.8	1117	58.0	89.2	477	0.0003
Urology	41.0	67.1	870	41.0	59.4	467	0.0832
Orthopaedics	146.0	202.3	802	103.5	147.0	284	<0.0001
Ear nose and throat	151.0	170.3	360	120.5	125.6	150	0.0001
Ophthalmology	141.0	159.0	984	116.0	147.5	402	0.0720
Oral surgery	94.5	94.5	2	-	-	0	-
General medicine	72.5	72.5	2	-	-	0	-
Gynaecology	70.0	100.9	805	61.0	89.2	383	0.0282
TOTAL	80.0	129.6	4942	62.0	103.7	2163	<0.0001
1995-96							
General surgery	84.0	130.6	846	87.0	127.7	487	0.6683
Urology	48.0	84.6	937	50.0	85.4	576	0.8797
Orthopaedics	173.0	222.6	747	149.0	189.8	415	0.0014
Ear nose and throat	135.5	184.6	296	129.0	175.4	179	0.5020
Ophthalmology	120.5	132.3	770	122.0	132.3	503	0.9935
Pain relief	7.0	7.0	1	-	-	0	-
General medicine	302.0	309.0	2	-	-	0	-
Gynaecology	79.0	99.2	629	74.0	99.2	427	0.9968
TOTAL	83.0	136.1	4228	83.0	127.7	2587	0.0075

At Worthing and Southlands, table 4.8 shows that differences were significant in all four years for the orthopaedic department, in three out of four for general surgery, in two out of four years for ophthalmology, gynaecology, plus ear nose and throat, then in only one for urology. Apart from a few cases in the last two of the four years, patients for general medicine were only categorised in the elective waiting list during 1992/93 and 1993/94.

As a general rule (although there were exceptions), the waiting times of patients in the urology departments at three of the four units (the Mid Sussex, Royal West Sussex, plus Worthing and Southlands providers) were lower than in the other major specialties. The reason why Crawley Horsham is excluded from this observation is the fact that they have no separate urology department.

It seems clear from the above tables that NHS patients at the four providers had the length of their waiting times determined to a significant extent by the type of purchaser commissioning the surgery on their behalf. In sum, patients of fund-holding practices had significantly shorter average waiting times than those registered with other GPs. In fact some of the differences are so large they would have remained statistically significant even if an alpha level had been used that produced a higher confidence level than 95 per cent. Nevertheless, this in itself is the most commonly used confidence level in social research (see Healey, 1996) and cannot reasonably be called over-cautious.

Links to other research

The finding of clear disparities in the waiting times of fund-holding and non fund-holding patients differ from judgements expressed by the Audit Commission (1996a). In a short passage on waiting times the point was made that although seasonal variations could have existed, these became evened out over the whole year and the waits of fund-holding and non fund-holding patients were usually similar on an overall basis. However, information elicited via personal communication with an author of this report explained how this verdict was reached, and doubts concerning the validity of the conclusion are provoked for three reasons.

First, the data used related to just one hospital over a single year, hardly an exceptionally comprehensive investigation. Second, the analysis included all NHS patients who had fund-holding operations at the hospital that year, so combined all three categories of the waiting list. As discussed earlier, if waiting times for planned and booked patients were not dependent on the purchaser representing them then this could tend to equalise differences between patients on the elective waiting list (despite the larger population). Third, the average waits of fund-holding and non fund-holding patients were calculated in accordance with the status of their practice, fund-holding or not, at the time of the operation. If that leads to counting the waits of patients who spent a long period on the list before their practice entered the scheme towards the average waiting times of fund-holders, this could corrupt the analysis (also highlighted previously).

To clarify the possible impact of these factors, tables 4.9 to 4.12 compare the waits of fund-holding and non fund-holding patients using precisely the same methodology as that adopted by the Audit Commission (1996a). Instead of there being significantly shorter waiting times for fund-holding patients at each provider in all years, the null hypothesis was not rejected in six out of sixteen computations. It therefore seems feasible that the Audit Commission's (1996a) approach might have hidden significant differences in the waiting times of patients on the elective waiting list. However, it must also be noted that in ten cases out of sixteen, fund-holding patients still had significantly shorter waits.

Tables 4.9 to 4.12 also seem to confirm that NHS hospitals did admit clinically urgent patients, defined as those on the elective booked list, within fairly short time-scales regardless of whether the procedure was commissioned by a GP fund-holder or health authority. According to the mean, such patients were usually admitted within two or three weeks at Worthing and Southlands, then after about one month at Mid Sussex plus Crawley Horsham (although at the latter non fund-holders did have to wait some three months in 1993/94). Booked patients generally had a wait of something around the two-month mark at the Royal West Sussex. This slightly longer average conforms to the idea, discussed earlier, that rather more patients with a less serious clinical urgency are placed in the booked list here than at the others.

Moreover, there is only one significant difference in waiting times between booked fund-holding and non fund-holding patients out of the sixteen cases. This was at the Crawley Horsham provider in 1995/96, where non fund-holders had the shorter waits. As such, the hypothesis that there is less variation between urgent patients than there is between routine patients is correct, and the directive that common waiting lists should have existed for urgent cases (see NHS Executive 1994e; 1996d) appears satisfied.

Tables 4.9 to 4.12 also indicate that patients requiring regular investigations, namely those on the elective planned list, do not appear to have the length of their waiting times determined by the purchaser type commissioning their services either. Again there was only one statistically significant difference, this time out of fourteen cases as comparisons were not possible for the Crawley Horsham provider in a couple of the years since no patients in one of the two populations had their waits recorded. Moreover, the numbers where waiting times were available for this provider in the other two years were also very low. The significant difference for the planned category occurred at the Mid Sussex provider in 1993/94 where fund-holding patients benefited from the shorter waits. From this, the general evenness between the waits of patients on the planned and booked lists, whichever agency acts as the purchaser, could feasibly tend to equalise the differences between fund-holding and non fund-holding patients on the elective waiting list.

Moving on to the individual providers, table 4.9 indicates how wide the waiting time differences were between fund-holding and other patients on the elective waiting list at the Crawley Horsham provider. This is because the variances remained statistically significant even when the other waiting list categories and patients who joined the list before their practice entered the fund-holding scheme are included in the analysis.

Table 4.9   **Waiting times (in days) over four years at the Crawley Horsham provider for operations covered by the fund-holding scheme on non fund-holding and fund-holding patients defined by the status of their practice at the time of the procedure**

Year and category	Non fund-holding patients			Fund-holding patients			ANOVA
	Median	Mean	No	Median	Mean	No	P-value
1992-93							
Elective waiting list	69.5	148.4	2655	64.0	123.2	552	0.0010
Elective booked list	20.0	31.8	117	18.5	30.0	50	0.8045
Elective planned list	23.0	23.0	1	-	-	0	-
OVERALL LIST	64.0	143.5	2773	56.0	115.5	602	0.0001
1993-94							
Elective waiting list	167.0	214.2	2067	85.0	149.5	1027	<0.0001
Elective booked list	35.5	97.7	76	13.5	63.7	48	0.1802
Elective planned list	29.0	46.0	9	50.0	37.4	5	0.7207
OVERALL LIST	154.5	209.4	2152	78.0	145.2	1080	<0.0001
1994-95							
Elective waiting list	132.0	193.9	1865	74.0	149.9	1547	<0.0001
Elective booked list	13.0	35.0	277	13.0	44.1	264	0.3493
Elective planned list	-	-	0	16.0	16.0	1	-
OVERALL LIST	86.5	173.4	2142	58.0	134.4	1812	<0.0001
1995-96							
Elective waiting list	168.0	194.6	1897	121.0	172.8	1381	<0.0001
Elective booked list	21.0	43.3	801	26.0	51.6	812	0.0306
Elective planned list	199.0	256.7	24	189.0	237.4	19	0.7106
OVERALL LIST	89.0	150.6	2722	65.5	128.9	2212	<0.0001

At the Mid Sussex provider, even when the whole waiting list is analysed together and the patients whose practice changed their status during the course of the wait are not excluded from the comparison, fundholders still had significantly shorter waits in three out of the four years (table 4.10). 1992/93 was the only exception. For two of the three years in which the differences were significant at Mid Sussex, 1993/94 plus 1995/96, it is noticeable that the variances between fund-holding and non fund-holding patients were very wide indeed.

Table 4.10   Waiting times (in days) over four years at the Mid Sussex provider for operations covered by the fund-holding scheme on non fund-holding and fund-holding patients defined by the status of their practice at the time of the procedure

Year and category	Non fund-holding patients			Fund-holding patients			ANOVA
	Median	Mean	No	Median	Mean	No	P-value
1992-93							
Elective waiting list	54.0	94.6	1788	53.0	88.6	595	0.2320
Elective booked list	23.0	33.3	507	21.0	30.3	138	0.5702
Elective planned list	209.0	239.5	129	196.0	232.6	49	0:7975
OVERALL LIST	48.0	89.5	2424	47.0	87.3	782	0.6330
1993-94							
Elective waiting list	62.0	112.9	1473	47.0	77.1	615	<0.0001
Elective booked list	15.0	29.2	301	13.5	22.3	194	0.1310
Elective planned list	186.0	237.5	81	112.0	164.0	47	0.0357
OVERALL LIST	52.0	104.7	1855	38.5	69.5	856	<0.0001
1994-95							
Elective waiting list	62.0	118.3	1666	50.0	96.9	1113	<0.0001
Elective booked list	11.0	28.8	289	13.5	23.6	130	0.4942
Elective planned list	170.0	265.9	80	112.0	243.5	66	0.5589
OVERALL LIST	51.0	111.4	2035	38.5	97.0	1309	0.0022
1995-96							
Elective waiting list	59.0	125.8	1737	48.0	89.1	1101	<0.0001
Elective booked list	12.0	39.2	365	13.0	30.5	224	0.1112
Elective planned list	164.0	215.1	97	154.0	239.5	71	0.4961
OVERALL LIST	49.0	115.4	2199	45.0	87.3	1396	<0.0001

For the Royal West Sussex provider, table 4.11 shows that adopting the same methods for the comparison as that used by the Audit Commission (1996a) reveals significantly shorter waiting times in two out of the four years, 1994/95 and 1995/96. With regards to the elective waiting list in 1993/94, there was still a statistically significant shorter waiting time for fund-holding patients, even when their average is increased by including those who spent part of their wait registered with a non fund-holding practice. This comment is verified by table 4.3 showing at this provider that year, over 70 per cent of the waiting times for patients whose practices became fund-holding during the course of their wait passed while the practices concerned where outside the scheme. But when the other two categories of the overall list are included in the analysis for that year, this difference is equalised to the point where the variation is no longer significant.

Table 4.11   Waiting times (in days) over four years at the Royal West Sussex provider for operations covered by the fund-holding scheme on non fund-holding and fund-holding patients defined by the status of their practice at the time of the procedure

Year and category	Non fund-holding patients			Fund-holding patients			ANOVA
	Median	Mean	No	Median	Mean	No	P-value
1992-93							
Elective waiting list	176.0	262.8	1179	278.5	304.1	68	0.1401
Elective booked list	26.0	57.7	2482	19.5	63.2	150	0.5216
Elective planned list	154.0	184.9	165	224.0	211.1	7	0.6066
OVERALL LIST	48.0	126.4	3826	46.0	140.6	225	0.2476
1993-94							
Elective waiting list	245.0	270.4	1037	95.0	235.4	347	0.0038
Elective booked list	23.0	61.4	2851	26.0	61.5	688	0.9965
Elective planned list	157.0	162.4	102	166.0	170.5	25	0.7472
OVERALL LIST	38.0	118.3	3990	48.0	121.0	1060	0.6404
1994-95							
Elective waiting list	284.0	282.0	1279	156.0	200.7	560	<0.0001
Elective booked list	26.0	53.1	3594	26.0	57.1	1416	0.1725
Elective planned list	136.0	183.6	97	172.0	202.8	27	0.5694
OVERALL LIST	37.0	114.5	4970	38.0	99.2	2003	0.0001
1995-96							
Elective waiting list	153.0	205.8	1751	89.0	155.6	1345	<0.0001
Elective booked list	25.0	51.4	2267	27.0	48.7	1942	0.2811
Elective planned list	34.5	68.9	298	31.0	64.1	272	0.4860
OVERALL LIST	44.0	115.3	4316	40.0	90.3	3559	<0.0001

For Worthing and Southlands, table 4.12 indicates that the Audit Commission's (1996a) methodology has reduced the number of years in which the overall differences among fund-holding and non fund-holding patients were significant to just one out of four, 1994/95. Nevertheless, the differences were significant for the elective waiting list alone in both 1992/93 and 1994/95. This is the case even though table 4.3 indicates that by including in the population those who spent part of their wait registered with a non fund-holding practice, the average waits for fund-holders were substantially increased.

Also, managers from the Worthing and Southlands provider have said that the only reason significant differences in 1995/96 did not emerge is because the health authority slowed its activity in the last quarter of that year, pushing many non fund-holders with very long waits into the next year. If an analysis were conducted for 1996/97, much shorter waits for fund-holders would probably be evident. However, it does seem fair to remark that in general the variances between fund-holders and other patients were somewhat narrower at this provider than at the other three.

Table 4.12   Waiting times (in days) over four years at the Worthing and Southlands provider for operations covered by the fund-holding scheme on non fund-holding and fund-holding patients defined by the status of their practice at the time of the procedure

Year and category	Non fund-holding patients			Fund-holding patients			ANOVA
	Median	Mean	No	Median	Mean	No	P-value
1992-93							
Elective waiting list	74.0	129.1	6555	64.0	116.4	661	0.0279
Elective booked list	5.0	16.4	1311	5.0	15.1	129	0.7393
Elective planned list	175.5	177.3	424	181.0	196.2	51	0.2996
OVERALL LIST	59.0	113.7	8290	53.0	105.7	841	0.1058
1993-94							
Elective waiting list	83.0	134.4	6221	83.0	131.6	1355	0.4967
Elective booked list	5.0	18.2	1282	5.0	18.7	287	0.8752
Elective planned list	147.0	173.8	547	147.0	162.2	125	0.3882
OVERALL LIST	64.0	118.6	8050	63.0	115.5	1767	0.3622
1994-95							
Elective waiting list	80.0	129.6	4942	75.5	123.6	2596	0.0436
Elective booked list	4.0	15.5	1186	4.0	13.2	666	0.3356
Elective planned list	92.0	126.3	690	90.0	124.6	399	0.8126
OVERALL LIST	60.0	109.4	6818	55.0	103.6	3661	0.0190
1995-96							
Elective waiting list	83.0	136.1	4228	87.0	132.6	2708	0.2544
Elective booked list	6.0	19.3	1410	6.0	21.7	818	0.3168
Elective planned list	103.0	141.0	748	98.0	145.2	426	0.6155
OVERALL LIST	60.0	110.9	6386	63.0	111.0	3952	0.9810

In summary, for patients on the elective waiting list, those from fund-holding practices tended to have significantly shorter waiting times for the elective surgery covered by the fund-holding scheme at the four providers featured in the research project. When the analysis is narrowed to patients whose GP practice did not change their status regarding membership of the scheme, fund-holders had shorter waits at all the providers in each of the four years. Even when the comparison was made according to the status of practices at the time of their patients' operations, in twelve cases out of sixteen the shorter waiting times of fund-holding patients were still significant. Indeed, there is not even a single example where non fund-holders had significantly shorter waits than their fund-holding counterparts.

Do shorter waits for fund-holders continue?

Nevertheless, there is still one final step that can be taken to eliminate any lingering doubts concerning the impact of keeping or removing from the analysis those patients whose general practice changed their status (fund-holding or not) during the course of their wait. That is to exclude the patients of fund-holding practices in their first year within the scheme from each comparison. Hence, for a computation pertaining to the 1992/93 financial year only patients from first wave fund-holders would have their waits compared to those of non fund-holders. For 1993/94 the fund-holding population would be those from first and second wave practices, from the first three waves for 1994/95, and from waves one to four in 1995/96. The rationale for this exercise is to show if shorter waits were a one year anomaly for new fund-holders that disappeared when they had been in the scheme a while, perhaps through losing their enthusiasm or the provider developing control over them. Table 4.13 details this comparison.

For this comparison, it seemed reasonable to include any fund-holding patients who joined the waiting list before their practice entered the scheme. After all, they would have had at least twelve months on the list as a fund-holding patient, so there is a diminishing likelihood that the wait before their practice entered the scheme would exceed the waiting period after it joined. Anyway, the practice would have had over a year to facilitate the patient's admission anyway, and consequently there should be a relatively small number of them that started waiting before their practice joined the scheme.

It can be seen from table 4.13 that in eleven out of sixteen cases, patients from practices in at least their second year within the scheme had significantly shorter waits than did non fund-holding patients. Out of the five where differences were not significant, in four of them the fund-holding population numbered fewer than 100 (and in two they were under 5), and small numbers make significant results less likely. Indeed, in these four cases the mean waits of fund-holders were still much lower than that of the non fund-holders, even though the results were not significant. The other instance that did not produce a significant result was Worthing and Southlands in 1995/96, and the circumstances making this a special case have already been discussed.

Table 4.13   Comparison of waiting times (in days) for operations covered by the fund-holding scheme on elective waiting list patients of non fund-holding GPs and those registered with fund-holders except for the latest wave of such practices in any year

Provider and year	Non fund-holding patients			Fund-holding patients			ANOVA
	Median	Mean	No	Median	Mean	No	P-value
Crawley Horsham							
1992-93	69.0	148.4	2655	64.5	123.5	550	0.0012
1993-94	167.0	214.2	2067	96.0	161.5	571	<0.0001
1994-95	132.0	193.9	1865	68.0	144.7	1052	<0.0001
1995-96	168.0	194.6	1897	121.0	172.6	1377	<0.0001
Mid Sussex							
1992-93	54.0	94.6	1788	50.0	72.4	77	0.0767
1993-94	62.0	112.9	1473	46.0	78.2	469	<0.0001
1994-95	62.0	118.3	1666	48.0	86.4	759	<0.0001
1995-96	59.0	125.8	1737	48.0	88.3	1067	<0.0001
Royal West Sussex							
1992-93	176.0	262.8	1179	223.0	223.0	1	0.8592
1993-94	245.0	270.4	1037	219.0	255.0	94	0.4700
1994-95	284.0	282.0	1279	152.0	199.1	403	<0.0001
1995-96	153.0	205.8	1751	74.0	125.2	718	<0.0001
Worthing and Southlands							
1992-93	74.0	129.1	6555	32.5	56.0	4	0.3036
1993-94	83.0	134.5	6221	71.0	118.1	601	0.0031
1994-95	80.0	129.6	4942	72.0	120.7	1402	0.0184
1995-96	83.0	136.1	4228	85.0	132.7	2465	0.2893

In short, the conclusion must be made that for non-urgent elective surgery, fund-holders generally had shorter waiting times than did non fund-holding patients. Yet these shorter waits may not necessarily be because practices were in the fund-holding scheme. As discussed in the second chapter, there could be suspicions that the practices joining the fund-holding scheme had always been able to get quicker admissions to hospitals for their patients.

DOES FUND-HOLDING SHORTEN WAITS?

The doubt over whether it really was something to do with the scheme that shortens the waiting times of fund-holding patients relates closely to a comment made by the Audit Commission (1996b, p. 1), the sentence written in bold type in the original document to emphasise the point being made. **'When differences appear between fundholders and practices outside the scheme, it does not necessarily follow that fundholding status is the cause'.** This statement was made in a digest of information about practices that joined the scheme in the first five waves, and a similar message was also put forward in another report on the scheme, published by the same organisation that corresponding year:

> ...GPs choose to become fundholders and they differ from those who choose not to in several important regards. Any success or failure could therefore be attributable either to fundholding as a system or to the nature of the particular GPs operating it... (Audit Commission, 1996a, p. 3)

If these points have any validity in the context of this research, it would mean that the shorter waits of fund-holding patients in West Sussex would not have been a consequence of their practices' participation in the scheme. If this really was the case, those practices which entered the scheme during the first five years of the internal market would surely have achieved shorter waiting times for their patients, relative to the waits endured by patients of the continuing non fund-holding practices, before they became fund-holders.

On the face of it, the Audit Commission's (1996a; 1996b) argument looks a little far-fetched. The spread of fund-holding in West Sussex was surely extensive enough to ensure that practices with diverse characteristics, including the working patterns and personalities of individual partners plus the demographic and social class profiles of their patients, had joined the scheme. Perhaps the clearest common denominator between them might have been no more than a simple willingness to participate in the scheme. Yet the Audit Commission (1996a; 1996b) still raised their doubts and the matter thus needs investigating.

Hence it is necessary to establish whether the shorter waiting times of fund-holding patients on the elective waiting list occurred once their practice joined the scheme, relative to the continuing non fund-holding population, or whether it was a continuation of an existing trend. To do this, the patients registered with practices in their last year outside the scheme were separated from the rest of the non fund-holding population using the same provider. Differences in the waiting times that year for procedures covered by the scheme of these two non fund-holding populations were again tested for statistical significance through ANOVA computations.

The waiting times in the following year for patients of these preparatory year practices, their first inside the scheme, were then compared with the waits of the continuing non fund-holding population using the same provider over the equivalent period. As such, the waits of patients from the same practices prior to and after fund-holding status are compared to those of the continuing non fund-holding population using the provider in those two years, in effect the latter being used as a control group.

The logic of the methodology rests on the principle that if it was something specifically to do with fund-holding status that had lowered waiting times, two findings would be predicted. First, it would be expected that for practices in their last year outside the fund-holding scheme the waiting times of their patients would not normally be shorter than the waits of patients from other non fund-holding practices. Second, in the following year once these new fund-holders had joined the scheme it would be anticipated that the waiting times of their patients would fall below the level experienced by those of the continuing non fund-holding practices. If these two phenomena were evident, it would surely be legitimate to conclude that it was something to do with membership of the scheme that reduces waiting times for patients of fund-holding practices.

The four-year run of data (April 1992 to March 1996) that was available meant details concerning the preparatory year (1991/92) of those practices that entered the scheme in 1992/93 were not accessible. Because the approach compared the waits of practices' patients over a two-year period, this part of the study was necessarily confined to those practices (and their comparators) which joined the scheme in 1993/94, 1994/95 and 1995/96. Table 4.14 itemises the first stage of the approach, comparing the waits of patients from continuing non fund-holders with those from practices in their last year outside the scheme.

Table 4.14 shows that in ten cases out of twelve there was not a significant difference between the waiting times of patients from continuing non fund-holding practices and those registered with practices in their final year outside the scheme. The other two cases went in different directions. At the Royal West Sussex provider in 1993/94 the patients of non fund-holders in their preparatory year had shorter waits than those registered with practices staying outside the scheme from April 1994. For the other case, 1994/95 at Worthing and Southlands, the patients from practices in their last year outside the scheme were significantly longer than those registered with GPs who were continuing their non fund-holding status in 1995/96. Hence with just one exception out of a dozen cases future fund-holding practices were not reducing their patients' waiting times prior to their entry into the scheme, relative to the other non fund-holders.

The inclination of the second stage of this investigation is obviously to discover whether the waiting times of these practices' patients fell, relative to those from continuing non fund-holders, after they had joined the fund-holding scheme. However, when the fund-holding population embodies patients only from first year fund-holding practices there is a complication, again linked to the changing status of some patients as their practice joins the fund-holding scheme. The effect of either removing from or keeping within the population those people that started their waits prior to the practices entry into the scheme will have a greater influence on the outcome of the analysis than was the case with the previous comparisons which used practices from all waves.

Table 4.14 **Waiting times (in days) for operations covered by the fund-holding scheme of elective waiting list patients from continuing non fund-holding practices and those from practices in their final year outside the scheme**

Provider and year	Continuing non fund-holders			Final year non fund-holders			ANOVA
	Median	Mean	No	Median	Mean	No	P-value
Crawley Horsham							
1992-93	74.0	149.9	2202	58.0	141.1	453	0.3042
1993-94	159.0	211.0	1646	188.0	227.0	421	0.1210
1994-95	132.0	194.0	1863	163.0	163.0	2	0.8073
Mid Sussex							
1992-93	54.0	95.0	1712	53.0	85.3	76	0.4494
1993-94	62.0	114.0	1244	64.0	106.8	229	0.4306
1994-95	62.0	118.8	1630	61.5	97.8	36	0.3402
Royal West Sussex							
1992-93	181.0	266.7	997	165.0	241.5	182	0.1642
1993-94	257.0	274.8	953	138.5	220.4	84	0.0167
1994-95	282.0	282.5	938	296.0	280.6	341	0.8658
Worthing and Southlands							
1992-93	74.0	129.0	5825	74.5	129.7	730	0.9052
1993-94	84.0	134.1	4991	83.0	135.9	1230	0.6652
1994-95	78.0	128.2	4700	121.0	156.6	242	0.0005

If patients who started waiting before their practice became fund-holders are included, this could well mean that numerous long waits which may have been shortened if the practice had been in the scheme from the start of the wait will falsely amplify the average waits of fund-holders, perhaps enormously. Yet if the analysis was performed this way, with the waiting times endured before the practice joined the scheme counted towards the fund-holders' average and they still had significantly shorter waits than non fund-holding patients, this would be absolutely conclusive. But otherwise if all such patients who started waiting prior to their practice joining the scheme were excluded from the analysis, this may lower the average waits of the fund-holding populations too much. For some of the waiting period whilst registered with the practice when it was outside the scheme may also have been endured as a fund-holder.

Table 4.15 details the comparison after such patients have been excluded from the fund-holding population. It shows that patients of first year fund-holders had statistically significant shorter average waits at every provider in all years. This covers eleven comparisons as no operations on patients of first year fund-holders were performed at Crawley Horsham in 1995/96, which seems entirely consistent with table 4.14 showing that just two had been received by patients of preparatory year practices the year before. Yet if the results in table 4.15 are not too surprising, it is necessary to assess the position of all patients of first wave fund-holders whether or not they might have spent much time on the list before the practice joined the scheme.

Table 4.15   **Waiting times (in days) for operations covered by the fund-holding scheme for elective waiting list non fund-holding patients and those from practices in their first year inside the scheme who spent the entire duration of the wait as a fund-holding patient**

Provider and year	Non fund-holding patients			First year fund-holders' patients			ANOVA
	Median	Mean	No	Median	Mean	No	P-value
Crawley Horsham							
1993-94	167.0	214.2	2067	45.0	64.5	279	<0.0001
1994-95	132.0	193.9	1865	42.0	62.6	289	<0.0001
1995-96	168.0	194.6	1897	-	-	0	-
Mid Sussex							
1993-94	62.0	112.9	1473	39.0	50.5	107	<0.0001
1994-95	62.0	118.3	1666	36.0	62.2	222	<0.0001
1995-96	59.0	125.8	1737	22.0	52.2	20	0.0136
Royal West Sussex							
1993-94	245.0	270.4	1037	76.0	101.0	113	<0.0001
1994-95	284.0	282.0	1279	77.5	99.0	84	<0.0001
1995-96	153.0	205.8	1751	52.5	82.3	338	<0.0001
Worthing and Southlands							
1993-94	83.0	134.5	6221	52.0	78.4	418	<0.0001
1994-95	80.0	129.6	4942	53.0	80.0	768	<0.0001
1995-96	83.0	136.1	4228	72.0	95.9	147	0.0002

Table 4.16 details the comparison in this format and if anything it backs-up the deduction that the waiting times of patients normally fell if their practice entered the fund-holding scheme. In six cases out of twelve, they still had significantly shorter waits. In five the differences were no longer statistically significant, and in one the non fund-holders had significantly shorter waits. Moreover this latter case, Crawley Horsham in 1995/96, reveals how the inclusion of patients from practices whose status changed during the wait can often pervert the inquiry by overstating the

waits of fund-holders. There was only one relevant fund-holding patient for this comparison, and the circumstances of the analysis closely mirror the earlier examples.

This patient had a waiting time of 509 days, but started it well before the practice (which does not come from the provider's catchment area) joined the fund-holding scheme, hence the individual's exclusion from table 4.15. The patient started waiting on 17 February 1994, so 407 days passed until 31 March 1995, the practice's last day outside the scheme. The patient had the operation on 11 July 1995, which was 102 days after the practice joined the scheme on 1 April. Yet it is the 407 days that accumulated prior to the practice gaining fund-holding status which makes the waiting time significantly longer than the average for continuing non fund-holders. In brief, if ever there was a case where the shorter waiting times of fund-holding patients were going to be hidden, the circumstances of the analysis pertaining to table 4.16 was surely going to be it. Yet there still seems enough to show that there are repeatedly genuine significant differences between the waits of fund-holders and other patients.

Table 4.16 Waiting times (in days) for operations covered by the fund-holding scheme on patients from the elective waiting list registered with non fund-holding GPs and those of fund-holders in their first year inside the scheme

Provider and year	Non fund-holding patients			First year fund-holders' patients			ANOVA
	Median	Mean	No	Median	Mean	No	P-value
Crawley Horsham							
1993-94	167.0	214.2	2067	73.0	135.3	451	<0.0001
1994-95	132.0	193.9	1865	83.0	160.5	488	0.0002
1995-96	168.0	194.6	1897	509.0	509.0	1	0.0381
Mid Sussex							
1993-94	62.0	112.9	1473	49.5	70.3	136	0.0001
1994-95	62.0	118.3	1666	59.5	119.6	354	0.8653
1995-96	59.0	125.8	1737	64.0	114.6	34	0.6270
Royal West Sussex							
1993-94	245.0	270.4	1037	182.0	228.1	253	0.0021
1994-95	284.0	282.0	1279	160.0	204.9	157	<0.0001
1995-96	153.0	205.8	1751	126.0	190.3	627	0.0473
Worthing and Southlands							
1993-94	83.0	134.5	6221	97.0	142.2	708	0.1382
1994-95	80.0	129.6	4942	79.0	127.4	1189	0.5819
1995-96	83.0	136.1	4228	97.0	131.5	243	0.5879

Although various anomalies pertaining to this section have had to be taken into account, the balance of evidence strongly suggests that the shorter waiting times of fund-holder patients, relative to those of other GPs, had something to do with the participation of their general practices in the fund-holding scheme. The doubts concerning the Audit Commission's (1996a; 1996b) claim that it is difficult to establish whether something has changed due to fund-holding as a system or simply the nature of the GPs participating in the scheme have surely been overcome. As such, fund-holding did lessen the waiting times of patients on the elective waiting list who were registered with practices inside the scheme, relative to those who had their surgery commissioned by a health authority.

CONCLUSION

This chapter has dealt with two principal inquiries. The first was to demonstrate whether patients of GP fund-holders enjoyed shorter waiting times for the elective surgery covered by the scheme than their non fund-holding counterparts. For the sake of thoroughness, the inquiry into this question was performed on a number of slightly different levels. Although providers can differ in the way they rank people into the various bands of the list, consistent contrasts between the waits of fund-holding and other patients only appear in the category largely devoted to those with a routine clinical status, the elective waiting list (see tables 4.9 to 4.12). Such variations were scarce for the booked and planned categories of the waiting list, so fund-holding does not appear to make a significant difference to the waiting times of clinically urgent patients nor those requiring regular investigative procedures.

Moreover, those patients on the elective waiting list who began their wait before their practice entered the fund-holding scheme but had the operation after it joined generally spent much longer on the list as a non fund-holding than fund-holding patient (table 4.3). That seems perfectly compatible with a tendency for fund-holders to have shorter waits than their non fund-holding counterparts. After all, there is no other obvious reason why it should happen. This particular analysis covered people who, at the extremes, joined the waiting list both the day before their practice entered the scheme as well as those having the operation the day after it joined. If fund-holding had made no difference, it could sensibly be expected that the percentage of the overall waiting times for all such patients would be divided evenly between the periods before and after the date of the relevant practices' entry into the scheme.

However, this also means that when the criterion for nominating a patient as either fund-holding or not is whether their general practice was in the scheme at the time of the operation, this will commonly lead to the average waits of fund-holders being overstated. When the analysis is restricted to those patients whose practice did not alter their status (fund-holding or not) during the course of their wait, fund-holders had significantly shorter waiting times in all sixteen cases (table 4.4). Even when patients on the elective waiting list were identified as fund-holding or not in line with the status of their practice at the time of the operation, fund-holders still benefited from significantly shorter waits in twelve cases out of sixteen (tables 4.9 to 4.12).

Regarding the four cases where the differences lost significance, the influence of including patients in the fund-holding population who spent part of their wait before their practice joined the scheme on inflating the waits of this group is emphasised by looking at tables 4.10, 4.11 and 4.12 alongside table 4.3. At Mid Sussex in 1992/93, the Royal West Sussex in 1992/93 plus Worthing and Southlands in 1993/94, patients whose practice joined the scheme during their time on the list spent the substantial majority of this overall period before the date of entering the scheme. The only exception was Worthing and Southlands in 1995/96, where patients on the waiting list at the time their practice became fund-holders on 1 April 1995 generally waited longer after this date than before it.

Furthermore, in ten of the sixteen cases the differences for the elective waiting list were so wide that fund-holding patients still had statistically significant shorter waits even when the other two categories of the list, the planned and booked groups, were brought into the comparison as well. These results for the whole list as a unified amalgam are also given in tables 4.9 to 4.12.

The second primary concern of the chapter was to evaluate if the shorter waiting times of fund-holding patients on the elective waiting list had anything to do with the participation of their general practices in the scheme, to which the answer was shown to be yes. The waiting times of patients from practices in their last year outside the scheme were rarely different to the average waits of patients from general practices that would be continuing their non fund-holding status the subsequent year. In just two cases out of twelve were the variances significant, and in one of these it was the continuing non fund-holders' patients that had the shorter waits (table 4.14).

Yet when the waits of patients from the same blocks of practices were compared in the following year, it became perceptible that the waiting times of patients from the first year fund-holders often fell below the level experienced by the continuing non fund-holders' patients (tables 4.15 and 4.16). Therefore, the balance of evidence strongly indicates two main conclusions. First, fund-holding patients on the elective waiting list commonly had shorter waiting times than those registered with GPs outside the scheme. Secondly, it was something to do with the fund-holding status of their general practices that brought this about.

To close, equality should preferably be measured by contrasting one specific variable, whatever it may be, between two persons or groups (Sen, 1992). When waiting times for the non-urgent elective surgery covered by the fund-holding scheme is the chosen variable, at four providers over four years they were regularly unequal with fund-holders customarily having shorter waits than other patients. From this, establishing that there were differences in waiting times between the two groups of patients is just one issue being considered. Another equally important aspect is to discover the reasons why this happened, and it is this objective to which the book turns next.

5 Fund-holders' Budgets via Historic Activity: Who benefited?

The evidence from the previous chapter showed that the average waiting times of fund-holding patients on the elective waiting list who received operations covered by the fund-holding scheme were generally shorter than the waits endured by other patients. But in the context of comparing the internal market's primary purchasers, that finding alone says little about the effectiveness of fund-holders as commissioners, relative to the health authority, if they had received overgenerous budgets to purchase elective surgery.

As such, this chapter focuses on the question of whether fund-holding practices in West Sussex were funded over generously. It reports on the outcomes of the budget setting system for elective surgery, covering the effect of fixing fund-holders' budgets in line with historic data and the opportunity for such practices to inflate activity. Also discussed is the division of extra funding allocated to the NHS in the county, plus the likely impact of changes in hospital prices. Fund-holders' actual budgets are then compared against the resources they should have received according to a capitation formula.

BUDGET SETTING IN WEST SUSSEX

The first task is to examine how the budgets of GP fund-holders in West Sussex were actually set for the hospital services covered by the scheme in respect of the four years relevant to this research project, 1992/93 through to 1995/96. This information was obtained from senior managers in the finance department of the county's health authority. Two distinct methodologies, capitation techniques and historic activity, were adopted for different types of services.

Capitation techniques

The budgets of GP fund-holders for pathology, x-rays, and physiotherapy[14] were largely set through a simple non-weighted capitation formula. Local NHS providers supplied details of the activity for all practices within its catchment area during the first half of a financial year. The health authority, or prior to the amalgamation of such bodies the family health services authority, collated this data and valued it according to the fund-holding tariff of the specific provider for the following year. This total was divided by the number of people registered with all practices in the relevant locality, and each one joining the scheme in the forthcoming April received an allocation set by multiplying the per capita amount by the total of patients registered with it. The amount was, of course, doubled to annualise it.

In itself this was a fairly unsophisticated methodology. Although the practices concerned accepted it, the system took little account of their demographic profile. As a precaution, practices that felt they were special cases through having a demanding list of patients were formally protected by having the opportunity to discuss their circumstances, with a view to negotiating extra funds. Yet there was seldom any real success for the practices that had tried to use this safeguard. Health authority staff claimed that a minimal amount of money had been added to fund-holders' budgets in this way.

Additionally, on the occasions when practices had such activity performed on their patients at another hospital during the first half of their last year outside the scheme, meaning one that was not their principal acute provider, the prospective fund-holder was welcome to record this. The data had to be agreed by the specific provider that supplied the service and if the hospital did not do this, the practice was not funded for it.

As mentioned in the second chapter, this methodology suggests that it is going to be very unlikely that new fund-holders would be systematically over funded for these services. If practices preparing for fund-holding status inflated their activity deliberately, the financial consequences of the increase would be spread around all the practices in a provider's catchment area. Essentially, the opportunity for fund-holders to have gained from the system was therefore negligible.

---

14. Prior to the scheme's extension in April 1996, these services accounted for some 9 per cent of all fund-holders' hospital and community health services budgets (Audit Commission, 1996a).

Historic activity

The principal hospital services for which fund-holders' budgets were set on the basis of historic activity were elective surgery and outpatient appointments.[15] In brief, practices preparing for fund-holding status would record all the elective operations and outpatient activity provided for their patients which appeared relevant to the scheme during the first six months, April to September, of their last year as non fund-holders. The providers also catalogued the activity applicable to each of the relevant practices and on a monthly basis the two parties were asked to compare their records in the expectation that every month would be agreed as it passed. The idea was to avoid the extremely onerous task, and dare one say panic, that would have occurred if all six months had to be agreed together in the ensuing October and November. The activity was valued in line with the price lists of the various providers for the following year and doubled in order to annualise it.

Because the hospitals had details of the precise codes of the operations given to patients, practices were highly dependent on the provider accepting that a procedure was covered by the fund-holding scheme. Conversations with managers at practices and providers confirmed that the hospital data was the primary source of information used to agree the activity, meaning it was what the provider claimed to have happened that was routinely agreed. Nonetheless, if a practice discovered that it had received a discharge notice for a patient who had not appeared on the provider's list, the hospital investigated that episode to establish whether it should be counted towards the budget.

Regardless of this safeguard, if a discharge summary was despatched, the strong odds were in favour of the episode being on the provider's listing. Managers at various practices thought it far more likely that applicable procedures might have taken place where no notice had been sent out by the hospital. Practices would thus be unlikely to know about such treatments, which consequently may not have been recorded, leading to them being under funded on joining the scheme. Even so, it is possible that such practices might not be invoiced for an equivalent number of episodes the following year, which could balance out the problem. Yet it is also feasible that if the administrative efficiency of providers improved, practices may have been charged for a growing number of procedures,

15. Prior to the scheme's extension in April 1996, these services accounted for some 69 per cent of all fund-holders' hospital and community health services budgets. Elective surgery covered 29 per cent of the total, and outpatient appointments 40 per cent (Audit Commission, 1996a).

relative to the total that might have been missed in the year prior to becoming fund-holders. On balance, it seems the most likely probability was that fund-holders' budgets might have been set below the true level of historic activity.

Dixon's (1994) inference that the poor discharge information of hospitals may result in practices recording too much activity therefore looks to have an inverse logic. Because practices were so dependent on the data supplied by providers, it looks more likely that their activity could be under rather than overstated if insufficient treatment summaries or discharge notes were sent out to cover all the care provided. If that line of thought is correct, on entering the scheme practices may have been under funded. Although reports from practice and hospital managers suggests the monthly agreement process was essentially a harmonious affair, one of the main complaints of the practices was that this was the case.

Moreover, if a practice and provider were unable to reach agreement over activity levels, the local policy deemed that the hospital's records would be used to calculate the budget offer. For this reason too, Dixon's (1994) claim that practices who recorded more activity than providers would receive overgenerous funding is simply not applicable to the budget setting system in West Sussex.

For treatments which occurred at hospitals other than practices' local or main providers, the principles were the same but normally the agreement between the parties was left until the six-month period was over, due to the smaller volume of activity. For example, though it represents only a minority of such practices' activity, it is not too uncommon for consultants based at the West Sussex providers to make tertiary referrals to London teaching hospitals. In such cases, practices were again dependent on providers making them aware of such activity, and then agreeing that it had occurred, to have it counted towards their budget. If these conditions were not met, the practice would not have received funding for the treatment.

Similarly, when treatments were newly brought into the scheme, the sums allotted to existing fund-holders were set in the same way. Hence with operations, for the year prior to their inclusion in the scheme, episodes that practices and hospitals agreed had occurred in the first six months were valued in line with the providers' fund-holding price list in the ensuing year and annualised. The allocations for other less common services covered by the scheme, like domiciliary visits, were also set in accordance with the activity during the data collection period agreed between the practice and provider.

The final point to make in describing the historic data methodology is the very strict way in which the precise dates of the first six months of the financial year were adhered to. Even the episodes of care counted as taking place on the last day of March or the first day of October, just one day either side of the data collection period, were not included in the treatments used to calculate the budget offers. Moreover, since any money allocated to fund-holders was taken from the districts' cash limit, as far as was possible health authorities had every reason to set the budget setting rules to their own advantage rather than that of the fund-holders. For all the reasons just discussed, it is feasible that the baseline budgets of GP fund-holders were more likely to have been set against an under rather than overestimate of their true historic activity.

Community extensions

Although the two methods for allocating resources in respect of hospital services have now been discussed, there were other elements of fund-holders' hospital and community health services budgets, the community extensions covered by the scheme.[16] Because the discharge information from the providers to practices for aspects of care like outpatient appointments for mental health and learning disability patients was notoriously poor, it was not considered worthwhile for historic data to be agreed by the parties. Instead, providers supplied their own record of each relevant practice's activity levels (this was shared with the prospective fund-holders), and the health authority set the budgets according to these details produced by the provider.

For community nursing, new fund-holders in West Sussex received budgets in line with the number and grades of district nurses and health visitors already allocated to the practice, plus their on-costs. Therefore, if inequity had existed between fund-holders and other practices, this would have been a continuation of a pre-existing state of affairs unrelated to the scheme. It was also likely that overgenerous budgets for community nursing would have been passed back to the employing provider in a non-attributable block contract, so would not extend the resources available to purchase extra acute services like elective surgery.

---

16. Prior to the scheme's extension in April 1996, expenditure on community extensions accounted for some 22 per cent of fund-holders' hospital and community health services budgets. Of this figure, 16 per cent was taken up by the community nursing services covered by the scheme (district nursing and health visiting), and 6 per cent by other community services, mainly mental health outpatient consultations (Audit Commission, 1996a).

SOURCES OF OVER FUNDING: SEASONAL VARIATIONS

The presumption that fund-holders will be over funded therefore seems questionable in principle. However, was it in practice? For example, was the six-month data collection period likely to bias the calculation of the annualised costs of historic activity and if so, in what direction? The basis for this hypothesis is that if the provision of activity covered by the scheme to non fund-holding patients is skewed towards the first half of the year, new fund-holding practices could enter the scheme with overgenerous allocations. A large proportion of their budgets would have been set on the basis of the six months in their preparatory year in which most of their activity occurred.

For the analyses in this section, it should also be noted that the data relates to the elective surgery performed on all applicable NHS patients, not just the elective waiting list that was the main focus of the investigation performed in the fourth chapter. The justification for this is that the budgets of GP fund-holders for elective surgery were set according to the number and value of operations covered by the scheme performed on each of their NHS patients in the data collection period. As such, patients from the elective waiting, planned and booked lists were all covered by the methodology, including those who did not have their waiting times recorded. Consequently, the totals from table 5.1 correlate with the overall numbers in table 4.1 from the previous chapter.

Table 5.1 gives the breakdown per half year of operations covered by the fund-holding scheme provided to NHS patients from the elective waiting, planned and booked lists registered with practices both inside and outside the scheme at the providers and years relevant to this study. It is noticeable that for both the non fund-holding and fund-holding populations as a whole, there was a slight tendency for more operations to occur in the second half of the year. Moreover, the aggregated totals reveal only a tiny difference between the two groups of patients in the ratios for their activity between the halves of the year, and in some cases the activity trends for each group looks very similar. The Royal West Sussex plus Worthing and Southlands providers in 1994/95 are good examples of this, with more operations on both populations happening in the second six months than in the first.

Yet there are some cases where profound differences exist. For instance, in 1993/94 at Crawley Horsham, whilst the fund-holding activity was spread quite evenly, practically 59 per cent of non fund-holding work occurred in the second half of the year. At the same provider a year later, substantially more of the operations on non fund-holders took place in the last six months, while this trend was reversed for fund-holders. As such, with regard to seasonal variations it appears that the balance in the activity of the two populations suggest there sometimes are differences in the priority given to each group at alternative times of the year, but by no means does this look a consistent finding.

Table 5.1 **Breakdown per half year of operations covered by the fund-holding scheme performed on patients from the overall waiting list registered with non fund-holding and fund-holding practices at four providers over four financial years**

Provider and year	Period	Non fund-holding patients		Fund-holding patients	
		No	%	No	%
Crawley Horsham					
1992-93	April-September	1775	48.5	451	51.5
	October-March	1888	51.5	425	48.5
1993-94	April-September	1187	41.1	727	49.8
	October-March	1701	58.9	734	50.2
1994-95	April-September	1229	45.0	1237	52.6
	October-March	1505	55.0	1115	47.4
1995-96	April-September	1636	51.7	1304	51.3
	October-March	1531	48.3	1239	48.7
Mid Sussex					
1992-93	April-September	1289	52.5	349	44.6
	October-March	1168	47.5	434	55.4
1993-94	April-September	941	50.2	392	45.4
	October-March	933	49.8	471	54.6
1994-95	April-September	1013	49.4	608	46.4
	October-March	1039	50.6	703	53.6
1995-96	April-September	1180	53.4	672	47.9
	October-March	1031	46.6	730	52.1
Royal West Sussex					
1992-93	April-September	2184	49.6	138	54.5
	October-March	2220	50.4	115	45.5
1993-94	April-September	2514	51.5	626	49.6
	October-March	2366	48.5	635	50.4
1994-95	April-September	2395	46.0	946	45.0
	October-March	2812	54.0	1154	55.0
1995-96	April-September	2181	48.1	1827	49.6
	October-March	2349	51.9	1857	50.4
Worthing and Southlands					
1992-93	April-September	4150	48.6	414	48.2
	October-March	4396	51.4	445	51.8
1993-94	April-September	4122	48.6	918	49.1
	October-March	4356	51.4	950	50.9
1994-95	April-September	3435	47.6	1820	47.7
	October-March	3779	52.4	1995	52.3
1995-96	April-September	3484	51.7	2053	49.5
	October-March	3258	48.3	2094	50.5
Aggregate 4 years					
	April-September	34715	48.9	14482	49.0
	October-March	36332	51.1	15096	51.0

So what does table 5.1 say about the likely impact of differences between the first and second halves of the year on the budgets of GP fund-holders? Across all sixteen cases, four providers over four years, more operations on non fund-holders took place between October and March than from April to September. With all else being equal this would suggest most fund-holding practices in West Sussex were, if anything, somewhat under funded by way of seasonal variations, having been budgeted on the basis of the half year in which less of their patients' surgical activity occurred.

Additionally, it is noticeable from table 5.1 that in 1995/96 more operations on non fund-holders were performed in the first half of the year than in the second, 8,481 against 8,169. A reason for this was the situation at Worthing and Southlands, discussed in the previous chapter. Non-urgent activity in the last quarter of that year on non fund-holders from the elective waiting list was slowed to just over 19 per cent of the annual number for that specific waiting list category (against an even spread of 25 per cent).

As such, for the three earlier years, 1992/93, 1993/94 and 1994/95, the tendency for more non fund-holding work to take place in the last six months was even more striking than the difference which is perceptible in the aggregated rows for four years in table 5.1. And this is the period relevant to the budget setting process for the practices that acted as fund-holders during the time-span of this study. At the four providers in these three years, 54,397 operations relevant to the scheme were performed on non fund-holding patients. Of these, 26,234, slightly more than 48 per cent, were performed in the first half of the year and 28,163, approaching 52 per cent, in the second. The gap is thus widened if 1995/96 is excluded.

Whilst the point was made that with all else being equal, this might indicate that fund-holders as a group will be somewhat under funded, other things are not always equal. It is therefore necessary to analyse the balance between the two halves of the year for those practices formally preparing for fund-holding status in 1992/93, 1993/94 and 1994/95. The last of the four years included in the database, 1995/96, is not included as it has no significance on the budgets offered to fund-holding practices during the four year time span of the study. The practices for which this was their preparatory year will not have entered the scheme until 1996/97, the sixth wave. Yet it is still worth mentioning that most sixth wave fund-holders in West Sussex could well have had their budgets for elective surgery set on the basis of the half year in which the majority of their activity occurred. A logical interpretation from this is that if all else were equal, these practices would generally have been over funded for elective surgery.

Seasonal variations for preparatory year practices

The West Sussex practices that prepared for fund-holding status during either 1992/93, 1993/94 or 1994/95, and used the Crawley Horsham, Mid Sussex, Royal West Sussex, plus Worthing and Southlands providers in that year were identified and separated from the other practices outside the scheme. The elective surgery received by their patients, whichever category of the waiting list they were called in from, was divided into two blocks. Those relevant to the period running from 1 April to 30 September, which would have been used to calculate their budgets for the next year once they joined the scheme, and those from 1 October to the following 31 March. In line with the local budget setting methodology, every one of the procedures that were applicable to each half of the year were valued according to the relevant providers' price list in the ensuing year.

The rationale for this venture was to compare the allocations received by practices for elective surgery at the four providers to what would have been received had the annual costs of the work been spread evenly between the two halves of the year. Table 5.2 provides this information and to clarify the investigation its format is now described in some detail. The number and value of operations performed on patients of practices preparing for fund-holding status in each half of the applicable year are given and requires no further explanation. The column headed 'budget effect' is the April to September total doubled, and relates to the genuine funding of such practices for elective surgery at local hospitals. The column denoted as 'activity value' represents the sum of the values for April to September and October to March, and portrays the real costs of the practices' surgery covered by the fund-holding scheme at local providers that year.

The figure in the 'over + under -' column is the difference between the budget effect and the activity value. If the latter, the activity value, exceeds the former, the budget effect, the total is a negative figure and denotes an under funding. This is because the practices involved generally lost out, at least as far as their allocations for operations at local providers is concerned, by having their budgets set on the basis of the half year in which their surgical activity was at its lowest level.

Alternatively, if the total in the right-hand column is a positive figure, meaning that the budget effect was a greater amount than the activity value, it signifies that the practices concerned were generally over funded for the elective surgery received by their patients at local providers. In line with the previous definition of under funding, the reason for this is that the costs of their activity in the data collection period tended to be higher than in the second six months of that year. The totals for the sum of the three years are also given for each provider, along with the aggregate figures.

Table 5.2 shows that the activity for elective surgery covered by the fund-holding scheme of preparatory year practices at the providers is inclined to reflect that of the wider non fund-holding group (table 5.1). Hence GP fund-holders in West Sussex tended to lose out to an extent by having their budgets set on the basis of a six-month activity window. The consequences of this on practices' budgets were unevenly distributed in different localities. For example, in the catchment areas for both the Mid Sussex plus Worthing and Southlands providers, the overall effects were fairly marginal. Moreover, in one year at each the costs of the activity for practices in their preparatory year were even higher in the data collection period than in the second six months.

Table 5.2   Effect at four providers over three years of setting new fund-holders' allocations for elective surgery by doubling the value of their activity in the first half of their last year outside the scheme

1	2	3	4	5	6	7	8	9
		April-September		October-March		Budget	Activity	Over +
Provider	Year	No	value	No	value	effect	value	under -
Crawley	1992-93	273	199302	326	227066	398604	426368	-27764
Horsham	1993-94	251	168375	382	284015	336750	452390	-115640
	1994-95	2	1372	1	652	2744	2024	+720
	Total	526	369049	709	511733	738098	880782	-142684
Mid Sussex	1992-93	58	55155	59	47490	110310	102645	+7665
	1993-94	155	117750	118	123190	235500	240940	-5440
	1994-95	18	14945	25	25045	29890	39990	-10100
	Total	231	187850	202	195725	375700	383575	-7875
Royal West	1992-93	335	232852	340	255277	465704	488129	-22425
Sussex	1993-94	237	148290	200	107870	296580	256160	+40420
	1994-95	655	402497	746	482645	804994	885142	-80148
	Total	1227	783639	1286	845792	1567278	1629431	-62153
Worthing and	1992-93	457	388720	455	376085	777440	764805	+12635
Southlands	1993-94	854	617109	868	618469	1234218	1235578	-1360
	1994-95	144	105732	161	125234	211464	230966	-19502
	Total	1455	1111561	1484	1119788	2223122	2231349	-8227
Aggregate		3439	2452099	3681	2673038	4904198	5125137	-220939

[a] Column 4 is the value of the number of operations shown in column 3.
[b] Column 6 is the value of the number of operations shown in column 5.
[c] Column 7 is double the value of the April to September activity shown in column 4.
[d] Column 8 is the true value of operations over the whole year (column 4 plus column 6).
[e] Column 9 is the difference between the budgets and activity (column7 less column 8).

Yet the negative outcomes of the budget setting methodology were far more serious for fund-holders local to the Crawley Horsham and Royal West Sussex providers. At the former, practices lost a significant amount of money through having their budgets set in accordance with activity in the first half of the year, a circumstance that had quite severe consequences for those joining the scheme in April 1994. At the Royal West Sussex, practices entering the scheme that same year, its fourth wave, actually did quite well out of the methodology, with most of their activity during 1993/94 falling in the data collection period. However, this effect was reversed in the years either side of 1993/94, with the practices in their preparatory year during 1994/95 losing out particularly badly.

These findings comply with answers given during interviews with the chief executives of both the providers and health authority, plus the public health director of the latter. The health authority commonly raised its financial commitment to hospitals in the second half of a financial year. Whilst the huge majority of this money commissioned more elective surgery, three of the provider chief executives maintained that modest numbers of extra outpatient consultations had occasionally been purchased later in the year. This could suggest that some fund-holders may have been budgeted for outpatient services on the basis of the six months during their preparatory year in which least activity was provided to their patients, albeit to a lesser extent than was the case with elective surgery.

In sum, as far as elective surgery at local providers is concerned, West Sussex fund-holders were generally disadvantaged by the use of their historic activity over a six month period in the year prior to them joining the scheme, rather than gaining from this methodology. The aggregate under funding of such practices from waves three to five for surgical activity at four providers, using the techniques for measuring this as detailed in the earlier description of table 5.2, totalled £220,939.

SOURCES OF OVER FUNDING: INFLATED ACTIVITY

As discussed in the second chapter, suspicions have been raised in the literature that GPs preparing for fund-holding status may have tried to manipulate the budget setting system. The idea is that they could have inflated the usage of hospital services by their patients during the year prior to their entry into the scheme to surreptitiously increase the budget they receive for purchasing such services. This possibility was investigated by comparing the rates of surgical activity for practices in the two years prior to their entry into the fund-holding scheme. By doing this it should be possible to assess whether the elective surgery performed on patients registered with practices in their last year outside the scheme was higher than would have been expected from the level of activity in their penultimate twelve months as non fund-holders.

However, this task is not as straightforward as simply comparing the number of operations performed on patients of such practices over a two-year period.   Three of the providers underwent major rebuilding programmes during parts of the four years covered by the database that, when finished, increased their capacity for patient throughput.   And even without such capital projects, events like the appointment of new consultants and other changes in the medical staff establishments at hospitals would be expected to alter the number of operations performed. Shifts in the priorities of purchasers could also make a hospital modify the overall volume of elective surgery it provides.   Otherwise, part of a hospital's operating theatre complex could be closed down for a lengthy period of refurbishment, which is liable to reduce surgical activity during that interval.

Consequently a large rise, or decrease, in the surgical activity of practices in their last year outside the fund-holding scheme may on its own be nothing more than a reflection of a change to the circumstances and capacity of their local hospital.   Moreover, there are a number of factors that could cause this change.   A control group is thus required in order to legitimise any comparison and fortunately there is a suitable party equipped for this function: the continuing non fund-holding population over the two years.   After all, if the activity of one non fund-holding group is going to vary because of changes in the capacity of a hospital during that period, then surely it will also shift for the other.   The trend in activity rates between continuing non fund-holders and prospective fund-holders can thus be compared for the two years prior to the latter group's entry into the scheme.

The four-year run of data that is available (1992/93, 1993/94, 1994/95 and 1995/96) means that comparisons between the two groups of non fund-holding patients can be performed twice.   For the fourth wave practices that entered the scheme in April 1994, the data is available for their final two years as non fund-holders, their penultimate year of 1992/93 and also their preparatory year of 1993/94.   Likewise, for the fifth wave practices that became fund-holders in April 1995, the data is available for both their penultimate year outside the scheme, 1993/94, as well as their last, 1994/95.   Obviously the third wavers whose first twelve months inside the scheme was 1993/94 have to be excluded from this exercise because their penultimate year as non fund-holders, 1991/92, is not included in the database.

Table 5.3 gives the number of operations that were performed in both 1992/93 and 1993/94 at the four providers on patients registered with both continuing non fund-holders (those who remained outside the scheme in 1994/95) and those from practices that joined the scheme in April 1994. The totals include patients from all categories of the waiting list that received operations covered by the scheme in those years, whether or not their waiting time had been recorded.

Table 5.3 shows that for the operations covered by the fund-holding scheme performed on non fund-holding patients in the 1992/93 and 1993/94 financial years, the proportions relevant to practices who became fourth wave fund-holders and those who stayed outside the scheme during 1994/95 changed very little. To ensure the same practices should remain in each group for both years, the analysis pertaining to 1992/93 excluded those patients registered with practices that joined the scheme in April 1993, the third wave.

Table 5.3   Change in the percentage of elective surgery covered by the fund-holding scheme performed on patients of fourth wave future fund-holders (FHs) in their last two years outside the scheme against the overall non fund-holding activity in that period

	Future 4ᵗʰ wave FHs No	1992-93 Ongoing non FHs No	%	Future 4ᵗʰ wave FHs No	1993-94 Ongoing non FHs No	%	Variance %
Crawley Horsham	599	2465	19.5	633	2255	21.9	+2.4
Mid Sussex	309	2031	13.2	273	1601	14.6	+1.4
Royal West Sussex	390	3339	10.5	437	4443	9.0	-1.5
Worthing and Southlands	1607	6027	21.1	1722	6756	20.3	-0.8
Aggregate	2905	13863	17.3	3065	15055	16.9	-0.4

Indeed, on a proportional basis the overall activity of fourth wave fund-holders was lower in their last twelve months outside the scheme than in the penultimate year, though individually neither Crawley Horsham nor Mid Sussex fit into this generalisation. The movements in the activity of either group, at the level of individual providers and on an aggregate basis across them all, do not look remotely sufficient to warrant a conclusion that practices in their preparatory year inflated the elective surgery performed on patients. Additionally, a chi square analysis (confidence level 95 per cent) of the changes in both prospective fourth wave and continuing non fund-holding practices' activity between 1992/93 and 1993/94 is provided in table 5.4.

Table 5.4   Significance in the movement of elective surgery covered by the fund-holding scheme on patients registered with continuing non fund-holding practices and fourth wave fund-holders in the two years prior to the latter joining the scheme

1992-93				1993-94				
Future 4th wave FHs		Continuing non FHs		Future 4th wave FHs		Continuing non FHs		
Actual	Expected	Actual	Expected	Actual	Expected	Actual	Expected	χ^2
No	No	No	No	No	No	No	No	P-value
2905	2869.2	13862	13897.8	3065	3100.8	15055	15019.2	0.3089

This chi square test for independence (table 5.4) has been performed to ascertain whether the movements in the elective surgery supplied to the patients of both groups of practices were statistically significant. Because the hypothesis relates to the change in activity for the fourth wave practices in general, the totals of the operations cover all four providers (even though these were separated in table 5.3). The analysis reinforces the impression that fourth wave fund-holders did not inflate activity in their preparatory year. The changes over the two-year period were not significant.

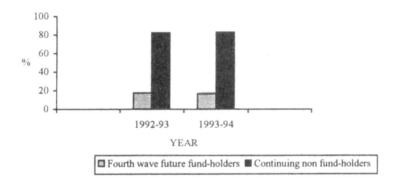

Figure 5.1   Two year chart of elective surgical procedures covered by the fund-holding scheme performed at four providers on patients registered with practices who became fund-holders in April 1994 and those registered with practices that remained outside the scheme in 1994-95

This verdict is reinforced by figure 5.1 which compares the percentage movement in the operations performed on patients of practices who eventually became fourth wave fund-holders with those who retained their non fund-holding status in 1994/95. No obvious contrast is apparent. The judgement must therefore be made that fourth wave fund-holders in West Sussex did not inflate the level of elective surgery that was received by their patients at the four featured providers prior to joining the scheme, relative to other non fund-holders. Even if such practices had attempted to do this, it seems they failed.

Table 5.5 presents exactly the same analysis as that performed for the production of table 5.3, apart from everything having moved on a year (so patients from practices that joined the scheme in April 1994 are excluded from the analysis). The movements between the 1993/94 and 1994/95 financial years in the percentage of activity covered by the scheme on patients registered with fifth wavers (who eventually became fund-holders in April 1995), and on patients from practices that remained as non fund-holders during 1995/96, are compared. In this case, a slightly greater proportion of the overall non fund-holding activity was performed on patients of fifth wave practices in their final year outside the scheme, 1994/95, than in the previous year, 1993/94. But the point must also be made that this was only a very marginal increase, just over one-quarter of a single percentage point.

Table 5.5   Change in the percentage of elective surgery covered by the fund-holding scheme performed on patients of fifth wave future fund-holders (FHs) in their last two years outside the scheme against the overall non fund-holding activity in that period

	Future 5th wave FHs	1993-94 Ongoing non FHs		Future 5th wave FHs	1994-95 Ongoing non FHs		Variance
	No	No	%	No	No	%	%
Crawley Horsham	4	2251	0.2	3	2731	0.1	-0.1
Mid Sussex	31	1570	1.9	43	2009	2.1	+0.2
Royal West Sussex	1157	3286	26.0	1401	3806	26.9	+0.9
Worthing and Southlands	300	6456	4.4	305	6909	4.2	-0.2
Aggregate	1492	13563	9.9	1752	15455	10.2	+0.3

The same analysis of the statistical significance in the activity movements for future fifth wave and continuing non fund-holders is performed in table 5.6, as was shown by table 5.4 for the fourth wavers and their comparators. It confirms that the changes between 1993/94 and 1994/95 for each group of practices were not statistically significant.

Moreover, the lack of movement in the activity of practices in their last year outside the scheme during 1994/95, relative to the continuing non fund-holders, is again clearly shown by the chart in figure 5.2. There is no observable difference in the relative size of the bars representing the activity of fifth wave practices and continuing non fund-holders in the two years prior to the former group's entry in the scheme. If future fifth wavers had inflated surgical activity, the expectation would be that their bar for 1994/95 should have been visibly higher than the one for 1993/94.

Table 5.6   **Significance in the movement of elective surgery covered by the fund-holding scheme on patients registered with continuing non fund-holding practices and fourth wave fund-holders in the two years prior to the latter joining the scheme**

1993-94				1994-95				
Future 5th wave FHs		Continuing non FHs		Future 5th wave FHs		Continuing non FHs		
Actual	Expected	Actual	Expected	Actual	Expected	Actual	Expected	χ^2
No	No	No	No	No	No	No	No	P-value
1492	1513.8	13563	13541.2	1752	1730.2	15455	15476.8	0.4184

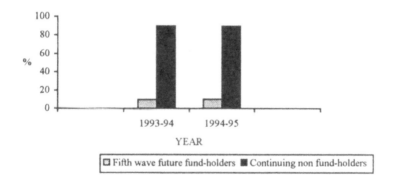

Figure 5.2   **Two year chart of elective surgical procedures covered by the fund-holding scheme performed at four providers on patients registered with practices who became fund-holders in April 1995 and those registered with practices that remained outside the scheme in 1995-96**

In fact when the two cases pertaining to tables 5.3 and 5.5 are combined, the surgical activity of fourth and fifth wave fund-holders in their penultimate years outside the scheme amounted to 13.8 per cent of the overall non fund-holding activity. Fourth and fifth wavers then had 13.6 per cent of the non fund-holding surgical activity that was covered by the fund-holding scheme in their final year outside the scheme. Hence on an aggregate basis the practices in their preparatory year during 1993/94 and 1994/95 proportionately had slightly less surgery performed on their patients during their last year outside the fund-holding scheme than in the previous twelve months, relative to the continuing non fund-holders.

As such, from the two cases that were open to examination, the only conclusion that looks appropriate is that practices in their final year outside the fund-holding scheme did not inflate their surgical activity, relative to the other non fund-holders, to surreptitiously increase their budget.

SOURCES OF OVER FUNDING: INFLATION, PRICES AND GROWTH

There are other issues related to the fairness of the budget setting methodology that were briefly mentioned in the second chapter. One is that fund-holders' budgets should be adjusted for inflation in a similar fashion, and to the same extent, to those of health authorities. With all else being equal, it would be unfair if one purchasers' budget was increased for inflation more than that of the other. This point has strong connections to the prices charged by providers to separate purchaser types, and that topic will also be discussed.

Another issue relates to the possibility that a health authority could have a diminishing cash limit as the years pass, whilst fund-holders might have been allowed to retain the budgets they had on joining the scheme. The effect of this would be to upgrade the resources available to fund-holding practices in the local NHS economy, relative to the health authority. Further to this, even if a health authority had an increasing cash limit through the receipt of growth funds, the additions made to fund-holders' budgets should not by comparison be excessive (similar to the point just made about inflation). Each of the issues of inflation, prices, and the growth or decline of the health authority's cash limit are discussed in turn with the last topic also being linked to the rise in the demand for emergency services.

Inflation

Discussions with various senior managers from the finance department of the West Sussex Health Authority provided a straightforward answer to the query concerning inflation. Whatever percentage increase for inflation was received by the health authority in a particular year for the purchase of health care services, the same percentage was passed on to the overall hospital and community health care budgets held by fund-holders.

For example, say that in a single year the overall resources available in West Sussex for commissioning health care services were £250 million. If an uplift of 2.5 per cent had been applied that year for inflation, an addition of £6.25 million would be received. Out of the £250 million, if fund-holders had budgets for purchasing health care services totalling £50 million, then altogether they would get an addition of 2.5 per cent to this figure, an extra £1.25 million. The health authority would keep the other £5 million, which also equates to 2.5 per cent of their £200 million. Therefore, on an overall basis the allocations for inflation were most unlikely to change the relative funding position of the two purchaser types. If fund-holders started off in the scheme as under funded, they were likely to remain so, with the reverse also being true.

However, while the increase for fund-holders mirrored the percentage received by the health authority in global terms, all such practices did not necessarily receive the same proportional uplift to their budgets. As far as possible the rises reflected the price changes of local providers. For example, with all else being equal, say one hospital raised its prices by 3 per cent and another by 2 per cent in a year when the relevant uplift for inflation was 2.5 per cent. The budget increases to fund-holders in each provider's catchment area would mirror the price rises of the local hospital. In this case one group of practices would get an addition of 3 per cent and the other 2 per cent. For the overall balance of resources between the health authority and fund-holders, this does not imply any systematic over (or under) funding for inflation for either party.

Price differentials

The arrangements for inflation link to the prices different purchasers are charged. The global percentage that went to existing fund-holders for inflation, whatever it was in a particular year, was supposed to cover rises in hospital prices. If the uplift received was not sufficient to do this, then fund-holders were expected to shape their non-urgent activity levels accordingly, or send patients to cheaper providers. In West Sussex it was thus only for the budgets of new fund-holders where resources tended to automatically follow in full any price increases by providers, formally to enable them to afford the same activity levels previously received by their patients. After that first year price rises had to be met out of the global uplift for inflation, despite the attempts to cover those of particular hospitals within the overall sum.

This might contradict the likelihood that providers would have hiked their fund-holding tariff to extract more money from local practices for the same level of work. While this could have worked for those embarking on their first year inside the scheme, it may have endangered business with existing fund-holders. This was especially likely as five providers encompassing seven acute hospitals were compressed into a county that also had big hospital complexes in Brighton, Guildford, Redhill, and Portsmouth within commuting distances of its boundaries. The location of the inter-county hospitals was given in figure 3.1. In line with this possibility, senior finance managers at the health authority claimed there was nothing to suggest that local providers' had exorbitantly hiked their fund-holding tariffs to get more money from practices. On balance, therefore, differential prices look anything but a safe bet as to the reason why fund-holders in the county might have been over funded.

However, could the reverse be true in the context of which purchaser was charged the higher prices? This is a rather delicate issue as a hospital's prices should have been based upon its costs (see Bartlett *et al.*, 1994), with no planned cross-subsidisation of contracts (see MacKerrell, 1993). Because there is no obvious reason why the cost of supplying the same treatment to fund-holding and non fund-holding patients would deviate, providers were not supposed to charge different prices for the same service to alternative purchasers. Nevertheless, Dixon (1994) was probably correct in claiming that the setting of prices by hospitals was an imprecise science and there could have been scope for providers to charge varying prices to each commissioner. So, in line with the thoughts of Propper and Söderlund (1998), might the health authority have been charged the higher prices?

Unfortunately, it is impossible to prove this for West Sussex one way or the other. A direct comparison of the prices to different purchasers is impracticable because hospitals did not issue a price list for specific treatments to health authorities in the same way that they did to fund-holders. For surgical procedures the contracts between the health authority and its local NHS providers detailed a single amount to be paid per specialty for all day cases, then another total for elective and emergency inpatients. Both figures represented an imprecise amalgam covering a whole range of treatments both inside and outside the fund-holding scheme. A price per individual treatment did not exist and discussions with health authority staff indicates this made it impossible for them to distinguish what was being paid for distinct services within the scheme, plus episodes outside it. Providers are in an advantageous position in any asymmetry of information (see Propper, 1993a; 1993b), and this may reinforce the idea that health authorities could be seen as 'captive' purchasers.

In such circumstances it seems feasible that providers may have taken advantage of this and charged health authorities more than fund-holders for the same services. If this proposition is correct it raises the question as to what, if anything, should have been done about it. If the health authority was paying higher prices, should it have retained more funds at the expense of fund-holders' budgets?   A problem with this idea is that it was impossible to prove whether the health authority was paying higher prices. And even if it were verified the same dilemma would have existed as if fund-holders' budgets had been uplifted for the same reason.   If fund-holders should not have been funded in full for providers' extortionate price rises because this would have unfairly lessened the amount left for the health authority, then the same point can be made about districts bailing themselves out by taking more money from practices.   It may also have removed, or at least reduced, any economic incentive for a hospital to improve its efficiency and lower its running costs in order to cut prices.

The share of capitation growth

The point was made in the second chapter that inequitable funding between fund-holders and health authorities could feasibly have developed from the latter having a diminishing cash limit, if fund-holders were able to retain their original budgets set when a district had more funding.   The purchasing power of the two commissioner types could gradually move in opposing, or at least not the same directions.   Funding for the health authority would have been squeezed, without the same disadvantages falling upon the practices within the scheme.   This hypothesis has less to do with the mainstream debate about any alleged under funding of the service than the change in the early 1990s to the way health authority cash limits were set (when RAWP was discontinued in favour of a weighted capitation formula).

This would have benefited some districts but not others, according to whether the new capitation formula had showed a health authority to be under or over funded through RAWP.   The custom was for the districts defined as under funded against their capitation target to be awarded supplementary increases to their annual cash limits.   The intention was to move all areas towards their capitation targets and progress with this was usually gradual over a number of years.   This actually worked in favour of West Sussex, with the county being appreciably short of its capitation target.   As such, the county received significant increases for capitation growth over a number of consecutive years during the 1990s, so NHS funding in West Sussex was anything but shrinking during the decade.

However, is it feasible that GP fund-holders in West Sussex might have received an unfairly large proportion of the extra funding for capitation growth that came in to the county?   Perhaps the health authority could have felt obliged by the desire of the government at that time to attract practices into the scheme to hand an inappropriately large proportion over to the budgets of fund-holders.

For this reason, details concerning the capitation growth received by the NHS in West Sussex during the 1990s, and how much of this went to the budgets of GP fund-holders, were required. The division of funds to distinct health authorities was performed at the regional level (see Smee, 1996), and the information concerning the capitation growth received by the county in the earlier years of the decade was obtained from the South Thames regional office. The West Sussex Health Authority director of finance provided this data for the later years, plus the division of these funds between health authorities and GP fund-holders for the whole period. As such, the capitation growth that came to West Sussex, and the amount that went to fund-holders in the county, was successfully acquired for 1992/93 through to 1995/96, and indeed for 1996/97 plus 1997/98 as well.

Nevertheless, even with this information there is still a major query to be addressed. Of the growth received each year, what would have been a fair allocation to fund-holders? Critics of the scheme might feel that if fund-holding patients were benefiting from shorter waits, their practices should not receive any additional growth monies, whatever their funding position to start with. However, this view might be flawed for two reasons. At the time the decisions were being taken about how much of the growth money should go to fund-holders there was no evidence about waiting time differences. Alternatively, others may think that if fund-holders were acquiring quicker services, it might have been inefficient to leave more money with a health authority that was perhaps the less effective purchaser.

The Audit Commission (1996a, p. 6) provided a useful guide as to what would have been a fair division of growth money. Without citing a year to which the remark was attributable, the comment was made that 'fundholders purchase about 20 per cent of their patients' hospital and community healthcare by value'. Also, the document later stated that 'by 1994/95, 41 per cent of the population were covered by the scheme, and about 8 per cent of health services' annual revenue expenditure was channelled through fundholding practices' (Audit Commission, 1996a, p. 107). The statistics in this second quote match neatly with the fund-holding practices having purchased 20 per cent of the value of their patients' hospital and community health care services, so this percentage can be taken as relevant to 1994/95. Hence if every GP were fund-holding, that year practices would have controlled some 20 per cent of such expenditure.

The two years in which major extensions to the scheme, in the context of the scope of services within it, were enforced are 1993/94 when the community extensions became incorporated and 1996/97 when a great deal more elective surgery was brought into the remit of standard fund-holding. Therefore, it seems reasonable to suggest that for 1993/94 through to 1995/96, the 20 per cent figure is as good as any to use as a guide to what fund-holders should have received out of the capitation growth in those three years. In 1992/93 the county received no capitation growth anyway, so there is something to work from in assessing if fund-holders were over or under funded for capitation growth in the years relevant to this project.[17]

Considering that the data was available, this exercise was continued for 1996/97 and 1997/98. However, because of the large extension to the fund-holding scheme in April 1996, the 20 per cent share loses its relevance. A larger portion would be applicable. The Audit Commission (1996a) stated that about half the population would have been registered with fund-holders in 1996/97, when their practices would manage some 15 per cent of expenditure on hospital and community services. Of this percentage, GP total purchasers controlled 4 per cent. If about 3 per cent of this quota were for the services outside the standard scheme post-March 1996, this leaves some 12 per cent of overall expenditure channelled through fund-holding practices covering around half the population. Hence if the entire population was registered with standard fund-holders, such GPs might have controlled 24 per cent of expenditure in 1996/97 and 1997/98.

Of course, the appropriate percentages might vary in separate areas due to a number of factors, including the demographic profile of the local population. For example, the proportion of the available resources spent on services covered by the standard fund-holding scheme in West Sussex might have been different to the ratio in Lancashire, Cumbria, Birmingham, East Anglia, or anywhere else. Yet this does not change the point that the Audit Commission's (1996a) percentages are still the most valuable source of data there is to use.

Capitation growth net of emergencies

Table 5.7 compares what would be expected to go to fund-holders in the county for capitation growth, using the percentages calculated above, against what actually was assigned to them. For clarification, table 5.7 will now be explained in some detail. The total growth that came to West Sussex per year is detailed in the first two columns. The third column

---

17. If growth had been received in 1992/93, the Audit Commission (1996a) enabled the percentage due to fund-holders for that year to also be calculated. They identified 22 per cent of the 20 per cent (so 4.4 per cent of the overall total) as relevant to the community extensions. Taking this 4.4 per cent from the 20 per cent leaves 15.6 per cent for the services inside the scheme during 1992/93.

represents the percentage of patients registered with fund-holding practices in the county (see table 3.1). For 1997/98, that percentage includes the 5.3 per cent of patients registered with the East Grinstead GP total purchasing project because they purchased all the services in the standard fund-holding scheme. However, it excludes the 1.3 per cent that were on the lists of community fund-holders to restrict the analysis to the potential over or under funding of those commissioning hospital services.

The next column provides the percentage of hospital and community services covered by the standard fund-holding scheme (methodology just explained). The column depicting the expected growth to fund-holders uses the data in the previous three. For example, in 1993/94 if every West Sussex practice was in the scheme, it was estimated that 20 per cent of the £5,448,000 growth should go to fund-holders, £1,089,600. Since 28.9 per cent of patients were registered with such practices that year, the total in the fifth column is 28.9 per cent of £1,089,600, or £314,894. The next column details the actual growth passed on to fund-holders that year, and the column on the far right represents the difference between the expected and actual amounts to such practices.

Table 5.7   Comparison of the capitation growth received by fund-holding (FH) practices in West Sussex against what would have gone to them if allocations had been in line with the published quota of services covered by the standard fund-holding scheme over a six year period

Year	Growth received	% patients on FH lists	% services in FH scheme	Expected growth to FH	Actual growth to FH	Difference
1992-93	-	16.5	15.6	-	-	-
1993-94	5448000	28.9	20.0	314894	-	314894
1994-95	3555000	41.1	20.0	292221	-	292221
1995-96	5985000	47.4	20.0	567378	503000	64378
1996-97	19706000	62.8	24.0	2970088	499000	2471088
1997-98	7637000	68.9	24.0	1262854	1012000	250854
TOTAL	42331000	-	-	5407435	2014000	3393435

Table 5.7 shows the fund-holders that joined the scheme during the time span of the research, 1992/93 to 1995/96, as being under funded for capitation growth by £671,493. Although not relevant to the budgets of such practices in the four years covered by this study, their situation deteriorated over the next couple of years with a serious shortfall occurring in 1996/97. Over the whole period detailed in table 5.7, West Sussex fund-holders may have missed out on funding worth something approaching £3.4 million.

The impact of emergency admissions

However, it may be that accepting the above figures without any 'fine-tuning' could lead to a less than wholly fair conclusion. For instance, the health authority might have been liable for expenditure on non fund-holding services that could have grown at a far quicker rate than the costs of treatments within the scheme. Perhaps the most prominent service for which this argument was likely to be used is that of emergency admissions. Despite the lack of specific prices for distinct emergency services, perhaps health authorities financed the increase in demand for such care by reducing the resources originally earmarked for the elective care of non fund-holding patients. Also, Keeley (1997) felt fund-holders may have admitted more patients as emergencies to induce savings on their budgets, though Mays (1997) denied this by citing Toth *et al.* (1997) as finding no contrast in emergency admission rates for fund-holding and other patients.

Yet even if fund-holding was not implicated in any increase to the demand for emergency services, the impact of such a trend could have been the same. It might conceivably have eaten into the resources for purchasing elective care for non fund-holding patients. A persuasive argument can thus be made that it would have been reasonable for the health authority to make the increased costs of emergency services, of which the precise rise was unknown, the first charge on the capitation growth monies coming into the county. Therefore, it seems germane to consider what the impact of emergency admissions was in West Sussex although, unfortunately, the available data on this subject was somewhat vague due to the point made in the previous section devoted to prices. The health authority had little insight into the prices that it paid for any specific treatments inside or outside the fund-holding scheme, including emergencies.

Hence there are huge and perhaps even insurmountable complications in computing precisely what the financial consequences of emergency admissions have been in West Sussex during the lifetime of the internal market. Yet the PID data held by the West Sussex Health Authority provides a record of the number of emergency admissions for residents of the county. Table 5.8 details the number of emergency admissions to the county's five public providers that supply acute services, over a five-year period. While it covers only the activity at providers within West Sussex, including the Queen Victoria Hospital, the totals will represent the vast majority of the health authority's liability for emergency admissions over the period. Although some West Sussex residents will get admitted as emergencies in other parts of the country, like those who fall ill or suffer accidents when on holiday, the incidence of this type of event is likely to be limited.

Table 5.8 shows that there was indeed a steady growth in the number of emergencies over the five years, with the overall difference between the number in 1992/93 and 1996/97 representing an increase of more than 17 per cent. By far the largest single increase occurred in 1994/95 when there was a rise of some 7.5 per cent against the previous year, due mainly to the position at Crawley Horsham. Indeed, this rise made the health authority perform some work on the costs of emergencies at the time. Although emergency costs are not identified separately, they estimated their expenditure on such admissions that year at something around £21.2 million. Although it must be remembered that this was an imprecise estimate, it is still the best approximation they could come up with. Basically, it is the nearest thing there was to information on the costs of emergency services.

Table 5.8   Number of emergency admissions for West Sussex residents at five providers over five financial years

Provider	1992-93	1993-94	1994-95	1995-96	1996-97
Crawley Horsham	8186	8246	9584	9627	10101
Mid Sussex	4571	4776	5086	5355	5723
Royal West Sussex	8813	9308	10015	10755	11302
Worthing and Southlands	14172	14752	15252	15046	14863
Queen Victoria	753	547	522	813	856
AGGREGATE	36495	37629	40459	41596	42845

Source: West Sussex Health Authority PID.

If this figure is adequately reliable and the uplift to the health authority's annual cash limit for inflation is taken to cover any price increases (despite emergency services not being attributed to separate charges in the contract), increases in the expenditure on such services can be estimated. Expenditure of some £21.2 million in 1994/95 for 40,459 admissions gives an average cost of nearly £524. Ignoring price changes because the assumption is made that the effects of these are cancelled out by uplifts to the health authority's cash limit in respect of inflation, this makes the cost in 1992/93 about £19.1 million (for 36,495 episodes). In 1993/94 emergencies may have cost a little more than £19.7 million (for 37,629 episodes), and in 1995/96 the charge could have risen to almost £21.8 million (for 41,596 admissions). While that covers the four years of this study, because the growth funding is available for 1996/97, the cost of 42,845 admissions that year might have been around £22.5 million.

As such, from the available data the best estimate of the growth in emergency costs is an increase of £600,000 in 1993/94 (from £19.1 million in 1992/93 to £19.7 million), £1.5 million in 1994/95, £600,000 in 1995/96, and £700,000 in 1996/97. From this, table 5.7 can be updated by making these rises the first charge on the extra funding year on year for capitation growth that was received in West Sussex. Although that table also included the amount for 1997/98, because the number of emergencies for the whole of that year was not available when this book was written, it is excluded from table 5.9. It is also worth noting that the health authority's estimated expenditure of about £21.2 million on emergencies in 1994/95 relates to the aggregate costs on such services, not just those at its local hospitals. As such, by attributing the gradual rise in admissions at the West Sussex providers to this overall figure, an implicit assumption is being made that the local trend was a fair representation of the admission rates for West Sussex patients as emergency cases outside the county. There is no obvious reason why this should not be considered a justifiable presumption.

From this, whilst the lack of firm data relating to the exact spend on emergency services has forced a greater reliance on conjecture than would have been ideal, the assumptions that have been made seem reasonable. Keeping in mind such qualifications, table 5.9 still shows that it looks exceedingly likely that fund-holders in West Sussex did not receive the share of capitation growth that may have legitimately been due to them. For the period up to 1995/96, the term relevant to the previous waiting time comparison, such practices appear under funded by some £457,000 (from the totals in the column on the far right), even though there was a very small difference for the last of these years. Their position appeared to get even worse in 1996/97, when a very small proportion of the overall growth found its way to fund-holders' budgets.

Table 5.9   Comparison of the capitation growth received by fund-holding (FH) practices in West Sussex against what would have gone to them if the estimated cost of emergency admissions were the first call on the growth received

Year	Growth received	Rise in cost of emergencies	Growth net of emergencies	Expected growth to FH	Actual growth to FH	Variance
1993-94	5448000	600000	4848000	280214	-	280214
1994-95	3555000	1500000	2055000	168921	-	168921
1995-96	5985000	600000	5385000	510498	503000	7498
1996-97	19706000	700000	19006000	2864584	499000	2365584
TOTAL	34694000	3400000	31294000	3824217	1002000	2822217

It thus becomes quite a challenge to understand how the rising burden of the emergency costs in West Sussex can be blamed for the longer waits of non fund-holders (though this may not necessarily have been the case in other areas). Could expenditure on emergencies have been underestimated, or might there have been other unavoidable rises in the charges applicable to non fund-holding services? To test such suspicions, the cost of emergencies, plus anything else that might have been beyond the health authority's control, can be inflated to a level far beyond the previously used totals. If the £21.2 million for 1994/95 is uplifted by 300 per cent to £63.6 million, the figures in table 5.9 are modified to those in table 5.10. The rate of the growth in expenditure on such services is taken as identical to that shown in table 5.10, and over the whole period comes to £10 million.

Table 5.10 Comparison of the capitation growth received by West Sussex fund-holders (FH) against what would have gone to them net of generously estimated increases in the cost of emergency admissions

Year	Growth received	Rise in cost of emergencies	Growth net of emergencies	Expected growth to FH	Actual growth to FH	Variance
1993-94	5448000	1800000	3648000	210854	-	210854
1994-95	3555000	4400000	-845000	-69459	-	-69459
1995-96	5985000	1800000	4185000	396738	503000	-106262
1996-97	19706000	2000000	17706000	2668648	499000	2169648
TOTAL	34694000	10000000	24694000	3206781	1002000	2204781

Table 5.10 indicates that even when the rising costs of emergencies are increased to a level way beyond the health authority's own estimates, fund-holders are still revealed as having been 'short changed'. For the period up to 1995/96 the accumulated negative effect of this for fund-holders, £35,133, was due to the situation in 1993/94 although the position of such practices again worsened from 1996/97. There is consequently a great deal to suggest that fund-holders were under funded with regard to capitation growth. Further, because table 5.10 might represent a large overestimate of emergency costs, the apparent shortfall in the growth funding apportioned to them looks as though it could have been very significant indeed.

In retrospect there have been a few unavoidable 'ifs and buts' in this investigation into the way capitation growth was distributed. Beyond those already discussed, no attention was paid to the demographic characteristics of the non fund-holding and fund-holding populations. Nevertheless, there is no obvious reason why such factors would make a telling difference to the analysis. During the lifetime of the internal market areas of relative social deprivation, neighbourhoods densely inhabited by both the elderly and young, plus the more wealthy areas of the county were all well served by fund-holding and non fund-holding practices.

Summary

Hence an examination into the impact of prices, inflation and growth does little to show that fund-holders in West Sussex had received overgenerous budgets. This coincides with the division between the two halves of the year for the surgical activity of practices in their preparatory year for fund-holding status, and no clear increase in the number of operations performed on their patients in the last year outside the scheme (relative to continuing non fund-holders). In view of these findings, the evidence is beginning to mount that the hypothesis about practices in the scheme being over funded may not offer a valid explanation for the shorter waiting times of their patients.

However, there is one further line of inquiry to perform regarding the funding issue. What does a capitation analysis suggest about the budgetary position of fund-holding practices in West Sussex? That question is the topic addressed in the next section.

ANALYSIS BY CAPITATION FORMULA

It has already been mentioned that it was always the previous government's intention to set GP fund-holders' and health authority budgets in the same way (see Department of Health, 1989a). The use of historic data in the allocation of resources to fund-holders was planned as a temporary measure, and the intention was to fix their budgets for hospital services by way of a capitation methodology. Consequently, devolving budgets to general practices has meant the composition of a capitation formula that is efficient for allocating resources in respect of small populations was given much attention during the internal market era. For example, the Welsh Office and former Mid-Glamorgan Family Health Services Authority hired a consultancy firm named London Economics to examine variations in practice expenditure on hospital services and derive targets to be used in determining allocations to fund-holders.

The priority given to the evolution of a sound capitation formula is not surprising. After all, the evidence revealed in this chapter suggests that the setting of budgets to practices partly on the basis of past activity has tended to make the process something of a lottery. Although West Sussex fund-holders that had their preparatory year in 1992/93, 1993/94 and 1994/95 were usually disadvantaged through the historic activity methodology, there are exceptions at particular providers in specific years (see table 5.2). And even though fund-holders in all the providers' catchment areas lowered their patients' waiting times relative to non fund-holding patients, this may suggest that not all such practices in the county were given the same opportunity to make savings on their budgets.

A number of consistent themes were put forward about the desired properties of such a formula in both governmental and academic publications. It should have promoted equity between fund-holders and other patients (Sheldon *et al.*, 1994; NHS Executive, 1996a). It should also have taken account of the genuine needs and characteristics of people, rather than variables which were endogenous to the system like hospital prices, the volume of existing supply, plus referral habits (Glennerster *et al.*, 1994a). Sheldon *et al.* (1994) considered the breakdown of populations in the contexts of age and sex to be the most vital weightings for the development of an equitable capitation model.

Such issues overlap with the reasons cited for the historic variations between practices in an official document issued under the last government (see NHS Executive, 1996a). Demography and the relative morbidity of patients correspond with their sincere needs and attributes, whilst factors like a possible surplus of locally available facilities and differences in medical practice correspond with the endogenous variables. Beyond this, Martin *et al.* (1997) placed the causes of variations in health care utilisation into four groupings. First there were those due to the features of individual patients, such as age. Second were those created by factors not automatically covered by a formula, like the presence of diabetes, but which in principle can be predicted. Third, there were those that arise from clinical practice. Fourth, there was a random element, specifically the chance incidence of illness.

Martin *et al.* (1997) claimed that the first of these factors could be captured comfortably by a capitation formula for small populations, and that in principle the second can be predicted. By contrast, any formula should not attempt to cover the third factor and no capitation methodology can adequately compensate for the fourth, because it is a random element. From this, the crux of their argument was that there is considerable random variability in the demand for health care of small populations numbering 10,000 which becomes less significant as the group increases, becoming very small for bodies of 100,000 and microscopic for those of 450,000. This randomness cannot be readily captured by any budgeting system for GP practices, making their expenditure subject to serious deviations from the allocation. To counter this, ideas were put forward on how the problem could be resolved, like setting budgets for longer than a single year.

Yet whether or not there are major obstacles in setting budgets for individual general practices by a capitation methodology, the factors which have just been discussed do not seriously undermine the forthcoming analysis. This is because it is concerned with demonstrating what a capitation formula suggests about the funding apportioned to GP fund-holders as an overall group, rather than the breakdown of resources between individual practices.

The capitation methodology

The work towards developing a capitation formula for allotting sums to individual general practices for the services covered by the fund-holding scheme resulted in national guidance on budget setting for fund-holders and GP total purchasers eventually being produced (see NHS Executive, 1997a). Although this was formally issued in 1997, the West Sussex Health Authority used a very similar formula to test the amounts apportioned to their local fund-holders in the 1996/97 financial year. The one difference between the formulas was to count the population as the aggregate body of patients registered with general practices in the county, rather than scaling them back to account for list inflation. This is because list inflation did not differ between fund-holders and non fund-holders within the county.

Because detailed advice on the use of capitation methods for setting budgets to fund-holders was provided in the official document, there is no point in rewriting it here. While the process is abbreviated into the single paragraph below, a full description of the techniques can thus be traced in NHS Executive (1997a).

In brief, expenditure on fund-holding treatments was sub-divided into the services covered by the scheme because each, such as community nursing and elective surgery, will have a diverse age-cost curve and needs weightings. Data on the spending patterns between practices on the various treatments were then obtained, including indicative amounts for non fund-holders, and from this the total pot to be allocated for each category of fund-holding service was determined. The aggregate list size of general practices in the county was counted, then sub-divided between the distinct practices. The national 'weighted' capitation formula for health authorities incorporates need drivers to account for area wide characteristics. Estimation techniques were used to attribute these, most obviously but not exclusively adjustments for the age and sex breakdown, to specific practice populations. The 'weighted' population per practice was then attributed to the total pot allocated to fund-holding services. This gave a notional budget per practice.

From this, each practice both in and outside the fund-holding scheme would have a capitation based indicative budget that weighted crude populations to factors connected to the relative need for, and cost of, health care services covered by the fund-holding scheme. If the formula is accepted as a rational method for measuring the fairness of allocations, it enables a judgement to be made about whether the actual budgets received by fund-holders were equitable.

The position against capitation

The West Sussex Health Authority used the above methodology to compare the funding position of fund-holding and non fund-holding practices for the 1996/97 financial year (see table 5.11). Whilst the table concerns the year after the period relevant to this study, the full range of data required to calculate the position prior to 1996/97 was no longer accessible.

Table 5.11 Comparison of 1996-97 fund-holders' (FHs) hospital and community budgets and the total apportioned for the same services to non fund-holders (non FHs) against the allocations implied by a capitation funding methodology

Group	List size	Actual allocation		Capitation allocation		Differences	
		Funding	Per capita	Funding	Per capita	Overall	Per capita
FHs	487382	56938000	116.82	56887000	116.72	51000	0.10
Non FHs	273102	32850000	120.28	32901000	120.47	-51000	-0.19
Aggregate	760484	89788000	118.07	89788000	118.07	-	-

[a] List sizes are registrations with West Sussex GPs, as cross border patients balance out.
[b] Actual funding for non fund-holders was valued from providers' fund-holding price list.

Source: West Sussex Health Authority capitation modelling papers.

Nevertheless, the results for 1996/97 should convey a valuable signpost to the position in prior years. It is unrealistic to imagine that the characteristics of practices that have a bearing on the weightings attached to a capitation methodology are going to dramatically alter in a short time span. If a practice has, against the norm, an elderly list size, this is part of its nature and may well be permanent. They will not have that characteristic one year and the next have a very low proportion of old patients. Patient turnover between general practices, particularly in a county like West Sussex, is not that extreme. Even if there was a shift in the characteristics of a practice's profile, it will be gradual. Any change would, if it happens at all, ordinarily occur over a long period.

As such, it appears from table 5.11 that an analysis of the financial position of GP fund-holders in West Sussex by way of a capitation formula also fails to suggest that such practices were budgeted over generously. If they were over funded, by the health authority's own calculations this came to about ten pence per patient.   For a practice of 10,000 patients this translates into £1,000, about one-quarter of the average cost of a single hip replacement operation announced by Warden (1998a), and hardly a material sum.   If non fund-holders were under funded, the health authority reckoned this came to £51,000 on an aggregate basis in 1996/97, some nineteen pence per patient.   To put this into context, details supplied by a local community trust implies that would have paid for less than one and a half full-time health visitors plus their on-costs like travel expenses.   Not a great deal to share between practices covering more than 270,000 patients.

Yet the capitation analysis, indicating that funding for the two groups was quite even, leads to a slightly different understanding of the financial balance between the purchaser types to certain other issues investigated in this chapter.   Some suggested that fund-holding practices might well have been under funded.   This warrants a further consideration of the groundwork on which the judgement derived from the capitation analysis was based.

The capitation analysis revisited

The various kinds of analyses performed for this chapter lead to two distinct views.   The capitation assessment showed fund-holders to be budgeted quite fairly.   Alternatively, examining the effects of setting fund-holders' budgets by historic activity and evaluating the division of growth monies between the purchasers indicates that practices within the scheme may have tended to be somewhat under funded.   However, there are factors that could explain these contradictory findings.   But before these are discussed, it is also necessary to recognise the unavoidable limitations on the study.

The inquiry into the six-month balance of surgical activity for practices in their final year outside the scheme covers just one element of their hospital and community health care services allocations, elective surgery. Altogether this service accounted for just 29 per cent of that budget (Audit Commission, 1996a).   Yet the database contained no data about the minority of operations that would have occurred at providers other than the four featured in the study.   Hence the activity available for analysis will have represented a slightly smaller percentage of the budgets for elective surgery.   The data necessary to facilitate investigations into the other components of fund-holders' budgets was not accessible.   Hence the evaluation that was possible had no direct relevance to something more than 71 per cent of fund-holders' hospital and community services budgets.

For this reason, the theoretical likelihood of over or under funding for other hospital services such as outpatient consultations, physiotherapy appointments plus investigations like x-rays and pathology was discussed at some length (see also the second chapter). Whilst the point was made that there might be good reasons for believing that over funding in these areas may not have occurred, this conclusion is inevitably based upon theory rather than firm evidence, simply because the data required for hard proof is not retrievable.

Yet beyond the unavoidably limited scope of the analyses is another reason, and perhaps a more convincing one, why fund-holders looked under funded by seasonal variations and growth money, but budgeted at the right level under a capitation analysis. To examine these differing outcomes, it is necessary to move the debate towards the way in which the capitation comparison was performed. The source of concern about the reliability of the capitation analysis relates to one of the notes to table 5.11, how the costs of the services to non fund-holding patients were valued.

The health authority used the providers' fund-holding price lists to determine the costs of services covered by the scheme that they purchased for non fund-holding patients. The official line of the health authority was that this was justifiable. There was no firm evidence of any variation in the prices charged by the same provider to different purchasers, and no doubt this is absolutely correct. Yet, as inferred earlier, could the reason for this be that nobody was, and the way the contracts are arranged perhaps no one could be, sure of what was being paid by the health authority for specific treatments. In short, the budgets to each group by way of a capitation methodology cannot be weighted against any difference in the prices that might have been charged to alternative purchasers.

Hence the following hypothesis can be volunteered. If the health authority was paying 10 per cent more than the prices GP fund-holders were charged for the same treatments, then table 5.11 would look rather different to the way it turned out. As it currently stands, using the fund-holding price lists to cost the activity of non fund-holding patients, the actual allocation per non fund-holding patient was a little higher than the spend on their fund-holding counterparts, maybe because of case mix or demographic variations, but still broadly similar. But if the real price paid by the health authority for items of care was on average 10 per cent higher than the fee for equivalent treatments charged to practices, the allocation to non fund-holding patients would be raised from £32.85 million to £36.135 million. This new total equates to £132.31 for each non fund-holding patient, £15.49 more than the per capita amount attributed to fund-holders.

Therefore, if the health authority was paying 10 per cent more than the practices, the overall pot would be increased from £89.788 million to £93.073 million (the fund-holders' £56.938 million plus the non fund-holders' new allocation of £36.135 million). This would also alter the appearance of the right hand side of table 5.11. Table 5.12 shows the way the table changes. The proportional split between the capitation allocations to fund-holders and non fund-holders calculated by the health authority and shown in table 5.11 has been transposed in the equivalent column in table 5.12. Hence in table 5.14, £56.887 million (some 63.4 per cent of the £89.788 million) was attributed to fund-holders and £32.901 million (about 36.6 per cent) was attributed to non fund-holders. Similarly, around 63.4 per cent of the new pot of £93.073 million, nearly £59 million, becomes defined as the capitation allocation for fund-holders, while approximately 36.6 per cent, over £34 million, is attributed to non fund-holders.

Table 5.12 Comparison of 1996-97 West Sussex fund-holders' and non fund-holders' hospital and community health services budgets if the health authority was charged 10 per cent more for treatments than GP fund-holders

Group	List size	Actual allocation		Capitation allocation		Difference	
		Funding	Per unit	Funding	Per unit	Overall	Per unit
Fund-holders	487382	56938000	116.82	58968278	120.99	-2030278	-4.17
Non fund-holders	273102	36135000	132.31	34104722	124.88	2030278	7.43
Aggregate	760484	93073000	122.39	93073000	122.39	-	-

* List sizes are registrations with West Sussex GPs, as cross border patients balance out.

Source: West Sussex Health Authority capitation modelling papers.

The capitation allocation to fund-holders thus becomes about £2 million more than their actual allotment, with the reverse being true for non fund-holders. Hence if table 5.11 did represent a 10 per cent underestimate of the amounts paid by the health authority for fund-holding services, a completely different complexion is put on the capitation analysis. Whilst this percentage is an estimate, the same principles apply for any other judgement. If the price differentials were 5 per cent, then against the formula fund-holders would have been under funded by about £1 million, by some £0.5 million with a 2.5 per cent differential, and so on. Whichever percentage is applied, the point can still be made that it is no more dependent on 'guesswork' than the prices estimated by the health authority.

CONCLUSION

The central goal of this chapter was to assess, as far as the accessible data allowed, whether the shorter waiting times for elective surgery commonly enjoyed by patients of GP fund-holders in West Sussex corresponded with practices in the scheme being over funded. This question was partly approached by investigating the timing of the surgical activity that was used to calculate the budgets of new fund-holding practices. It was shown that more operations on patients from practices preparing for fund-holding status at local NHS providers tended to occur in the six month window that was disregarded for budget setting purposes. This is one of the findings that make allegations about fund-holders having overgenerous budgets look rather frail.

After all, what type of circumstances could compensate the practices who 'lost out' in this way? Perhaps their activity with other more distant providers, which was not available for examination, was heavily slanted towards the work mainly taking place in the period used for budget setting. It might be possible to think of a few peculiarities like this, but in the final analysis, they are all likely to be rather far-fetched. For even if this did happen, it would only have had relevance to a minority of the activity for such practices. The large majority of the elective surgery received by patients registered with GPs in West Sussex will surely occur locally. Moreover, it appears that practices preparing for fund-holding status did not inflate their surgical activity in the last year outside the scheme, relative to other non fund-holding practices.

Further to these findings, it also seems possible that fund-holding practices in West Sussex did not receive a fair share of the capitation growth that came into the county for patients of all types of GP, fund-holders and non fund-holders alike. This looks to be the case even after subtracting the increasing costs to the health authority for emergency admissions, which had to be estimated, from the total received. There also seems little or no reason to deduce that inequitable funding would arise through the techniques adopted for apportioning funds in respect of inflationary pressures.

Another important approach to the funding issue concerned the move towards capitation formulas for setting budgets at the level of general practices. The comparison between actual and capitation based allocations for GPs inside and outside the scheme, performed by the health authority, implies that the budgets of fund-holders were at about the right level. But the accuracy of this discovery would seem dependent on the health authority and fund-holding practices having been charged the same prices for the individual services that were covered by the scheme. Yet there are reasons to suspect that the ambiguous contracting arrangements between the health authority and providers, particularly concerning the prices for specific treatments, could have made this doubtful. If the health authority had been paying higher prices than fund-holders, a capitation analysis might show such practices to be under funded.

This is not to say that providers charging hidden but higher prices to the health authority would have absorbed all the capitation growth. Some of it, and doubtless plenty of it, would have facilitated additional clinical activity in the county. A rising trend in the overall provision of elective surgery covered by the fund-holding scheme in the years and at the providers featured in this project, reflecting a national tendency highlighted by Le Grand *et al.* (1998), supports this claim (see table 5.1). Yet this rise fails to guarantee that the health authority was not paying higher charges than fund-holders for the same services. And if they had, it goes some way to explaining why the health authority perhaps needed to retain a greater share of the capitation growth than would otherwise appear reasonable.

A question that arises from this possibility is whether it justifies the health authority dominating the partition of growth funds between the purchasers beyond a level that would otherwise look even-handed. After all, fund-holding patients benefited from shorter waiting times for non-urgent elective surgery, so why should they have got more funding? On the face of it this response has an elementary appeal. However, the point that there was nothing beyond anecdotal evidence about waiting time differences at the time the growth was divided up, plus the risk of undermining efficiency incentives to providers, makes this option less attractive.

It is also worth contemplating how many critics of fund-holding would, if practices in the scheme were paying higher prices and achieving longer waits for their patients than the health authority, had argued that this should have been balanced by giving fund-holders a disproportionately large share of any growth funding. If the answer is not very many, then the same response seems applicable if the reverse is true. Thus the health authority might not be entitled to a larger share of growth funds just because it is obtaining longer waits and possibly paying higher prices.

To close, the focus of this chapter was to demonstrate whether fund-holders in West Sussex were over funded, and perhaps the most salient comment about this question was a remark made by the health authority's director of public health during an interview conducted for this research. "It is most unlikely that anyone from the health authority would even attempt to claim that our fund-holders have been over funded. We are all quite aware that they have not been". Considering that observation, it does not appear necessary to 'sit on the fence'. If the nearest thing to making such practices look over funded is a capitation analysis indicating they were budgeted at an appropriate level, which itself may be based upon a dubious assumption that might have hidden their under funding, the following conclusion looks justified. The evidence strongly supports the rejection of the hypothesis that fund-holding patients in West Sussex enjoyed shorter waiting times due to the overgenerous funding of their practices.

6 Case Mix: Critical or an Irrelevance?

The hypothesis that contrasts in the waiting times of fund-holding and non fund-holding patients might have been a consequence of differences in case mix was advanced, albeit very briefly, in the letters pages of the *British Medical Journal* (see Black, 1998). It is therefore necessary to respond to this speculation. As such, the focus of this chapter is an investigation into the effect of the surgical case mix on the waiting times of both the fund-holding and non fund-holding populations. It will demonstrate whether sufficient discrepancies existed in the assortment of the range of operations given to each group of patients, and the waits applicable to them, to explain the contrasts in their waiting times.

There are three prominent reasons for suspecting case mix could have had a major influence on average waiting times, and one seems less likely than the others. The least probable is the impact of randomness in the need for certain types of operations. The logic behind this idea is the fact that there will always be a degree of randomness in the demand for health care, and differences in medical practice by doctors can amplify the variability in the utilisation of services (see Newhouse *et al.*, 1989). Yet even without contrasts in medical practice, a level of random variability must surely exist in that the precise range of care two groups of patients need over a year will customarily differ to some extent, regardless of any contrasts in the demographic profile of the populations.

Yet on its own this may be the least probable cause why case mix might have had a critical impact because the degree of randomness in the demand for health care is not prone to always be skewed one way. After all, is it likely that something perhaps driven by pure chance will predominantly work in a one-sided manner? Why should it invariably have been non fund-holding patients who, on a proportional basis, needed to utilise services that had the longest waits? If such randomness did have a significant impact in some instances, is it not just as likely that fund-holders would proportionally have required procedures for which waiting times were lengthy as often as non fund-holders? Therefore, if randomness had consistently caused shorter waiting times for fund-holding patients, it would seem to have as much to do with one-sided chance or bad luck for non fund-holders, than anything else. This somehow seems a rather far-fetched proposition.

Yet rather than relying on randomness to provide a convincing rationale for the case mix hypothesis, there are two other reasons to attach validity to it, both also linking to the notion that certain operations at providers will have longer waiting times than others. The first depends on fund-holders having sent their own patients who needed treatments for which there were long waiting times at their local hospital elsewhere. This could have been either to another NHS hospital with a shorter waiting list or, connected to the point of Harrison *et al.* (1997) that the private sector can under certain conditions relieve pressure on the NHS, a non-public establishment. Either way, fund-holding GPs may have followed a policy of 'pick and choose' between hospitals to enable their patients to go to providers offering shorter waits for the treatments required.

If this had been a widespread response amongst fund-holding GPs to services offering long waits it could feasibly have made a difference to the average waits of their patients who were treated at local public providers, relative to other patients. They would have tended to receive services for which waits were shorter. Of course, an idealistic view held by disciples of market systems would be that this should have created incentives for NHS hospitals to try and improve the speed of access to those services which had long waiting times. However, even if this did happen it may still be the case that, at least in the meantime, fund-holding patients would have been sent elsewhere for those services with long waits locally, so the shorter waiting times of fund-holding patients could still be elucidated by a case mix comparison.

The other reason why case mix might have had relevance to waiting times is the impact of demography. After all, it is true that some procedures are often applicable to certain types of population. For instance the provision of cataract surgery, plus hip and knee replacements, is usually associated with older patients. If these operations had long waiting times at a hospital and younger patients from the locality were concentrated onto the lists of fund-holding GPs, or vice versa, that may well have an effect. Alternatively, gynaecology services are obviously gender rather than age specific. With all else being equal if fund-holders, relative to other practices, proportionally had twice as many middle-aged female patients on their lists it could be expected that they would have had double the incidence of hysterectomies in their procedure case mix. If the average waits for hysterectomies were abnormally long or short against the par for other operations performed at the hospital, this might have contributed to waiting time differences.

THE ANALYSIS

The possibilities discussed above lead to a fundamental question. How should a comparison of the case mix of fund-holders and non fund-holders be discharged? In very broad terms, Black (1998) addressed this issue. It is noteworthy that he inferred it is the mix of surgical procedures that can particularly determine contrasts in waiting times. However, he also implied that this matter could be investigated by evaluating other characteristics of the fund-holding and non fund-holding populations, specifically mentioning age, sex and diagnosis.

Nevertheless, if case mix did have a tangible effect it will surely be contrasts in the waits for specific operations, more than anything else, that determined the differences in waiting times between patient groupings. Certainly if one population had, for example, proportionally more women or elderly than the other, the incidence of some conditions were likely to be more common in that band. But that should be reflected in the mix of operations. Yet it is also possible that the populations might have had a diverse age and sex breakdown, but their diagnosis trends could have been identical. Alternatively, diagnosis rates may have differed even without any discernible contrast in the structure of the groups' age and sex profile, due to the effect of random variability. Either way, whilst age and sex can sway the prevalence of certain types of conditions and the diagnosis of them will drive the demand for particular forms of operation, it is principally the contrasts in waiting times for specific procedures that might shape the average waits of two groups.

As such, simply showing that differences exist in the construction of the groups in the context of age or sex may do nothing more than hint at the surgical case mix variances that could exist. It does not provide hard evidence of this because there is no firm guarantee that the case mix of two populations with dissimilar characteristics will vary, nor that it will be the same for groups with similar profiles. Consequently, it seems logical to focus on the actual spread of operations more than the demographic features and diagnosis trends of the populations. This should give the strongest clue about the true role of case mix in waiting times because it focuses on the final outcome in the assortment of procedures, rather than the potential causes of it.

There is also another reason why diagnoses may have had less bearing on the difference in waiting times of non fund-holding and fund-holding patients on the elective waiting list than the actual mix of procedures. This is the partition of patients into separate categories of the overall list. It has already been reported that at the margins separate providers may use differing criteria for deciding which part of the list some patients are placed in (see figure 4.1). Yet despite this, the spread of diagnoses between people in the same section of the list will be far less wide than would have been the case if they had not been divided up into the elective waiting, booked and planned categories.

This remains the case even though dissimilar diagnoses can lead to the same operation. Though there will be others, an example of this are women who undergo hysterectomies, the surgical removal of the uterus. Some experience the event due to the diagnosis of a malignant disorder in that area of the body, while others have the same type of operation because of menorrhagia unrelated to any form of cancer. The first group will ordinarily go on the booked category of the list, while the second are more likely to join the elective waiting list. If a case mix analysis centres on a single element of the overall list, the diversity in the diagnoses of patients having the same operation type should be much restricted. As such, to reach the real crux of the case mix issue it again seems sensible to focus on procedures within a single category of the waiting list, rather than diagnoses.

Clustering elective surgery

Before undertaking the main analysis pertinent to the case mix hypothesis, it is necessary to consider how operations are grouped under various codes. These are conventionally termed OPCS codes because the latest edition of the manuscript which details the full range of all operation procedure codes, and their categories, is the Office of Population Censuses and Surveys (1990). For a valid contrast of the surgical case mix provided to the two bands of patients, it is essential to be aware of the potential complexity of the exercise. There was a large range and number of operations within the fund-holding scheme in the four years under review and one of the most common types of operation covered by the scheme were hip replacements. Yet there are actually nineteen distinct hip replacement operations in three main groupings. For instance, the OPCS code W37 covers six different operations categorised under the heading 'Total Prosthetic Replacement of Hip Joint Using Cement', namely:

W37.0 Conversion from previous cemented total prosthetic replacement of hip joint.
W37.1 Primary total prosthetic replacement of hip joint using cement.
W37.2 Conversion to total prosthetic replacement of hip joint using cement.
W37.3 Revision of total prosthetic replacement of hip joint using cement.
W37.8 Other unspecified.
W37.9 Unspecified.

Similarly the code W38 includes six types of 'Total Prosthetic Replacement of Hip Joint Not Using Cement', whilst the code W39 incorporates seven kinds of 'Other Total Prosthetic Replacement of Hip Joints'. Although some of the nineteen operations are far more common than other types, even for fairly large populations the number of episodes recorded under each of the nineteen codes can often be quite small. The example given for hip replacements is repeated for all other kinds of operation as well, with there being various forms of the same overall procedure types. Hence a case mix study which followed the precedent for all operations of taking each of the nineteen hip replacement procedures on an individual basis might be so detailed that it could become both hard to understand and also less meaningful.

This is illustrated by reference to just one provider in a single year, chosen at random. At the Royal West Sussex provider in 1992/93, exactly 1,179 operations were performed on non fund-holding patients from the elective waiting list who had their waiting times recorded (table 4.4). Ignoring all the sub-codes within the overall codes, thus taking, for example, all the W37 episodes as one operation rather than six, these were spread out between ninety-seven procedures. This gives a mean of only some twelve operations per code. If these were then broken down according to whether they were W37.0 or W37.1 and so on, the figures could often be so small, frequently with just one or two episodes per procedure, interpreting the results of a case mix comparison might become over complex. To bypass this obstacle some kind of compression between the operations must occur. The decision is, what level of convergence?

Concerning this question, there appears little point in looking at, for example, W37, W38 and W39 procedures as three distinct groups. After all, they are all hip replacements. Further, what is so specific about hip replacements that they have to be considered on their own? It seems sensible to band them with knee replacements as well, of which there are also nineteen types of procedure under the W40, W41 and W42 codes. Also, discussions with clinicians suggest that replacements of other joints should logically be included in this group of procedures, thus incorporating the nineteen operations under the W43, W44 and W45 codes. Conveniently, all these joint replacement procedures are included under the same sub-heading for operations on the 'Bones and Joints of Skull and Spine', namely that of 'Joint', for which the codes run from W37 to W92.

From this, it can be argued that the most rational course for this case mix comparison appears to be utilising the groupings in the OPCS manuscript that merges procedures on specific areas of the body, such as joints. The breakdown for the groups that at some point, up to the end of 1995/96, included an operation covered by the fund-holding scheme is given in the appendix. From this, the data can be further compressed into an understandable format by amalgamating the operations pertinent to the activity of the two purchaser types in a particular year at a provider into the ten most common procedure categories. This again means those relevant to specific areas of the body (joints were mentioned as an example of this).

The fund-holding population

Another important matter to consider is which of the fund-holding populations to use for the comparison. After all, the waiting time comparison in the fourth chapter was performed in a variety of formats. Most obviously this was between non fund-holding patients and all those registered with fund-holding GPs at the time of their operations, plus those who spent the entire duration of their wait as a patient from a fund-holding practice. Because the case mix comparisons will cover every year at each provider, the study represents quite a plethora of information. As there was a large degree of overlap in the results pertaining to the elective waiting list in the fourth chapter, whichever fund-holding population was used, it seems rather over-elaborate to execute the full analysis twice over with both models of the fund-holding population. So which fund-holding group should be used?

The first point is obvious. The comparisons will, of course, cover just those patients from the elective waiting list who had their waiting times recorded. But beyond this, perhaps the most attractive option would be to use the patients numbering the larger of the two groups, whose status as a fund-holder was determined by their registration with a practice participating in the scheme at the time of the operation. It can be recalled from the fourth chapter that there was a clear tendency for fund-holding patients who spent part of their waits while their practice was outside the scheme to increase the average waits of the overall fund-holding group (table 4.3). Yet despite this, that larger group still had significantly shorter waits in twelve out of sixteen cases (tables 4.9 to 4.12).

Moreover, a preliminary assessment of the four cases where significant differences were lost by including those patients who joined the elective waiting list prior to the practice entering the scheme suggested that it does not actually matter which fund-holding group is used. The results of the comparisons are not materially altered whichever fund-holding population is used for the comparison with non fund-holders' activity. For this reason, the option previously identified as the most attractive one, the patients registered with a fund-holding practice at the time of the operation, is to be used as the fund-holding population. Particularly as a further benefit of this decision is that every NHS elective waiting list patient that had their waiting time recorded will thus be involved in the analysis.

The search for evidence

For the shorter average waiting times of fund-holding patients to be explained by case mix differences, certain conditions would have to be met. There would have to be significant variation in the proportion of common procedure types provided to fund-holding and non fund-holding patients. However, finding such a contrast is on its own not enough. It could be that a greater ratio of fund-holding patients were admitted for the procedure types which had longer waiting times than the norm for a provider in a year. In this event, it would seem reasonable to conclude that the case mix differences actually increased the waits of fund-holding patients, relative to non fund-holders, to a higher level than might otherwise have been the case.

As such, for the case mix issue to have any firm validity it appears that the following circumstances would be required. Tangible differences in the case mix of fund-holders and non fund-holders would have to be accompanied by a strong tendency for the variances to have increased, and significantly so, the waiting times of non fund-holders or decrease the waits for fund-holding patients. In summary, the search is for an indication of the following kinds of circumstances.

Firstly, it is essential that clear case mix differences must exist. The second is derived from the first and can be slanted two ways. One is that patients registered with fund-holding practices tended to undergo a preponderance of operations, relative to those received by non fund-holders, which typically had shorter waiting times. The other is that the surgery received by non fund-holders was skewed towards those operations that customarily had long waits. The third vital piece of evidence that is required is whether these tendencies, if they existed, had a significant effect on increasing the waiting time differences between the two sets of patients. All three trends, including at least one although preferably both aspects of the second, is required to corroborate the case mix hypothesis.

CASE MIX COMPARISON: THE RESULTS

Differences in the case mix of fund-holding and non fund-holding activity, merged into the OPCS groupings for operations on zones of the body, for elective waiting list patients receiving procedures covered by the fund-holding scheme were tested for significance at the 95 per cent confidence level. The measurement of variances in the expected and observed frequencies of the operation groups was performed through the chi square test for independence. Because the structure of the relevant tables in the context of their rows and columns offer ten degrees of freedom, the obtained chi square statistic in every case is compared to a critical statistic of 18.307 (see Healey, 1996).

Stage one: were case mix differences significant?

Tables 6.1 to 6.4 reveal the case mix in the surgery covered by the fund-holding scheme of elective waiting list patients at each provider. As the first stage of a fairly technical analysis, it is worth explaining the structure of the tables. For each of the four years the actual number of operations applicable to the ten most common procedure categories at the provider is detailed for both non fund-holding and fund-holding patients. Also shown is the aggregate number for all the procedures not falling into one of the other ten, thus making eleven all told.

From this data, the chi square analysis is performed for every combination of actual and expected frequencies. Although only the actual frequencies are exhibited in the tables, the expected frequencies were calculated in line with the usual practice for the test for independence, the multiplication of the total row and column frequencies divided by the number of cases (see Fleming and Nellis, 1994). From the computations, a chi square statistic is provided for each combination, which are detailed individually. The aggregate obtained chi square statistic is the sum of the twenty-two totals resulting from the comparison of the actual and expected values for each group of procedures. As a side point, because of the rounding up and down to get these figures to two decimal places, the sum of the individual amounts do not always exactly equal the aggregate total shown in the tables.

If the sum comes to over 18.307, the variance between the activity of fund-holding and non fund-holding patients is significant at the 95 per cent confidence level. Where the difference was not significant, no further action is required as it is taken that the variation in case mix was not adequate to have driven any meaningful contrast in the average waiting times of the two bands of patients. As such, tables 6.2 and 6.3 show that no further analysis will be performed for the Mid Sussex provider in 1992/93 and 1993/94 plus the Royal West Sussex for 1992/93, 1993/94 and 1995/96. In the other eleven cases where the contrasts were statistically significant, the search for the first of the conditions outlined earlier is considered satisfied. Subsequently, for these cases the investigation will move on to assess whether the other two trends are also evident.

In short, tables 6.1 to 6.4 have streamlined the continuing analysis to eleven cases, due to the discovery of five instances where any difference in the case mix relevant to the two populations was not statistically significant. But even in these eleven cases, as discussed earlier, on its own this far from proves that the variations in the average waiting times of the two groups of patients can be put down to case mix contrasts. It is therefore an opportune time to move on to the second step of the investigation. Do the disparities applicable to the eleven cases tend to increase the waits of non fund-holders (abbreviated in the tables to Non FH activity) or shorten those of fund-holders (abridged in the tables to FH activity)?

Table 6.1   Surgical case mix at the Crawley Horsham provider

Year	Procedure category	Non FH activity		FH activity		χ^2
		No	χ^2	No	χ^2	P-value
1992-93	Uterus	448	0.52	75	2.51	
	Mastoid and middle ear	254	0.10	59	0.49	
	Joint	228	0.17	40	0.81	
	Tonsil and other parts of mouth	176	1.34	56	6.46	
	Abdominal wall	135	0.02	26	0.11	
	Bladder	129	0.34	19	1.65	
	Skin or subcutaneous tissue	123	0.00	26	0.00	
	Nose	121	0.19	31	0.89	
	Fallopian tube	99	1.44	7	6.93	
	Breast	87	0.58	27	2.77	
	Other	855	0.05	186	0.26	
	TOTAL	2655	4.75	552	22.88	0.0021
1993-94	Uterus	292	0.65	125	1.30	
	Joint	214	3.10	70	6.25	
	Tonsil and other parts of mouth	151	0.14	82	0.28	
	Fallopian tube	133	0.06	62	0.11	
	Nose	118	0.46	70	0.92	
	Abdominal wall	114	0.01	55	0.02	
	Mastoid and middle ear	108	2.64	81	5.32	
	Veins and other blood vessels	90	0.40	36	0.81	
	Breast	75	0.19	43	0.37	
	Skin or subcutaneous tissue	71	0.03	33	0.07	
	Other	701	0.29	370	0.59	
	TOTAL	2067	7.97	1027	16.04	0.0075
1994-95	Joint	233	3.37	145	4.06	
	Uterus	212	0.71	154	0.86	
	Mastoid and middle ear	135	0.41	126	0.50	
	Tonsil and other parts of mouth	123	0.02	105	0.03	
	Nose	117	0.12	104	0.14	
	Stomach pylorus	112	2.52	126	3.03	
	Abdominal wall	109	1.59	116	1.92	
	Veins and other blood vessels	85	3.23	43	3.90	
	Skin or subcutaneous tissue	69	0.40	48	0.48	
	Bone	65	9.08	17	10.95	
	Other	605	1.75	563	2.11	
	TOTAL	1865	23.20	1547	27.98	<0.0001
1995-96	Joint	232	0.95	144	1.31	
	Stomach pylorus	167	0.02	125	0.03	
	Mastoid and middle ear	152	4.18	158	5.75	
	Tonsil and other parts of mouth	149	1.14	132	1.57	
	Uterus	145	4.78	64	6.57	
	Nose	139	0.05	106	0.08	
	Abdominal wall	85	3.34	94	4.58	
	Fallopian tube	79	1.88	38	2.59	
	Bone	78	3.23	32	4.44	
	Veins and other blood vessels	68	0.01	51	0.01	
	Other	603	0.00	437	0.00	
	TOTAL	1897	19.58	1381	26.93	<0.0001

Table 6.2   Surgical case mix at the Mid Sussex provider

Year	Procedure category	Non FH activity		FH activity		χ^2
		No	χ^2	No	χ^2	P-value
1992-93	Stomach pylorus	342	0.04	109	0.12	
	Uterus	227	0.34	64	1.03	
	Bladder	167	0.23	64	0.69	
	Joint	141	0.19	54	0.58	
	Peritoneum	109	0.47	27	1.43	
	Skin or subcutaneous tissue	106	0.88	23	2.63	
	Colon	99	1.31	49	3.93	
	Veins and other blood vessels	73	0.00	24	0.00	
	Abdominal wall	67	0.06	25	0.18	
	Breast	67	0.00	23	0.01	
	Other	390	0.01	133	0.04	
	TOTAL	1788	3.53	595	10.64	0.1647
1993-94	Stomach pylorus	299	0.13	116	0.32	
	Joint	179	0.01	77	0.03	
	Uterus	144	1.13	79	2.70	
	Colon	122	0.02	53	0.04	
	Abdominal wall	78	1.14	20	2.72	
	Bladder	71	0.04	32	0.09	
	Peritoneum	61	0.02	27	0.05	
	Breast	55	0.24	18	0.57	
	Veins and other blood vessels	45	0.02	20	0.04	
	Gall bladder	39	0.15	13	0.35	
	Other	380	0.00	160	0.01	
	TOTAL	1473	2.90	615	6.92	0.4579
1994-95	Stomach pylorus	316	0.73	237	1.09	
	Joint	179	4.05	168	6.06	
	Uterus	180	0.47	136	0.70	
	Colon	125	0.13	77	0.19	
	Bladder	95	0.02	61	0.03	
	Abdominal wall	86	0.49	47	0.74	
	Fallopian tube	78	0.51	42	0.76	
	Veins and other blood vessels	59	0.01	38	0.02	
	Breast	56	1.14	25	1.71	
	Outlet of bladder and prostate	48	0.07	29	0.11	
	Other	444	1.64	253	2.45	
	TOTAL	1666	9.26	1113	13.86	0.0103
1995-96	Stomach pylorus	303	1.49	228	2.35	
	Joint	263	0.11	158	0.17	
	Uterus	170	0.15	116	0.23	
	Colon	118	0.00	75	0.00	
	Bladder	87	0.00	55	0.00	
	Abdominal wall	80	0.05	54	0.08	
	Veins and other blood vessels	77	0.31	57	0.48	
	Nose	69	0.56	34	0.89	
	Bone	54	5.08	11	8.02	
	Fallopian tube	40	0.00	25	0.00	
	Other	476	0.15	288	0.24	
	TOTAL	1737	7.88	1101	12.46	0.0261

Table 6.3   Surgical case mix at the Royal West Sussex provider

Year	Procedure category	Non FH activity No	χ^2	FH activity No	χ^2	χ^2 P-value
1992-93	Joint	329	0.00	19	0.00	
	Uterus	145	0.02	10	0.28	
	Abdominal wall	102	0.03	4	0.55	
	Veins and other blood vessels	70	0.05	2	0.95	
	Fallopian tube	70	0.01	5	0.20	
	Outlet of bladder and prostate	57	0.03	2	0.46	
	Bladder	55	0.05	5	0.91	
	Vagina	39	0.07	4	1.17	
	Fascia ganglion and bursa	35	0.00	2	0.00	
	Peripheral nerves	28	0.01	1	0.21	
	Other	249	0.00	14	0.01	
	TOTAL	1179	0.27	68	4.74	0.8901
1993-94	Joint	300	0.04	105	0.12	
	Bladder	100	0.07	30	0.21	
	Outlet of bladder and prostate	94	0.01	30	0.04	
	Veins and other blood vessels	91	0.60	21	1.79	
	Abdominal wall	72	0.11	28	0.34	
	Peripheral nerves	63	0.49	14	1.46	
	Uterus	56	0.02	20	0.05	
	Gall bladder	29	0.01	9	0.03	
	Fascia ganglion and bursa	24	0.33	12	0.98	
	Skin or subcutaneous tissue	24	0.70	3	2.10	
	Other	184	0.52	75	1.56	
	TOTAL	1037	2.90	347	8.68	0.3155
1994-95	Joint	313	0.19	126	0.44	
	Bladder	118	0.00	51	0.00	
	Abdominal wall	114	2.13	29	4.86	
	Veins and other blood vessels	110	0.08	44	0.18	
	Outlet of bladder and prostate	108	0.02	45	0.05	
	Uterus	83	0.41	45	0.93	
	Fallopian tube	73	0.03	34	0.06	
	Peripheral nerves	34	4.08	35	9.31	
	Vagina	33	0.03	16	0.08	
	Skin or subcutaneous tissue	32	0.63	8	1.43	
	Other	261	0.29	127	0.66	
	TOTAL	1279	7.89	560	18.00	0.0039
1995-96	Joint	345	0.08	256	0.10	
	Stomach pylorus	204	3.10	204	4.04	
	Bladder	178	1.09	113	1.42	
	Colon	128	0.72	82	0.93	
	Abdominal wall	105	0.02	83	0.02	
	Uterus	101	1.41	100	1.84	
	Veins and other blood vessels	89	0.20	76	0.26	
	Peripheral nerves	80	0.80	48	1.04	
	Fallopian tube	63	0.01	50	0.02	
	Outlet of bladder and prostate	61	0.00	47	0.00	
	Other	397	0.30	286	0.39	
	TOTAL	1751	7.73	1345	10.06	0.0586

Table 6.4 Surgical case mix at the Worthing and Southlands provider

Year	Procedure category	Non FH activity No	Non FH activity χ^2	FH activity No	FH activity χ^2	χ^2 P-value
1992-93	Anterior chamber of eye & lens	995	0.01	97	0.09	
	Uterus	701	0.21	84	2.03	
	Bladder	593	0.00	58	0.04	
	Joint	579	0.16	48	1.55	
	Fallopian tube	258	0.21	18	2.10	
	Colon	254	0.48	38	4.73	
	Abdominal wall	252	0.18	33	1.82	
	Stomach pylorus	229	0.66	37	6.55	
	Skin or subcutaneous tissue	215	0.01	23	0.07	
	Breast	179	0.00	19	0.04	
	Other	2300	0.24	206	2.42	
	TOTAL	6555	2.16	661	21.44	0.0087
1993-94	Anterior chamber of eye & lens	761	1.96	214	9.00	
	Uterus	617	0.42	115	1.94	
	Bladder	600	0.01	133	0.03	
	Joint	547	0.75	95	3.42	
	Abdominal wall	328	0.02	68	0.11	
	Colon	262	0.04	61	0.18	
	Tonsil and other parts of mouth	226	1.46	28	6.69	
	Veins and other blood vessels	215	0.00	47	0.00	
	Outlet of bladder and prostate	205	1.26	65	5.78	
	Fallopian tube	203	0.61	31	2.81	
	Other	2257	0.01	498	0.06	
	TOTAL	6221	6.54	1355	30.02	<0.0001
1994-95	Anterior chamber of eye & lens	711	1.08	332	2.06	
	Bladder	644	1.96	394	3.73	
	Joint	523	2.08	226	3.96	
	Uterus	440	1.33	269	2.52	
	Abdominal wall	196	0.05	98	0.10	
	Colon	192	0.00	102	0.01	
	Skin or subcutaneous tissue	176	0.40	80	0.76	
	Fallopian tube	170	2.82	58	5.36	
	Outlet of bladder and prostate	169	0.00	88	0.00	
	Veins and other blood vessels	126	0.18	59	0.35	
	Other	1595	0.72	890	1.37	
	TOTAL	4942	10.62	2596	20.22	0.0006
1995-96	Bladder	680	0.05	426	0.08	
	Anterior chamber of eye & lens	537	1.34	389	2.09	
	Joint	505	3.99	253	6.23	
	Uterus	340	2.53	268	3.95	
	Outlet of bladder and prostate	174	0.00	111	0.00	
	Abdominal wall	162	0.00	105	0.01	
	Colon	120	0.00	76	0.00	
	Tonsil and other parts of mouth	118	0.10	70	0.16	
	Fallopian tube	117	2.47	49	3.86	
	Skin or subcutaneous tissue	99	0.22	56	0.34	
	Other	1376	0.15	905	0.23	
	TOTAL	4228	10.85	2708	16.95	0.0019

Stage two: the direction of case mix contrasts

In the eleven cases where the obtained statistic exceeded the critical one, 18.307, this does not mean critical variances exist the whole way through the tables. The null hypothesis can be rejected due to very large differences between the actual and expected activity for only a few groups of operations, whilst for the rest there might be little or no variance. It is because of this that the advantage of recording the obtained chi square statistic for the comparison between each of the individual operation groups can be recognised. It indicates at a glance which of the contrasts for each procedure category was primarily responsible for the rejection of the null hypothesis and therefore which categories require subsequent investigation to substantiate whether the net effect of the variation was to increase non fund-holders' waits or shorten those of fund-holders. Correspondingly, each sample where the difference in the case mix of fund-holding and non fund-holding patients was most noteworthy will now be addressed.

The results of the research into this matter is exhibited in tables 6.5 to 6.8, a separate one devoted to each provider. In brief, the analysis revolved around separating the procedure groupings for either population that contributed most to the overall rejection of the null hypothesis. The average waits for these categories, which had an abnormally high or low activity relative to the expected number, was then calculated as was the mean waiting time for the rest of the operation groups for which the actual and expected number of procedures were broadly similar. From this, it is possible to assess what the effect on the aggregate waiting times for the relevant population would have been if the activity for the abnormally high or low categories had been commensurate with the expected number.

For example, say for the non fund-holding population one category stood out as being radically different to the expected number, and for this particular group they received 100 more operations than the norm would have been. If the mean wait for these types of procedures for non fund-holders was 150 days longer than the average for all the other categories together, then it is taken that case mix differences would have added to the aggregate number of days waited by this population. The analysis for Crawley Horsham in 1992/93 is explained in some detail so as to use a genuine example to further clarify how the inquiries were performed. Because the same methods of inquiry are used for the other cases, this detailed description will not be repeated.

In line with the above example, the first step in this investigation is to identify which of the procedure groupings were chiefly responsible for the case mix difference at a provider to be significant. Table 6.1 shows that for 1992/93 at the Crawley Horsham provider a couple of the twenty-two operation categories stand out as making the chi square obtained statistic exceed the critical statistic. Both of these were activity performed for fund-holding patients, one being the episodes on tonsils and other parts of the mouth (predominantly tonsillectomy procedures), the other were fallopian tube operations (primarily female sterilisation). Together they accounted for nearly half, 13.39, of the overall obtained chi square statistic of 27.65. It is therefore the waits of fund-holders for these two procedure categories that are most worth investigating.

Returning to the database used for the waiting time comparisons, fund-holding patients on the elective waiting list at Crawley Horsham in 1992/93 who underwent operations on parts of their body other than either their tonsils and mouth or fallopian tubes had a mean wait of 115.7 days. Furthermore, the average waiting time for fund-holding patients receiving operations on their tonsils and other parts of the mouth was 184.1 days, 68.4 days more than the mean for operations outside the tonsils and mouth plus fallopian tube categories. Table 6.5 shows that the actual activity for operations on the tonsils and mouth for fund-holding patients, 56 episodes, was 16.1 more than the expected number, 39.9. Therefore, if the actual activity reflected the expected activity, 16.1 fewer operations on the tonsils and mouth would have occurred. This means that the case mix variation for fund-holding patients in respect of tonsils and mouth procedures can be taken as increasing their waits by 1,101.2 days (68.4 multiplied by 16.1).

Meanwhile, fund-holding patients who underwent operations on their fallopian tubes waited an average of 162.7 days, which is more than the mean wait of 115.7 days for the rest of the procedures, excluding tonsils and the mouth, by 47.0 days. The actual activity for fallopian tube procedures was 11.2 operations less than the expected total (7.0 rather than 18.2). So by using the same methodology as with the tonsils and mouth group, if the actual activity for fallopian tubes had mirrored the expected numbers 11.2 patients would have waited 47.0 days more. This raises the aggregate waits of fund-holding patients by 526.4 days. As such, if the actual activity for fallopian tube plus tonsil and mouth operations had reflected the expected numbers, the aggregate waits of fund-holders would be lower by 574.8 days (1,101.2 less 526.4). Because the variation in the expected and actual procedures for the procedure groups will inevitably have consequences upon the activity for other categories, this 'other' group is always shown in forthcoming tables.

Table 6.5 Effect of case mix differences on the mean waits of fund-holding (FHs) and non fund-holding (non FHs) patients on the elective waiting list at the Crawley Horsham provider

Year and group	Category	Mean wait	Actual No	Actual wait	Expected No	Expected wait	Variance
1992-93							
FHs	Tonsil and mouth	184.1	56	10309.6	39.9	7345.6	2964.0
	Fallopian tube	162.7	7	1138.9	18.2	2961.1	-1822.2
	Other	115.7	489	56577.3	493.9	57132.7	-566.9
	NET EFFECT						574.8
1993-94							
FHs	Joint	237.8	70	16646.0	94.3	22424.5	-5778.5
	Mastoid and ear	119.8	81	9703.8	62.7	7511.5	2192.3
	Other	145.1	876	127107.6	870.0	126237.0	870.6
	NET EFFECT						-2715.6
1994-95							
Non FHs	Bone	255.5	65	16607.5	44.8	11446.4	5161.1
	Other	191.7	1800	345060.0	1820.2	348932.3	-3872.3
	Net effect						1288.8
FHs	Bone	295.6	17	5025.2	37.2	10996.3	-5161.1
	Other	148.3	1530	226899.0	1509.8	223903.3	2995.7
	NET EFFECT						-2975.4
1995-96							
Non FHs	Mastoid and ear	170.1	152	25855.2	179.4	30515.9	-4660.7
	Uterus	192.1	145	27854.5	120.9	23224.9	4629.6
	Other	197.2	1600	315520.0	1596.7	314869.2	650.8
	NET EFFECT						619.7
FHs	Mastoid and ear	160.4	158	25343.2	130.6	20948.2	4395.0
	Uterus	98.2	64	6284.8	88.1	8651.4	-2366.6
	Other	178.7	1159	207113.3	1162.3	207703.0	-589.7
	NET EFFECT						1438.7

Therefore, the nature of the actual case mix, relative to the expected case mix, appears to have lengthened the aggregate and consequently the average waits of fund-holding patients at Crawley Horsham in 1992/93. For this reason, the idea that case mix might explain the shorter average waits of fund-holding patients must be rejected in this case. In line with this judgement, Crawley Horsham in 1992/93 will not be carried forward to the third stage of the analysis. To close this explanation, the calculations just described are depicted in table 6.5, along with the inquiries pertaining to the same provider for 1993/94, 1994/95 and 1995/96.

Table 6.6   Effect of case mix differences on the mean waits of fund-holding (FHs) and non fund-holding (non FHs) patients on the elective waiting list at the Mid Sussex provider

Year and group	Category	Mean wait	Actual No	Actual wait	Expected No	Expected wait	Variance
1994-95							
Non FHs	Joint	194.8	179	34869.2	208.0	40518.4	-5649.2
	Other	109.1	1487	162231.7	1458.0	159067.8	3163.9
	NET EFFECT						-2485.3
FHs	Joint	145.6	168	24460.8	139.0	20238.4	4222.4
	Other	88.3	945	83443.5	974.0	86004.2	-2560.7
	NET EFFECT						1661.7
1995-96							
Non FHs	Bone	216.8	54	11707.2	39.8	8628.6	3078.6
	Other	122.9	1683	206840.7	1697.2	208585.9	-1745.2
	NET EFFECT						1333.4
FHs	Bone	203.6	11	2239.0	25.2	5130.7	-2891.7
	Other	87.9	1090	95811.0	1075.8	94562.8	1248.2
	NET EFFECT						1643.5

Table 6.7   Effect of case mix differences on the mean waits of fund-holding (FHs) and non fund-holding (non FHs) patients on the elective waiting list at the Royal West Sussex provider

Year and group	Category	Mean wait	Actual No	Actual wait	Expected No	Expected wait	Variance
1994-95							
Non FHs	Peripheral nerves	277.0	34	9418.0	48.0	13296.0	-3878.0
	Other	282.1	1245	351214.5	1231.0	347265.1	3949.4
	NET EFFECT						71.4
FHs	Peripheral nerves	154.6	35	5411.0	21.0	3246.6	2164.4
	Other	204.1	525	107152.5	539.0	110009.9	-2857.4
	NET EFFECT						-693.0

Table 6.8   Effect of case mix differences on the mean waits of fund-holding (FHs) and non fund-holding (non FHs) patients on the elective waiting list at the Worthing and Southlands provider

Year and group	Category	Mean wait	Actual No	Actual wait	Expected No	Expected wait	Variance
1992-93							
FHs	Stomach pylorus	21.2	37	784.4	24.4	517.3	267.1
	Colon	53.5	38	2033.0	26.7	1428.5	604.5
	Other	126.5	586	74129.0	609.9	77152.4	-3023.4
	NET EFFECT						-2151.8
1993-94							
FHs	Eyes and lens	151.5	214	32421.0	174.4	26421.6	5999.4
	Tonsil and mouth	243.1	28	6806.9	45.4	11036.7	-4229.8
	Bladder & prostate	159.6	65	10374.0	48.3	7708.7	2665.3
	Other	123.0	1048	128904.0	1086.9	133688.7	-4784.7
	NET EFFECT						-349.8
1994-95							
FHs	Fallopian tube	107.5	58	6235.0	78.5	8438.8	-2203.8
	Other	124.2	2538	315219.6	2517.5	312673.5	2546.1
	NET EFFECT						342.3
1995-96							
Non FHs	Uterus	101.3	340	34442.0	370.6	37541.8	-3099.8
	Fallopian tube	97.4	117	11395.8	101.2	9856.9	1538.9
	Joint	254.2	505	128371.0	462.1	117465.8	10905.2
	Other	122.9	3266	401391.4	3294.1	404844.9	-3453.5
	NET EFFECT						5890.8
FHs	Uterus	97.2	268	26040.0	237.4	23075.3	2964.7
	Fallopian tube	114.3	49	5600.7	64.8	7406.6	-1805.9
	Joint	225.3	253	57000.9	295.9	66666.3	-9665.4
	Other	126.4	2138	270243.2	2109.9	266691.4	3551.8
	NET EFFECT						-4954.8

With regard to the data in tables 6.5 to 6.8, two brief points are worth noting. First, by recording the figures to a single decimal point, a certain degree of rounding up and down has necessarily taken place. For this reason there will be slight differences in various cases if the mean waits shown in the tables for the itemised procedure categories are compounded for comparison against the averages detailed in tables 4.9 to 4.12. Second, if the net effect of the case mix difference was to increase the mean waiting time for a population, the actual wait would be a higher number of days than the expected wait. In such cases the figure in the variance column on the right of the table is a positive figure. Conversely, if the case mix reduced the average waiting time of a population, meaning the actual wait is a lower number than the expected wait, the total in the variance column is a negative total. The outcome of the above investigation will now be summarised.

In short, the objective was to identify which cases should progress on to the third stage of this study, that of ascertaining whether the impact of case mix in shortening fund-holders' waits or lengthening those of non fund-holders was substantial. It has already been explained that for Crawley Horsham in 1992/93, the case mix differences increased the waits of fund-holding patients, so this case does not graduate to the next stage. For the same provider in 1993/94, the case mix contrasts again centred just on the fund-holding population. The effect here was to decrease their waits, so this case will feature in the next stage. In 1994/95 case mix differences at Crawley Horsham both increased the waits of non fund-holders and reduced them for fund-holders, so this case will also be investigated further. In 1995/96 at Crawley Horsham case mix inflated the waits of both populations, but more for fund-holders in both a numerical and proportional context. This case is therefore not applicable to the third stage.

At Mid Sussex in 1994/95, case mix differences actually lowered the waits of non fund-holding patients but increased them for the fund-holders. Hence this case is clearly ineligible to be carried forward to the next stage of the inquiry. For the same provider in 1995/96, case mix extended the waiting times of both populations. Similar to Crawley Horsham in 1995/96, the increase to fund-holders' waits was both proportionately and numerically greater than for the non fund-holding population. As such, this case is also disqualified from the third stage of this examination. Indeed, this means the Mid Sussex provider will not have a role in the next step of this particular investigation.

For the Royal West Sussex provider in 1994/95, the outcome of case mix variation was a slight increase in the waiting times of non fund-holders, along with a decrease in waits for fund-holding patients. This case will therefore be admitted to the third stage.

The 1992/93 analysis for Worthing and Southlands concentrated on fund-holding patients and that population's waiting times were reduced by case mix contrasts. This trend was repeated at the same provider the following year, when the significance of case mix differences were mainly driven by operations on the eye and lens (cataract surgery), tonsil and mouth, plus the bladder and prostate of fund-holding patients. Once again the impact was to lower waits, so like 1992/93 this case shall be referred to the next stage of the inquiry. At Worthing and Southlands in 1994/95, case mix variation slightly raised the waiting times of fund-holders, so this case shall not have a role in the next stage of the process. For this same provider in 1995/96 the enquiry focused upon operations on the uterus (chiefly hysterectomies), fallopian tubes and joints of patients from both populations. The effect was to inflate the waits of non fund-holders and lessen them for fund-holders. This case will therefore be addressed in the third stage.

In sum, there were eleven cases where statistically significant differences emerged in the surgical case mix of fund-holding and non fund-holding patients. Six had a greater impact on abating the waits of fund-holders relative to people registered with practices outside the scheme whilst five appeared to have the reverse effect.

Stage three: were contrasts merely significant or important as well?

Five cases have been lost to the final stage in each of the first two steps of this study. As such, half a dozen out of sixteen cases have advanced to the final stage of this investigation into the gravity of case mix in driving the generally shorter waiting times of fund-holding patients. In each of these, the differences in the surgical case mix of patients registered with practices inside and outside the scheme were statistically significant, and the effect of this was to lower the waits of fund-holders, relative to non fund-holders. The issue to be addressed in this stage of the inquiry is the relevance of this trend. Was it likely to have been a consequential factor in driving significant discrepancies in the waiting times of the two populations?

The six cases under review each feature in table 6.9. For the relevant populations that were the basis for the analyses in tables 6.5 to 6.8, it provides the original aggregate waiting times upon which the comparisons in tables 4.9 to 4.12 were based. It also details what the impact on the original aggregate would have been if the actual activity had reflected the expected activity, as demonstrated in tables 6.5 to 6.8. The outcome from this is to display the extent to which the expected activity would have altered the mean waiting times of the specific population.

Regarding the Crawley Horsham provider, table 6.9 shows that 1,027 applicable fund-holding patients received operations in 1993/94. Their aggregate actual waiting time for these episodes was 153,535 to give a mean wait of 149.5 days. If their surgical case mix had reflected the expected case mix, calculated by the methodology explained earlier, the aggregate wait would be 2,715.6 days more than the actual total (see table 6.5). This increases the aggregate expected waiting times from 153,535 to 156,250.6 days. With the total number of procedures numbering 1,027, this will result in an expected mean wait of 152.1 days, an increase of 2.6 days to the actual average of 149.5 days.

From this, a decision needs to be made as to whether this difference can rightfully be considered as having a material effect in causing the contrasts in the average waiting times of fund-holding and non fund-holding patients (see table 4.9). A truly objective estimate via a recalculation of the ANOVA tests using the higher expected aggregate wait would be prone to subjective value judgements in constructing the individual components of the test, namely the discrete waiting time of individual patients. This is because results computed through ANOVA reflect the pattern of variation within the population groups and also between them (cases that have large variances within sub-samples are less likely to produce significant results). Consequently, spreading the additional 2,715.6 days between the 1,027 fund-holding patients equally, just over 2.6 days each, would give a different result to adding 2,715.6 to a single patient, or almost 13.6 days to 200 patients, plus any other possible combination.

To be fair, this is a somewhat extreme guide because the contrasts in the distinct categories of operations featured in table 6.5 have not been utilised, which they certainly should be. However, the point remains that the process of evaluating the genuine effect of the changes in the mean waiting times is not totally straightforward. Even so, it would still appear that the impact of the changes would have been very modest indeed.

For instance, in the case of Crawley Horsham in 1993/94, a mean wait of 152.1 days for fund-holders would still produce a statistically significant result against the non fund-holding average of 214.2 days (see table 4.9). Though not shown in table 4.9 (in common with broad practice), the original comparison produced an F critical statistic of 3.84 against an obtained statistic of 90.1. Just adding 2.6 days to the mean waits of fund-holders should lower the difference to a small degree, but would not stop the variance from being significant. Precisely the same point can be made about this provider in 1994/95. Subtracting 0.7 days from the actual mean wait of non fund-holders to give an expected average of 193.2 days and adding 1.9 to the actual mean of fund-holders to give an expected average of 151.8 is not going to make the original result in table 4.9 insignificant.

Table 6.9   Effect of case mix differences that would increase the mean waits (in days) of fund-holding (FHs) patients or decrease the mean waits of non fund-holding (non FHs) patients on the elective waiting list

Provider, year & group		No	Actual waits	Mean wait	Change to actual	Expected waits	Expected mean	Change to mean
Crawley Horsham								
1993-94	FHs	1027	153535	149.5	2715.6	156250.6	152.1	2.6
1994-95	Non FHs	1865	361677	193.9	-1288.8	360388.2	193.2	-0.7
	FHs	1547	231932	149.9	2975.4	234907.4	151.8	1.9
Royal West Sussex								
1994-95	Non FHs	1279	360690	282.0	-71.4	360618.6	282.0	-
	FHs	560	112413	200.7	693.0	113106.0	202.0	1.3
Worthing & Southlands								
1992-93	FHs	661	76967	116.4	2151.8	79118.8	119.7	3.3
1993-94	FHs	1355	178514	131.7	349.8	178863.8	132.0	0.3
1995-96	Non FHs	4228	575554	136.1	-5890.8	569663.2	134.7	-1.4
	FHs	2708	358953	132.6	4954.8	363907.8	134.4	1.8

Again, the same judgement looks applicable for the Royal West Sussex in 1994/95. Adding 1.3 days to the actual mean of fund-holding patients (from table 4.11) gives a new average of 202.0 days. Against a non fund-holding mean of 282.0 days it is nonsensical to imagine that the wide gap between the original F critical and obtained statistics, 3.85 and 87.0, is going to be narrowed to the point where the result no longer remains significant.

Regarding Worthing and Southlands, for two of the cases featured in table 6.9, 1993/94 and 1995/96, whilst fund-holders had shorter waits in both years the original results were not shown as significant in table 4.12 anyway. To be fair, for 1993/94 this was probably a result of 324 fund-holding patients at the time of the procedure spending nearly 56 per cent of their waiting time prior to their practices joining the scheme (see table 4.3). For 1992/93 at this provider, the actual mean wait of the fund-holding population would have been changed from 116.4 days (table 4.12) to 119.7 (table 6.9), against an average waiting time for non fund-holders of 129.1. Again, the relative closeness of these waits was driven by 205 fund-holders spending 64 per cent of their gross waits of 45,026 days on the list prior to their practice joining the scheme (see table 4.3). Taking this last point into account, it is hard to see how a change of 3.3 days to the mean waiting time of fund-holders could possibly undermine the significance of their shorter waits.

CONCLUSION

This chapter has dealt with the idea that waiting time differences between fund-holding and non fund-holding patients might have been caused by what is probably a more hidden factor than some of the other hypotheses investigated during this study. The inquiry focused on the contrasts in the surgical case mix of each population, with the relevance of the investigation being dependent on different sorts of operations at specific providers having varying waiting times. The definition of the case mix hypothesis as a more hidden factor can be justified on the following grounds. Firstly, if the case mix profile of fund-holding patients was set by chance or other random factors, it may have shortened their waits in an almost spurious manner. Secondly, other factors might have a more obvious potential impact on waiting times. For instance, it seems fair to suggest that the prospect of an imbalance in funding between the purchaser types probably 'springs to mind' as a possible reason for any discrepancies in waiting times before the case mix issue.

Although there may be various ways in which an investigation into case mix differences could be undertaken, the study concentrated on the mix of procedures rather than any contrasts in the age or sex profile of the fund-holding and non fund-holding populations. The reason for this is that if there were discrepancies in the waits for various kinds of surgery, it seems sensible to focus on the number of episodes received by each group of patients rather than some of the things that may influence the prevalence of certain types of operation. By doing this, the investigation converges straight away on the real crux of the matter instead of more peripheral side issues. A similar reasoning was behind the decision to concentrate on the mix of procedures rather than diagnosis rates, a judgement vindicated by the nature of the separate categories of the overall waiting list.

The methodology adopted for the inquiry showed that any differences in the surgical case mix of the fund-holding and non fund-holding populations were not significant in five out of the sixteen cases. In five of the remaining eleven cases, the contrasts in case mix tended to increase the waits of fund-holders relative to non fund-holders. In the other six cases where case mix had increased the waits of non fund-holding patients or decreased those of fund-holders, the effect looks too marginal to be accepted as a critical factor in explaining the disparities in the relative waiting times of each group. These cases seem almost perfect examples of the notion that statistically significant differences are not necessarily consequential.

As such, the overriding impression from this analysis has been that the shorter waits of fund-holding patients on the elective waiting list cannot legitimately be considered as driven by case mix differences. The hypothesis that contrasts in case mix might be a material factor behind the shorter waiting times of fund-holding patients must therefore be rejected. From this, and because the previous chapter indicated that fund-holding practices did not appear to receive an overgenerous level of funding, the genuine reason behind the lower average waits of their patients has yet to be established. The investigation into factors that have the potential to explain these differences thus continues in the next chapter.

7 Purchaser Performance in the Quasi-market

The last two chapters have demonstrated that the funding balance and case mix contrasts have both been found to be wanting in their capacity to explain the trend towards shorter waiting times for fund-holding patients on the elective waiting list at four West Sussex providers. The purpose of this chapter is to continue the investigation into the various other hypotheses mentioned in the second chapter that may account for this tendency. In doing this it will focus on the impact of contracts, the relationships between purchasers and providers, plus the information and incentives applicable to the commissioners. The chapter will then move on to the significance of the exit option whereby purchasers may have moved patients between alternative hospitals, or were at least perceived as able to do so by the providers themselves. Each of these issues shall be addressed in turn.

CONTRACTS

There are two main strands to the contract investigation. One relates to the idea that the shorter waiting times of fund-holding patients were determined by specifications placed in contracts between the practices and providers. The other concerns the notion that the use of alternative contract types by purchasers could have stimulated different responses by hospitals in admitting patients. In particular the widespread (although not universal) use of cost-per-case contracts by fund-holding practices might have been a vital factor in shortening the waits of their patients whilst health authorities persevered with block agreements that guaranteed local NHS providers a set income for a less specific level of service provision. If this were the case and contract type was the dominant factor in driving waiting time differences, it would seem reasonable to expect the waits of fund-holding patients admitted under block contracts to be longer than those from practices utilising cost-per-case agreements.

Contract specifications

The hypothesis that variances in waiting times resulted from distinct purchasers specifying different waiting time limits for their populations presumes a commissioner driven environment in probably its purest form. After negotiating a contractual agreement, providers would respond to whatever waiting time targets were in place. Hence if a provider's contract with the health authority defined a target wait of eighteen months for non-urgent elective surgery whilst agreements with fund-holders were for twelve months, the hospital keeping to these time spans would have produced clear contrasts between the discrete populations. From this scenario, if one fund-holder specified a goal wait of six months while another demanded ten months, differences would have arisen within the fund-holding population.

The idea that waiting times were a simple outcome of contractual demands represents an uncomplicated supposition. The question is, does it accurately reflect what tended to happen at four West Sussex providers between April 1992 and March 1996? The health authority, which holds copies of local fund-holders' contracts with providers, facilitated an inspection of these documents for the relevant period. Discussions were also held with the managers at each trust who had direct responsibility for contractual liaison with such practices. Both of these sources provided a compatible response. In short, the answer is no, this was not the reason behind waiting time differences.

For the years under review hospitals did not tend to negotiate differential waiting times between distinct fund-holders and the health authority. Managers at three providers said contracts were absolutely consistent in this respect, although one of them did start to allow individual fund-holders to specify their own targets after the four years relevant to this study. The manager at the other provider stated that occasionally they had, when a local practice insisted on setting differential waiting time targets, allowed them to do it. Yet this was followed with an observation that it was a purely "academic" exercise. "Even if we had tried, it would be a tremendous struggle to keep to different waiting time targets. Allowing contracts to occasionally be written this way had more to do with trying to keep a practice happy, and it really was just the odd one here and there, than anything else. In all honesty little or no attention was paid to it".

This corresponds with answers given by consultants at the providers. Whilst they were aware that fund-holders had the formal authority to try and specify shorter waits for their own patients in contracts, all denied this had a material influence in shaping waiting times. Nine of the twelve consultants declared themselves to be completely unaware of the contents of contracts, with a typical response being made by the consultant who described himself as "oblivious" to such issues. Another said it would have been a "nightmare" to attempt keeping to specific targets in different practices' contracts. In fact the only consultants who admitted to even being told by hospital managers that a practice had a waiting time target specified in their contracts were from the provider whose manager is quoted in the previous paragraph. Moreover, it was also noticeable that individual fund-holders' contracts did not even specify precise waiting time targets for elective surgery, beyond making some bland reference to meeting patient's charter standards.[18]

Whilst the collection of fund-holders' contracts held by the health authority was not absolutely complete, the very large majority were inspected. None were found where a practice had specified unique waiting times, so if it did happen at the above provider it must have been one of the contracts that were missing. In fact there appeared to be a common policy in the county in this respect. With minimal differences in punctuation and the use of upper and lower case letters, all the contracts seen contained the following sentence. 'The maximum waiting time will be as per the specification of the provider's district health authority and its requirements under the patient's charter'.

Hence it seems the most sustainable conclusion that can be reached is to reject the hypothesis that differential waits were a product of specifications that were formally stated in the contract document. But does the idea that hospitals respond differently to alternative types of contract offer more hope of finding the reason for contrasts in waiting times?

Contract type and waiting times

This inquiry used the waiting times of patients registered with fund-holders that commissioned elective surgery by way of different contract types as a guide to whether the trend towards longer waits for non fund-holders can be seen as a consequence of the health authority using block contracts. The logic of the analysis rests on the following principle concerning the way fund-holders commission surgery. Do the waiting times of patients from

---

18. Although the precise patient's charter targets were not formally mentioned in the contracts, from April 1992 nobody should have been on the waiting list more than two years (see Department of Health, 1991). Following an experiment in which this limit was reduced by six months for cataract surgery plus hip and knee replacements, the target of eighteen months was extended to most operations from April 1995 (see Department of Health, 1995b). The exceptions were coronary artery bypass grafts and angioplasty procedures, both of which had a target wait of twelve months (see NHS Executive, 1996d).

practices that utilise different sorts of agreement show similar tendencies to the contrasts in waits between fund-holders (on an overall basis) and non fund-holders? If they do, then the forms of contract employed by the health authority and most fund-holding practices could be at the root of the variances.

The type of contract used by specific fund-holders to commission elective surgery from the four providers featured in the research was established primarily by seeing the actual documents at the health authority's offices. In the few cases where the contract was not traceable, the information was obtained by telephoning the practices concerned. After excluding the East Grinstead fund-holders because the Queen Victoria Hospital was not applicable to this study, the remaining practices were separated into four groups on the basis of their local providers' catchment areas. The number of West Sussex fund-holders from each group that had used block, cost-per-case or cost and volume arrangements in each year to purchase surgery is shown in table 7.1. It is noticeable that cost-per-case agreements were the predominant contract type used by such practices during the four years under review.

Every fund-holder in both the Crawley Horsham and Mid Sussex localities used cost-per-case contracts, so these practices and providers have no further role in this investigation. With regard to practices whose main provider was the Royal West Sussex, the inquiry is confined to 1995/96 when just one had a block contract while all the others used cost-per-case agreements. The greatest mix in contract type was between fund-holders primarily using Worthing and Southlands, particularly in 1995/96 although there was a degree of variety in the two previous years.

Indeed, the mix at this provider in 1995/96 might even suggest that the contract type hypothesis may have some real substance to it, as fund-holders should not be considered to have had shorter waits in this particular case (contrary to the results shown in table 4.4). The analysis pertinent to table 4.4 had defined the fund-holding population as those patients whose practice had been in the fund-holding scheme over the entire duration of their wait. However, table 4.3 indicates that patients receiving operations at Worthing and Southlands in 1995/96, whose practice joined the scheme during the course of their wait, spent nearly two-thirds of their waiting period after the entry date. Excluding those patients from the fund-holding population can thus be seen as giving a false impression (too low) of the average waiting times of fund-holders in this case.

Table 7.1   Types of contract held by West Sussex fund-holding practices to purchase elective surgery at four providers over four financial years

Provider and year	Cost per case	Cost and volume	Block	Total
Crawley Horsham				
1992-93	2	0	0	2
1993-94	3	0	0	3
1994-95	5	0	0	5
1995-96	5	0	0	5
Mid Sussex				
1992-93	3	0	0	3
1993-94	3	0	0	3
1994-95	5	0	0	5
1995-96	5	0	0	5
Royal West Sussex				
1992-93	1	0	0	1
1993-94	4	0	0	4
1994-95	6	0	0	6
1995-96	9	0	1	10
Worthing and Southlands				
1992-93	2	0	0	2
1993-94	3	1	0	4
1994-95	7	1	1	9
1995-96	4	3	3	10

Whilst table 7.1 separates practices on the basis of their chief provider, that will not have been the only hospital where their patients were treated. Patients do not always receive services from the hospital that is geographically closest to their general practice. When someone registered with a fund-holding GP was seen at a provider that was not the nearest hospital to the practice's surgery premises, payment for the service tended to be made under one of two scenarios. If the practice was historically quite a heavy user of the less local provider, they may have had a cost-per-case contract with them. Otherwise, the admission was likely to be made on an extra contractual referral basis, meaning the practice paid for the treatment on a cost-per-case basis without holding a formal contract with the provider. The data in table 7.1 represents the contractual arrangements between providers and their local fund-holders, and covers all the cost and volume or block contracts held by such practices.

Table 7.2 provides a comparison of the waiting times of patients from practices using alternative types of contracts to purchase elective surgery. The patients applicable to the cost-per-case category include those registered with practices outside the provider's catchment area whose treatments were performed on an extra contractual referral basis, as well as people from practices that held a formal cost-per-case contract. The fund-holding population is defined according to the status of patients' practices at the time of the surgery in order to make the size of the cost and volume plus block groups as meaningful as possible. In this way it captures all fund-holding patients admitted under each form of contract that had their waiting time recorded. The analysis is unavoidably restricted to three years at Worthing and Southlands, plus one at the Royal West Sussex.

Of the four cases featured in table 7.2, only one shows a statistically significant difference between practices using alternative forms of contract. Patients of the practice that had a cost and volume contract with Worthing and Southlands in 1993/94 had significantly longer waits than those from fund-holders commissioning surgery on a cost-per-case basis. Yet the following year patients of this same practice had somewhat shorter waits than their cost-per-case counterparts, though not to a significant extent. Moreover, it is clear that patients from practices utilising block contracts at Worthing and Southlands in 1994/95 and 1995/96 did have longer waits that those admitted on a cost-per-case basis, even if not to a statistically significant extent. Yet this trend at Worthing and Southlands was reversed at the Royal West Sussex in 1995/96. In this latter case, patients from the practice using a block contract had shorter waits than those admitted under cost-per-case agreements, although again not to a significant degree.

Table 7.2 Waiting times (in days) at the Royal West Sussex (RWS) plus Worthing and Southlands (W&S) providers for operations covered by the fund-holding scheme on fund-holding elective waiting list patients admitted under alternative contract types

| | Cost per case | | | Cost and volume | | | Block | | | ANOVA |
	Median	Mean	No	Median	Mean	No	Median	Mean	No	P-value
RWS										
95-96	92.0	156.4	1194	-	-	0	88.0	149.0	151	0.5772
W&S										
93-94	82.0	127.6	1029	91.5	144.8	326	-	-	0	0.0302
94-95	76.0	122.8	2023	72.0	118.9	341	104.0	138.8	232	0.1368
95-96	87.0	130.4	1296	78.5	130.5	750	93.5	139.1	662	0.2828

As such, no consistent trend is apparent. A case exists where patients of fund-holders using block contracts had shorter waiting times than their cost-per-case counterparts (the Royal West Sussex in 1995/96), with the opposite being true elsewhere (Worthing and Southlands in 1994/95 and 1995/96). It is also possible to find a case where patients admitted under cost and volume agreements had shorter waits than those called in under cost-per-case contracts (Worthing and Southlands in 1994/95), with a statistically significant example going the other way to this (Worthing and Southlands in 1993/94). Hence the waits of fund-holding patients covered by different sorts of contract do not consistently reflect the trend that would support the contract type hypothesis. Patients called in under block contracts did not have significantly longer waits than those admitted on a cost-per-case basis. On balance, therefore, the hypothesis that waiting time variances were a result of the purchaser types tending to use different forms of contract lacks support.

RELATIONSHIPS

The foundation for the relationship hypothesis is the idea that different purchasers had varying levels of influence over the people at hospitals who decided which patients should be admitted when for their operations. In itself this raises a number of queries concerning, for example, the identity of whoever made this decision at the providers, which in itself connects to the administration of the admission process. Evidence linked to such issues came mainly from interviews with twelve hospital consultants and the four chief executives from the trusts, though six department managers were also seen at the providers. While the responses from each individual source were compatible, at the margins they exhibit some variance in practice. Yet on a general level, consistent policy trends were evident.

Admitting patients

Admission policies for elective surgery and outpatient appointments differed. Concerning outpatient services all of the dozen consultants confirmed that on receiving referrals they categorised patients according to the degree of urgency indicated by the GP's letter. This classification often determined whether they saw a patient themselves or passed them to a less senior colleague. Patients were then called in line with this urgency, with routine cases admitted in the date order of referral letters. All but one (eleven out of twelve) of the consultants said fund-holding status had no influence at all on the speed of admission for outpatient consultations. The exception claimed that in cases where the letter made it obvious the referral was not urgent, fund-holders may have been called in a little sooner.

Once seen in an outpatient clinic, those patients requiring operations were categorised according to their clinical urgency and entered onto the waiting list. At this point clerks marked every patient's notes and waiting list record according to whether or not they came from a fund-holding practice. Because of this every consultant indicated the latest they became fully aware of whether a patient on the waiting list was with a fund-holding practice was the time of their placement on the list. One made a typical response by stating, "quite simply, it would be impossible not to know". All twelve consultants remarked that fund-holding status made no difference whatsoever to the waits of clinically urgent patients and planned admissions, but confirmed that in routine cases fund-holders were called in sooner, regardless of who took the final decision.

Once people were on the waiting list with an urgency status, nine of the twelve consultants said they made the final decision as to which patients are called in when. The other three said their departmental manager, secretary or a waiting list clerk mostly made this decision for routine status cases, two of them saying they had relinquished this job since the internal market began. One was happy with this change, made for administrative convenience, and without complaint would have followed the line of admitting fund-holders sooner. The other also gave up the role willingly, but was uncomfortable with the expectation that he should admit fund-holding patients earlier and thus wanted such decisions taken out of his hands. As such, it appears that consultants admitted fund-holding patients sooner in order to take account of the interests of their trust. This issue will be explored later.

These accounts given by the consultants agree with the views of the chief executives of the providers, although an important qualification was strongly emphasised by them which particularly corresponds with the reason one consultant gave for choosing to limit his role in deciding the admission order of patients. All four remarked that consultants had the prime role in deciding which individual patients were called in when, although this was put into context by a set of additional comments. For example, their decisions must "comply with the rules of the game", their actions should be made "within an unwritten policy framework", they were "given advice about their decision making", and "their room for manoeuvring is restricted". In sum, a heavy majority of consultants felt they still retained the final responsibility for admitting non-urgent patients, even though some did not get too involved in this decision and preferred leaving it to non-clinical staff. Nevertheless, such specific decisions appeared to be shaped by wider organisational priorities.

It therefore seems feasible that if relationships had a major impact in driving waiting times, it was most likely to be the links purchasers had with consultants that was the fulcrum of the idea. After all, it is they who mostly decided which individual patients were called in when, even if they worked within a policy framework. Also, the relationships between GPs and hospital consultants, by way of the referral system let alone any contractual link, probably represented the closest point of contact between key purchaser and provider agents. Yet there is more than a single way of looking at the relationships between consultants and purchasers. One option is to examine their relationships with the agencies that were the actual commissioners of their services, the health authority and fund-holding GPs. Another is to evaluate the nature of the contact between consultants and the people who drove their business – all GPs, including non fund-holders.

Consultants, GPs and health authority staff

All the consultants denied that their personal relationships with individual GPs was in any way influenced by fund-holding, although one made a sweeping generalisation when he called non fund-holders "apathetic". The overriding view was that if there was any degree of friendship or hostility, it originated independently from the scheme. Also, eight of the twelve consultants said they had very good relationships with GPs in general, three making the point that it was in their interests to maintain such friendships for the sake of receiving referrals to their private practices. In short, the scheme did not appear to affect the nature of the personal relationship between GPs and consultants.

Moreover, every consultant also claimed that even in cases where the style of their relationship with individual GPs differed, it had no bearing on the speed or quality of care given to patients. In line with this, one made the following comment. "There is no way I would allow my relationship with specific GPs or practices to influence the way I look after patients. Besides, if I did get on badly with any I would be unlikely to see many of their patients anyway. They are going to send their referrals to one of my colleagues rather than me".

Also, only one of the dozen consultants felt he had more contact with partners of fund-holding practices than he did with GPs outside the scheme and claimed this had no effect on the waiting times of patients. Indeed, one of the other eleven commented that "fund-holding has increased the quantity and quality of dialogue between consultants and GPs in general, including non fund-holders". This complements the opinion of another consultant who stated that "today's non fund-holders are tomorrow's fund-holders. It would be pretty stupid for us to ignore them before they join the scheme as this would make it harder for us to keep their business once they are in it".[19]

---

19. This comment, like many of the others by consultants and GPs that are quoted verbatim in the book, was made in the context of the interviews taking place prior to the 1997 general election.

Therefore, as far as the relationships between consultants and GPs are concerned, the interviews with consultant staff at hospitals strongly indicate that personal relationships did not have a material effect on the relative waiting times of fund-holding and non fund-holding patients. In sum, fund-holding status allegedly made no difference to the relationships between individual consultants and GPs. Only one consultant out of twelve admitted that he had any more contact with fund-holding GPs than those outside the scheme, and like the other eleven claimed that his personal relationships with specific GPs made not the slightest difference to the care received by patients.

There were some discrepancies between the level of contact different consultants had with health authority staff. The clinical directors generally, although not always, had more interaction with them than did the other consultants. The dealings between health authority personnel and consultants usually occurred through contract discussions and monitoring, plus events labelled as 'strategy meetings'. One of the non-clinical directors claimed his main point of contact was as the recipient of "rude letters from dogmatic and uninformed people who haven't got a clue how to run a health service". In the single case where a consultant had no personal contact, his impressions were derived from the perceptions of clinical colleagues who had.

There was a substantial overlap in consultants' opinions about their relationships with the health authority managers, and it was not positive. The sole exception (out of twelve) to this trend called them "helpful". One defined his association with them as characterised by "antipathy", another thought they were "deeply unimpressive", while someone else said, "it is very them and us, I just don't rate them". Another claimed he would "cross the road to avoid them", whilst someone else volunteered the opinion that they were "complete wasters". Others suggested they "couldn't be much worse", and that "as individuals they are probably quite pleasant people, although I find them rather secretive and I do think the best thing might be for the health authority to go bankrupt", adding this would "get them off the scene".

The consultants were also asked to compare fund-holders and the health authority as advocates of patients' interests and classify each, taking their overall impression of fund-holders as a group, into 'good', 'medium' or 'bad' categories. Only one consultant rated the purchaser types equally, ranking them as 'medium'. The other eleven considered fund-holders to be better than the health authority, all placing such practices in the 'good' banding. Overall, four of them thought the health authority were worthy of a 'medium' classification and the other eight considered them to be 'bad', one reinforcing this view with the word "extremely". Interestingly the consultant who ranked both purchaser types as 'medium' qualified this by saying his opinion of fund-holding was untypical of his colleagues, and after the interview introduced the clinical director of his department. He also agreed to answer the same set of questions and felt fund-holders were 'good' and the health authority 'medium'.

Beyond this, the consultants were also asked about their general attitudes towards the fund-holding scheme. Remarks made previously by six departmental managers at the trusts that consultants had come to accept the scheme over time were confirmed. Seven out of twelve consultants were on balance supportive of it (indeed eight out of thirteen if the clinical director just mentioned in the previous paragraph is included in the total, and nine out of fourteen if the pilot interview is taken into account). One commented that it was a "potent force for producing positive change" and another said, "now everybody has got used to it, I and many of my colleagues would favour keeping it going". These kind of responses are perhaps a surprisingly positive response to the scheme, and it thus appears that what could have been initial bitter opposition from consultants might have mellowed quite drastically.

This idea may even be reinforced because out of the five consultants opposed to it, the stand of four was not really staunch. One said, "I would probably rather see it abolished, even though they are better than the health authority, simply because I am opposed to market mechanisms. The problem I have is not so much with fund-holding but the whole internal market. I would also like to see the health authority abolished, even more so". Another suggested, "it would be far more defensible if all practices were in it", an attitude repeated by the interviewee who said, "it geed things up a bit. I don't like it but it has improved over time. It should be abolished or made compulsory". Someone else said, "I honestly think fund-holding is a very good thing, though either everybody or nobody should be in it. It is a very close choice for me due to the good job most fund-holders have done in looking after their patients, yet I am a strong traditionalist regarding the order of our profession and I would vote to get rid of it, but only just".

In line with the above views, all of the consultants saw the opportunity that was encouraged by fund-holding to discuss service developments with other doctors as being preferable to dealing with the health authority. As a follow on to this response, one commented that "by giving GPs more influence fund-holding has made consultants try harder to achieve better services. We now do the type of things we should, looking back, have been doing anyway".

Yet while these results may be surprising considering the reputation fund-holding had for equalising the hierarchical status of consultants and

GPs, as referenced in the second chapter, the relationship hypothesis still seems to fall short of offering a valid explanation for the occurrence of waiting time differences. Only one consultant said the different nature of his relationships with the two purchaser types had any consequence at all on the relative waiting times of their clients, and he described the effect as "negligible".

In sum, the interviews with consultants strongly suggested that their relationships with health authority managers and GPs, both inside and outside the scheme, cannot be considered as a significant factor in driving the waiting time differences between fund-holding and non fund-holding patients. Even though consultants predominantly considered fund-holders to be better representatives of patients' interests than the health authority, there is no evidence that this was the reason for the shorter waits of fund-holding patients.

INFORMATION AND INCENTIVES

The kinds of information and incentives that were likely to be held by health authority staff and GP fund-holders in their commissioning functions were discussed in the second chapter. The ensuing section deals with the prospect that the information more readily available to GPs may be the type that lends itself best to commissioning elective surgery. Representatives from each purchaser type, fund-holding GPs plus the chief executive and director of public health for the health authority, were asked for their views on this matter. The investigation then progresses by assessing if specific incentives held by both GPs and health authority personnel has relevance to one purchaser type securing shorter waiting times for patients than the other.

Information

The first matter to consider is what kind of information would be required to secure shorter waiting times for elective surgery. Official publications have stressed the option of transferring patients to alternative providers when hospitals cannot offer satisfactory waits (see NHS Executive, 1996b; 1996d). The basic information required to utilise this action might be for a purchaser to hold accurate details of the waiting times for various operations at the hospitals in the surrounding area, so enabling them to switch referrals around accordingly. Nevertheless, on asking GPs about the extent of their knowledge of comparative waits at different NHS hospitals, the real situation fell short of satisfying this condition. This may well comply with the fairly limited differences in case mix for fund-holders and non fund-holders, discussed in the sixth chapter. GPs' attention to such issues was concentrated on those services with severely long waits at their local provider, not the position at competitors.

Moreover, only one out of the twelve fund-holders named an awareness of comparative waiting times as a meaningful piece of information for GP purchasers, along with the even more important personal knowledge of her patients. This last factor was named by eleven of the GPs as the most critical source of data held by fund-holding practices, one saying it was "information that cannot be replicated at the health authority". It was felt that seeing patients in the surgery and obtaining feedback from them on hospital services placed GPs in a unique position to understand their patients' needs and the standards of care at hospitals, even though they did not possess detailed knowledge on comparative waiting times. The one who did not select this factor as the most important information held by GPs for commissioning thought the comparative prices of alternative providers was more significant.

Beyond this, what is the position of the health authority in the context of information? Both of the health authority representatives felt their organisation held a crucial quality as a commissioner in that they were in a good position to see the broader picture of the health service in the area. One of them called this an "overview" which enabled them to piece things together. The other also maintained the health authority had a vital strategic function and had to retain a commissioning role for the sake of GPs who simply did not wish to get involved in purchasing.

Yet this raises the query as to what benefits any advantageous position in the context of strategic direction and overview provides for commissioning what services. After all, one of the health authority interviewees stressed that distinct services are best purchased at different levels, be it by individual practices, groups of practices, by single health authorities or at a grouped health authority level. This is an idea that appears to have a compelling logic. The inference made by a health authority representative to this was that "low volume high cost services for chronic conditions" were best commissioned by health authorities for the sake of risk sharing. But this was the only sort of care that both mentioned should ideally be placed firmly in the health authority's commissioning remit, apart from services for patients whose general practices choose not to participate in the commissioning function.

One made this point by saying, "GPs are closer to the action. Elective surgery should ideally be purchased at the level of general practice, along with just about all elective care. GP groups should also take responsibility for accident and emergency services. The health authority must, however, retain the authority to monitor their performance". The other representative of the health authority also considered the forms of information available to each purchaser made GPs the most appropriate purchasers of elective surgery, as well as many other things. Nevertheless, whilst putting forward the view that GPs must be fully involved in commissioning decisions, he did not see why they should need to actually hold the budgets for this role themselves.

On balance, GPs felt their closeness to patients gave them important impressions of the relative standard of care offered by alternative hospitals. However, they did not hold the form of information – a firm knowledge of the expected waits for common procedures at individual providers, that seems most applicable to reducing waiting times (even though they managed to do this). This suggests that there were other factors coming into play which were more important for lowering waits.

Incentives

This section examines whether the incentives of the purchaser types contribute to finding a convincing explanation for fund-holding patients tending to have significantly shorter waits for non-urgent elective surgery than their non fund-holding counterparts. The inquiry into this issue was once again undertaken through the interviews held with a dozen fund-holding GPs plus the chief executive and director of public health from the health authority.

The fundamental impression given by the health authority representatives was that many of the priorities for their organisation were essentially driven from what they called the "centre". The 'national planning guidance', issued on an annual basis by the NHS Executive, was seen as a critical document in shaping their purchasing decisions. As a broad generalisation, a strong impression was given that health authority commissioning was a reactive process in which "national priorities come first", followed by local targets. One of the interviewees also made the point that waiting times were a chief concern for them due to the patient's charter targets. "Waiting times are important to us because we are told to make sure nobody waits longer than eighteen months by the secretary of state and regional chairman. We adopt a crude unselective approach. That must be the maximum wait for all procedures and all patients". In sum, therefore, incentives at the health authority appeared driven by higher levels in the machinery of government.

This was also linked to what they felt represented the health authority's main leverage over NHS hospitals. One said, "trust boards and chief executives are personally accountable for meeting patient's charter standards. They can be sacked if they don't. We can call for outside objective audit if this happens, and can get the regional office involved". Yet beyond the patient's charter standards, the other admitted they held "very little" sway over providers in respect of reducing waiting times. "It is a sellers' market. We are beholden to the trusts to grant us what they want to give". From these comments, it looks as though the health authority possessed considerable leverage over providers to meet national targets, but not a great deal beyond that level. They admitted their power to reduce waits beyond targets imposed by the government was severely compromised. In short, it seems the health authority had the incentive and leverage to stop waits exceeding national targets, but not much else.

However, the opinions voiced by the health authority staff contrasted sharply with remarks made by the twelve GP fund-holders. Seven said that the objective to reduce waits for their patients was the major reason behind their practice's decision to join the scheme, and for three of the others it was the second most important reason. Of the two where waiting times had a less significant role in the decision to become fund-holders, at one it had since become a very important aspect of their fund-holding status. The other, who was the only fund-holder to even mention the patient's charter, tried to quantify the relevance of reducing waits in their decision to join the scheme. He said it accounted for 30 per cent of the decision, calling this a "smallish" consideration against the main reason, supporting the local hospital. For the other four practices where waiting times was not the biggest influence in making them join the scheme, two of whom were first wavers, keeping their referral freedom was the most important factor for them all.

Therefore, the clear impression is that the patient's charter waiting time standards which the health authority attempted to maintain for non fund-holding patients was not good enough for the large majority of practices coming into the fund-holding scheme. This seems the case even though that was the limit mentioned in the contracts between fund-holders and providers. When asked what the main cause of this motivation to reduce waiting times was, one responded that it was to achieve a greater level of equity between NHS and private patients. Five said it was primarily to avoid patients coming to them to moan about their long waits, which was described by one GP as creating "unnecessary work" for them. The other six made comments that are indicative of knightly behaviour (see Le Grand, 1997). It was chiefly because they wanted to better the lot of their patients. Various comments reflected an aim to reduce the time people "spend in pain", lessening patients' "frustration", and lowering their "hardship".

In sum, it therefore seems that the incentive to lower waiting times was stronger in the fund-holding community than at the health authority. At the latter, the strong impression was that the patient's charter drove their resolve to control waiting time standards. GPs appeared more determined to reduce the waits of their patients, the motivation for which complies with ideas discussed in the second chapter. There looks to have been a mix of wishing to improve the fortunes of their patients alongside a desire to make their own work routine less demanding by removing, or at least reducing, the likelihood of long-waiters complaining to them.

Moreover, this assessment of the incentives held by each purchaser conveniently moves the investigation towards the next section. Although GP fund-holders may have been the more motivated of the two commissioner types in wishing to reduce waiting times, they still needed a tool to enable them do this. That leads to the following question in the search for the reasons why fund-holding patients generally had shorter waiting times than their non fund-holding counterparts. What did fund-holders do to try and shorten waits, and how did hospitals react to them?

THE EXIT OPTION

When the twelve fund-holders were asked what they had done to try to shorten waiting times, the responses were very similar. The only exception was the answer given by the GP mentioned a little earlier whose practice were least concerned with lowering waits, this accounting for 30 per cent of their decision to become fund-holders. He said their patients' waiting times had fallen at the local provider "without us really doing anything to make it happen ourselves". All of the other eleven said their practice had been willing to move some of their referrals away from their local provider and had done this. "We do it to shake them up a bit", was a typical comment made by one interviewee. Three qualified their responses by saying this line had been taken primarily in the first couple of years in the scheme and had since redirected back to the local provider most of the workload they had initially moved away from it. Indeed, despite the tendency to move referrals, all the GPs stressed the loyalty of their practice to the local NHS hospital.

When asked where their practices had sent most of the referrals that had been directed away from their local hospital, only one said mainly to another NHS provider, and that was outside West Sussex. Six said that while they had sent the majority of these referrals to the non-NHS sector, a significant minority had gone to other public providers, though again the hospitals mentioned in this context were outside the county in Brighton,

Guildford, Portsmouth and Redhill. Five stated that it had largely been to non-NHS hospitals. Indeed, this use of non-NHS providers may also explain why the GPs did not give much priority to the relative waiting times of different public providers. It was surely safe for them to assume that waiting times in the private sector would be shorter than at public providers, so why concern themselves with memorising comparative waits at NHS hospitals? This finding may also update an observation of Mohan (1995) that there was little to suggest the private sector had received much income from fund-holders.

The fund-holding GPs interviewed for the research put forward three constraints on redirecting referrals between providers. Firstly, a concern not to destabilise their local NHS hospital. Secondly, the lack of mobility in many of their patients. Thirdly, the higher prices of competitors compared to the main provider. Nevertheless, because the interviewees had stressed that they do switch some referrals between providers, these factors should be seen as limiting rather than preventing such action. Indeed, three of the twelve believed there was little restriction on them spreading referrals between a number of providers, although they were all from the area that used to be covered by the Mid Downs District Health Authority. In addition to the local private sector, this had three separate NHS provider units covering four acute hospitals within its boundaries (see figure 3.1), along with public hospitals just to the north of the county in Redhill and not far to the south in Brighton.

In brief, despite a perceived lack of mobility in some patients, fund-holders tried to shorten waits by switching referrals to different providers, even though they did not have a firm knowledge of comparable waiting times and had loyalty to their nearest public provider. Shaking the local NHS hospital up seemed the major rationale behind this action. To assess whether that shortened waits for fund-holding patients, this point has relevance to the responses of interviewees representing the providers, to be reported shortly.

Were referrals switched?

So far it has been established that GPs said they tried to reduce waiting times by moving some referrals away from their local provider. It is, however, possible to put a little more 'flesh on the bones' regarding this declaration and assess whether there is any evidence that fund-holders did switch referrals. If fund-holders had moved work away from the NHS sector within the county, it could be expected that a lower ratio of fund-holding patients would receive operations at such providers than the number received by non fund-holders. This may still be the case, regardless of the greater throughput of such patients that is implied by their shorter waits. If fund-holding patients received a higher, or even a similar ratio of operations, this may cast doubts on the claims made by the GP interviewees.

Table 7.3 **Operations covered by the fund-holding scheme performed on patients from the elective waiting list at the Crawley Horsham, Mid Sussex, Royal West Sussex, plus Worthing and Southlands providers over four financial years**

Year	Non fund-holding patients			Fund-holding patients		
	Operations No	Patients No	Operations per 1000 patients	Operations No	Patients No	Operations per 1000 patients
1992-93	12358	629996	19.6	1894	124662	15.2
1993-94	11214	538304	20.8	3431	218374	15.7
1994-95	10008	446429	22.4	5933	311862	19.0
1995-96	9787	399639	24.5	6648	360845	18.4

Table 7.3 details the number of operations at the providers and years relevant to this study performed on NHS patients from the elective waiting list who were registered with fund-holding and non fund-holding practices at the time of the surgery. Because waiting times were not a consideration in this analysis, patients whose waits were not recorded are included in the totals. In every year there were less operations per thousand fund-holding patients than there were for non fund-holders. Whilst this is purely a numerical comparison with no weightings applied to the demographic profile of the populations, it conforms with the results that would be expected if fund-holders had moved work away from the featured providers towards the non-NHS sector, or other public hospitals. This also complies with a remark by one of the consultants interviewed. "When practices join the scheme, about 10 per cent of their work with us disappears".

Nevertheless, the point must also be made that rather than reflecting a trend for fund-holding practices to move patients to other hospitals, their lower rate of surgical activity at the four providers could signify a lower referral rate by GPs inside the scheme. The information required for testing that idea is not available. However, if the data is accepted as suggesting that referrals were switched to some extent, many of the patients go to either a non-NHS provider, or a public hospital other than those featured in this research. For instance, if a practice in Chichester referred a patient to the Mid Sussex provider instead of the Royal West Sussex and that person subsequently received an operation, this would not affect the aggregated procedures per thousand patients. Correspondingly, the interviews with GP fund-holders did suggest that many such movements in referrals were made to the non-NHS sector and this may account for a finding that was reported earlier, the views of the majority of consultants towards fund-holding.

The reason for this is that the lists of clinicians working at local private hospitals clearly indicates that consultants from nearby NHS trusts very largely comprise the medical staff at such non-public providers. Hence a cynical albeit perhaps quite a realistic view is that this could go some way to explaining the generally positive attitudes of the consultants interviewed for this study towards fund-holding. The scheme may well have extended the profitability of their private practices.

From this, the data in table 7.3 seems to support the hypothesis that a market did exist in West Sussex's health service between April 1992 and March 1996, complying with a viewpoint put forward by Glennerster *et al.* (1994a) following their research in other areas. GP fund-holders themselves saw many patients as not referable to hospitals other than their local provider (though some might live nearer a private institution anyway). But table 7.3 does suggest that proportionately more fund-holding patients were referred to a hospital other than the four featured in this study, even though it is not conclusive proof of this. By suggesting fund-holders did use the exit option in their commissioning strategies, this tightens the framework in which the interviews with hospital consultants and chief executives were conducted. It affords a greater degree of confidence in the notion that such practices utilised the exit option. The nucleus of the issue explored from this was whether it actually had an effect on waiting times.

Before moving on to the next stage of the investigation into the exit hypothesis, it should be noted at this point that the health authority representatives did not feel the movement of referrals between different providers was a realistic option for them. One explained the reason for this with the following example. While a strategic decision could be made, for instance, to open a new breast cancer centre at a trust, diverting relevant work to this service and away from the hospital that previously received such referrals was a matter for GPs. Hence the exit option, "in the final analysis", was not seen as applicable to the health authority. The point was made that they "cannot stand over GPs when they make referrals and force them to move a certain percentage of their patients to a different provider".

The inquiry into the exit hypothesis was continued when consultants and chief executives at the four providers were asked what they considered to be their own and the hospitals' key priorities. In addition to this, they were asked why they routinely admitted fund-holding patients with a routine clinical status sooner than such patients from non fund-holding practices. The responses thus provide the key information regarding the thought processes behind admission policies. In deciding to differentiate between fund-holders and other patients, who was striving for what?

Hospital priorities

All four chief executives identified the financial well being of their organisation as having the utmost importance in their working lives, one describing this as "maintaining the financial viability of the trust". Other named priorities included "sustaining emergency services" and "building the reputation of the trust as a quality provider", this last point linked by the interviewee to securing income through attracting referrals. Ten of the twelve consultants cited financial survival as the main priority for their trust. Many of those mentioning finance as the most crucial priority also followed that up with a desire to be seen as providing good quality services. Indeed, the other two referred to the goal of being perceived as providing a good service as the chief concern, although they added that this did have implications for attracting business and money. Four of the consultants also mentioned a desire to "look after" or "stick up for" their department and to develop its status by attracting referrals.

Additionally, eight consultants saw their own priorities as closely matching this concern with financial viability. One gave an example of this attitude by saying, "if we fail to attract referrals the hospital loses income. The conclusion of that could ultimately be the trust going out of business. That would put me out of a job and immediately connects my own priorities with the financial well being of the trust". The other four interviewees believed their own priorities were, as a whole, more 'patient centred' than those of their trusts' management. However, three of this four, making a majority of eleven out of twelve, felt that on balance there was a still a high level of compatibility between their own and the organisation's priorities. One of them said, "they have to be similar. I'm going to be working here for the next twenty years".

The comments of three consultants that mentioned the financial well being of the trust as their major priority seemed orientated towards the survival of personal careers. One said "we all want busy departments, otherwise there is a danger of appearing dispensable", while another claimed that consultants who "don't appear busy can fall by the wayside". The single consultant who did not perceive much overlap between his own and the provider's priorities, whilst stating he had retained some loyalty to the hospital, admitted to hoping that the "trust system burns in hell". The weight given to the finance issue was passed from management to hospital clinicians by a network of meetings, internal memorandums, and by 'word of mouth' through informal discussions. A concern for the financial health of the organisation thus seems a working priority embracing both the chief executives and many consultants at the providers.

Moreover, this connects to the work of Harrison and Pollitt (1994). They claimed attempts had been made to incorporate clinicians into the wider financial goals of the NHS. Through a policy known as the resource management initiative, doctors had been made budget holders in order to create explicit financial responsibilities for them, but reported this as having only a limited impact. Yet they also saw the introduction of the quasi-market as compatible with attempts to incorporate clinicians, and the evidence here suggests it had a more substantial effect. It would appear that many consultants shared the financial objectives of their trusts. All of this puts a framework around the responses to the most fundamental question asked during their interviews. For the non-urgent elective surgery covered by the fund-holding scheme, why were fund-holding patients generally admitted sooner than their non fund-holding counterparts?

The rationale for waiting time differences

Every consultant stressed the central impact of financial considerations in the admission procedures at their trust for non-urgent surgery, all citing this as the dominant reason why fund-holders were called in sooner. The point was unanimously made that the need to maintain and preferably increase fund-holding income was the driving factor behind such patients' shorter waits because of their capacity to transfer referrals to competitors. One described this as having a "very great effect". Another said, "fund-holding money is the major 'at risk' element of our income. They do not actually have to become macho and threaten to move work away. Despite some patients' lack of mobility, we know they can move enough at the margins to concern us, even fairly small practices. The shorter waits of fund-holding patients are designed to both nip this danger in the bud, and where it has started to stop it spreading".

Moreover, the declaration that fund-holders did not need to explicitly threaten to move work, or actually refer elsewhere, to shorten their patients' waiting times was a blanket point from the consultants. Even though four of the consultants said some local fund-holders had threatened to redirect referrals away from them, with one refusing to name them and another forgetting their identity, they all claimed this had not made them handle these particular practices' patients any differently to those registered with other fund-holders. Administrative convenience meant all fund-holding patients were taken as a block. In making this point, one said "we have not called their patients in any quicker, or slower, than anybody else's. We were already fast tracking their patients because they are in the scheme. What more did they want and what more could we have done? Throwing threats around has no effect at all".

Straightforward membership of the scheme therefore appears to have automatically reduced the waiting times of fund-holders' patients, regardless of practices resorting to coercive threat tactics which, according to the consultants, appeared to be ignored. Indeed, the GP that claimed his fund-holding practice had not redirected referrals away from the local provider also said their patients' waits had fallen. The opportunity fund-holders had to refer elsewhere and the prospect that such a pattern could spread, an apprehension which may have been amplified when consultants noticed a decline in the referrals they received, looks far more important in shortening waiting times than formal threats, idle or otherwise. It was the potential that practices had to refer patients elsewhere that appears the critical factor, with hospitals having perceived fund-holding work as equating with their income. In other words, if providers were to fulfil their potential income, they must at least have retained (or preferably increased) the volume of fund-holding work they performed.

The consultants' answers to this issue also reflected the responses of the providers' chief executives. As one remarked, "the shorter waits of fund-holders' patients is completely driven by the aim of stopping them referring elsewhere. Otherwise, we lose income. For this reason we also hold down our prices to them, especially as we know they are under funded. We have also paid more attention to other aspects of service quality, like the turnaround in pathology tests, although this has benefited all GPs". Another commented that "short waiting times are our main attraction to them, although we accept they are a pretty loyal lot round here. We don't want to see any fund-holding work go elsewhere, and in truth we cannot afford to see it go elsewhere. We need to get their money in and even a marginal loss of fund-holding work is a problem".

A further comment along the same line was made by the chief executive from the same trust as the consultant quoted earlier that used the term 'at risk' when talking of fund-holding income. Such phraseology has apparently caught on at that provider. "We call fund-holders' patients in earlier because we have to stop them referring elsewhere. Fund-holding work represents our 'at risk' income. We cannot lose their referrals, and we also try to avoid this by making our fund-holding prices competitive". The same point was made as well by another chief executive. "We wish to stop them referring to other hospitals to maintain our income. Shorter waits for their patients are one way of doing this, along with building up the quality of our services. Fund-holding balanced the power between consultants and GPs and made us sharpen up our act, though the system should be simplified as it is rather fragmented. Even so, by comparison the health authority is not strong on commissioning".

This last view was not a unique opinion amongst the provider chief executives. One of the others remarked that "fund-holding is far better than health authority commissioning. It is because of them we had to get our act together to attract referrals. Fund-holders have brought the positive changes. Consultants used to like long NHS waiting lists for the sake of their private practice, but that has had to change. Clinical as well as financial viability means we cannot stand still. While there must be some grouping together I'd like to see the whole budget in the hands of GPs, away from the health authority. There is no evidence they've achieved anything. They had their chance and lost it". Similarly, another made the following comment. "We are in a purchaser driven environment and fund-holding has been a good thing and driven most improvements, but allocating resources to individual practices is difficult to get right. GP commissioning is the way forward, but in groups of practices as fund-holding needs to be streamlined".

Therefore, the exit option of fund-holding GPs is the basic reason why their patients were admitted sooner for non-urgent elective surgery than non fund-holders. The extent to which specific practices used this option looks immaterial. Administrative convenience and the potential of any fund-holding practice to refer patients to competitors resulted in there being a blanket approach to the fund-holding population. They were routinely admitted sooner regardless of other factors. Further, the provider representatives claimed they also tried to restrain their price increases to fund-holders while improving the quality of services. Moreover, whilst shorter waits and price controls were specifically aimed at fund-holders, each respondent that mentioned service quality maintained that this also benefited non fund-holding patients. As one consultant said, "after patients are admitted, there is no differentiation between them. Non fund-holders have to wait longer, but once they are in they get exactly the same level of care as fund-holders".

CONCLUSION

Many findings reported in this chapter were detected through the core of the qualitative research applied in this study, complementing the use of a quantitative approach to investigate the effect of varying contract types. For that enquiry a clear trend in the waits of fund-holding patients called in under different forms of contract did not arise. Where fund-holders used a mix of contract types, there were instances when patients admitted under each form of agreement had the shortest waits, though such a difference was statistically significant in only one out of four cases. This hardly looks conclusive proof that cost-per-case arrangements automatically drive shorter waits than the other forms of contract. Further, the idea that waiting times might have been an outcome of formal demands in contracts does not appear sustainable due to both the lack of precise specifications in the actual agreements and also the answers given during the interviews with hospital consultants.

There is no evidence to suggest that contrasts in waiting times were determined by the relationships between representatives of the purchasers and providers. Moreover, fund-holding GPs did not appear to hold the most obvious piece of information for shortening the waits of patients, the comparative waiting times of different providers. However, the determination of each purchaser type to reduce waits did appear explicitly stronger in the fund-holding community than at the health authority. Incentives to GPs derived mostly from two potential benefits. First, improving the lot of their patients. Second, lowering the likelihood of frustrated patients complaining to them about the length of their waits. The motivation to shorten waits at the health authority went as far as meeting national standards.

Fund-holders attempted to reduce waiting times by referring to other providers. Whilst they did not claim to know how public hospitals compared in this respect, at least beyond their knowledge of what services had very long waits at the local provider, a large proportion of such redirected referrals allegedly went to the non-NHS sector. Moreover, this links to the reasons given by the chief executives and consultants of the featured providers for admitting routine status fund-holding patients more quickly than their non fund-holding counterparts. They could not afford to lose the income related to this work, so gave priority to bringing fund-holding patients in earlier to avoid their GPs sending them elsewhere. The interviewees from providers saw this as the main way in which they could attract fund-holding work and income, although the control of prices and service quality issues were not ignored either.

From this, there may have been rather paradoxical incentives influencing the behaviour of key agents within the quasi-market. On the one hand fund-holders used the exit option to reduce their patients' waiting times, often referring to the non-NHS sector to do this. Yet at the same time they frequently stressed a desire not to destabilise the local NHS provider. Meanwhile, consultants tended to admit such practices' clinically routine patients earlier than those from non fund-holders to safeguard their NHS hospitals' budgetary position. Alongside this, most of the financial benefits from fund-holders using the non-public sector when exercising the exit option could well have passed to NHS surgeons. Trust consultants seem to comprise much of the medical staffing establishment of many private providers. Consultants and GPs thus appeared to perform a balancing act in which they weighed up the interests of hospitals, themselves and patients in their decision making.

The next chapter will draw together the evidence detailed in this and previous chapters in order to outline what the research says on a theoretical level about purchasing leverage and hospital behaviour in the quasi-market, as well as efficiency and equity. It will also deal with the issue described in the last paragraph in which GPs and consultants may have balanced not only competing pressures, but also contrasting or even conflicting interests. In light of the development of primary care groups, the findings of this study are then used to put forward a set of policy recommendations.

8 Policy Implications: Lessons from the Internal Market

This study moved the debate about the possibility of a two-tier service between fund-holders and other patients beyond the former reliance on anecdotal evidence. Fund-holding patients on the elective waiting list at four public providers did tend to have shorter waiting times for the operations covered by the fund-holding scheme than non fund-holders. Various hypotheses were investigated that could have explained this phenomenon, ranging from an idea that GP fund-holders systematically received overgenerous budgets, the case mix differences of the populations, and contrasts in the way each purchaser type performed their role. The reason was a component of the last of these factors. Whilst GPs had more desire than health authority managers did to shorten waits beyond national standards, motivation and incentives alone were not enough. They needed to be backed up with a 'tool' to do the job and this was supplied by the exit option, their capacity to refer to alternative hospitals, or at least being perceived as able to do so by providers.

A key task of this chapter is to use that finding to consider the policy implications of the research. With regard to this objective, important characteristics of the quasi-market will be explained in a theoretical context, in particular covering the concepts of purchasing leverage, hospital behaviour, efficiency and equity. The evidence from this study in the light of these factors will then lead to a discussion concerning the implications of the research for the primary care groups that were formally introduced in April 1999 to succeed fund-holding and the internal market.

PURCHASING LEVERAGE

The objective of the 1991 reforms to increase the responsiveness of NHS providers was discussed in the first chapter. This research indicates that fund-holders acquired shorter waits for their patients by increasing the responsiveness of hospitals more than the health authority were able to do, despite such practices being individually and collectively the smaller commissioner of elective surgery. Because it is tempting to associate purchasing leverage with resource capacity, under normal circumstances this might not be expected. If both a large and a small commissioner used the same provider for the supply of a good or service to an extent that correlated with their relative sizes, it may often be anticipated that the larger one would usually negotiate a 'better deal'. From this, the bigger purchaser could perhaps secure a quicker delivery, cheaper price, or a higher quality product. Indeed, that inference looks to be a fundamental belief behind Light's (1998) argument that the NHS needed large and strong purchasers rather than the small, local and weak ones which he felt GP fund-holders had been.

To take an example from the commercial world, Rees (1969) implied some three decades ago that Marks and Spencer, a very large retailer, had developed considerable influence over its suppliers. If, as seems likely, the company has grown since then, this influence has probably also swelled. Although such relationships may be conducted on very good terms, they could conceivably incorporate a degree of domination. Hence if Marks and Spencer used the same manufacturer that supplies one of its best selling dresses as a number of independent single shop boutiques that sell an identical garment, it seems rational to presume the following. The manufacturer will be more dependent on its trade with Marks and Spencer for its survival or growth. In turn, the supplier would give the greatest priority to maintaining its custom with Marks and Spencer, who should thus be able to negotiate or demand gains that may not be available to the individual boutiques.

Although the NHS was a quasi-market for a completely different type of commodity to this example, in terms of size and financial resources it seems appropriate to think of the health authority as the Marks and Spencer of the two purchaser types and fund-holders as the single shop boutiques. Nevertheless, to use an analogy, within the West Sussex internal market the boutiques were often getting better delivery dates for elective surgery than Marks and Spencer. Holding the larger budget failed to give the health authority the purchasing leverage to reduce patients' waiting times below national standards, regardless of how much motivation they had to do this. Interviewees from the trusts also implied that attempts were made to limit the prices charged to fund-holders and improve the standards of services, although benefits arising from the latter were carried through to non fund-holding patients as well.[20] Indeed, the idea that trusts would try to attract referrals by enhancing service quality was discussed by Barker *et al.* (1997). Yet it is still essential to expand upon the exit hypothesis to explain the true nature of purchasing leverage. The greater distance between health authorities and their client population than the relatively limited gap between GP fund-holders and their patients was discussed in the second chapter. The theory was that this could have enabled partnerships to decide to send patients to a range of alternative hospitals whereas health authorities may have had to second-guess the demand for services at various providers, or persuade (perhaps force) non fund-holders to refer within set guidelines. But during their interviews fund-holding GPs revealed that they sent the large majority of their patients to the local hospital. The exit option was therefore probably utilised for a minority of fund-holding patients. It was thus only at the margins that such practices directed referrals between alternative providers, making it necessary to clarify why the exit option may have worked for fund-holders but not for health authorities.

For although the fund-holding GPs had indicated that the maintenance of referral freedom was a consideration in the decision of some practices to join the scheme, the potential to switch referrals also rested with non fund-holders. This was because the annual *Contract Directories* of the West Sussex Health Authority showed that it had formal contractual agreements with numerous providers around the south east of England. Considering this broad spectrum of hospitals that non fund-holding GPs could use, they had the opportunity to switch referrals. While they might have been more restricted than fund-holders through feeling constrained by health authority managers to only use the public sector when doing this, the chance to 'shake up' their local NHS hospital should still have existed.

Some practices may have been reluctant to do this, perhaps not being too concerned about their patients' waiting times or loyal to a provider. However, the first attitude was evident in one of the interviews with a fund-holding GP, and he reported their patients' waits had been lowered without them doing anything specific to make this happen, whilst others also claimed to be very loyal to their local provider. Yet hospital representatives said that no differentiation was made between patients of

---

20. Representatives of the trusts made no claims that they tried to constrain their charges to the health authority. This, alongside the attempts to check the prices charged to fund-holders, could support a hypothesis advanced in the fifth chapter that the health authority might had paid more than fund-holders for specific episodes of elective care.

distinct fund-holding practices for any reason at all, so the same principle could have applied to non fund-holders.

A question that arises from this is why the exit option worked for fund-holding practices but not for non fund-holders. A comprehensive understanding of purchasing leverage thus needs to go beyond a simple acceptance that the exit option applied only to fund-holding GPs, because non fund-holders were not always tied to just one hospital. Hence it is sensible to again consider the nature of the contractual relationships between the purchaser types and providers.[21] This may clarify why budget size in the NHS might not have had the same relationship with purchasing leverage as in the private sector, assuming that in the latter, abundant financial resources enable a greater degree of control over suppliers. This was the basis for the idea that Marks and Spencer will enjoy a much stronger negotiating position with a clothing supplier than single shop boutiques.

Part of the explanation for this might be the fact that there is a constant cycle of firms of various sizes in the private sector going out of business. In many cases the only people who are really going to take any great notice are the creditors, staff and shareholders, and such news is rarely worth extensive media coverage. If Marks and Spencer decided to move its custom away from a supplier, this could conceivably close it down. If this happened, it is feasible that there would not be enough negative publicity about such an event to make Marks and Spencer reconsider the decision and persevere with the existing arrangements. Hence in this kind of scenario companies like Marks and Spencer could have enormous power over their suppliers.

But this example has important differences to the NHS. If a hospital was closed down the media coverage and public outcry may create considerable embarrassment for politicians. It is thus difficult to imagine that any such decision would be taken locally without prior approval from higher levels in the NHS structure, at which there may also be a reluctance to grant permission for an action of this type. If such a decision was made independently at local level, it could endanger the careers of individuals involved in making the unpopular decision. This view was validated in managerial jargon by one of the health authority interviewees who said that

---

21. Flynn and Williams (1997) suggested that modes of contracting in the NHS internal market were divided into two camps, hard and soft contracting. Hard contracts were the more prescriptive, embodying close surveillance and sanctions. Soft contracts functioned symbolically as a general statement of intent, so providing a framework for collaborative work. Lapsley and Llewellyn (1997) have discussed the use of soft contracts in social care.

closing a public acute hospital could be seen as an "unwise career move". This can now be considered alongside the relative financial resources of the chief purchaser types in the internal market.

Because most, indeed the large majority, of the resources available for commissioning health care services was in the hands of health authorities, the contracts such bodies held with their local providers would have been of a substantial size. Probably so large that any decision by a health authority to take a large amount of money from a provider may well have threatened the financial security of the trust. Yet while health authorities yielded a decisive influence on the survival prospects of local trusts, the political sensitivity attached to the closure of NHS hospitals meant that this could have weakened their purchasing leverage. As such, health authority purchasing strategies might have been locked into safeguarding the survival of local NHS hospitals, regardless of whether non fund-holding GPs spread their referrals around alternative providers.

The role of health authority agreements, which were not attributable to definite costs for specific treatments like fund-holders' block, cost-per-case, or cost and volume contracts (Dixon *et al.*, 1994), can be seen as covering most of the fixed running costs of local NHS providers. Hence they might have had less to do with obtaining added patient benefits, like shortening waiting times beyond national targets. And because health authority agreements gave less priority to equating payments with the level of service provision than fund-holders' contracts, if non fund-holding GPs moved patients away from a hospital, this might not have concerned its management nearly as much as if fund-holding practices did this. No direct or immediate loss of cash would have resulted for the provider. Health authority money was not 'at risk' in the same way that fund-holding income had been, so the relevance of contracts was linked more to money following the patient than different contract types (see the seventh chapter).

Competition between providers in the quasi-market may thus have existed at the margins for a limited number of fund-holding patients. Hospitals gave them quicker access times for non-urgent elective surgery to avoid their GPs sending them elsewhere. Hence the size of a purchaser's budget seems less relevant to purchasing leverage than a capacity or willingness to execute the exit option, but only when money follows the patient. But the way in which the quasi-market worked in this respect does not mean the purchaser types operated under different regulations. There is no published rule that formally bans health authorities from closing NHS providers, even though in reality there are factors that can stop this happening. Health authorities and fund-holders tended to perform their roles as commissioners in dissimilar circumstances, not under different regulations.

The competition over a relatively small number of patients may also explain how fund-holding GPs performed a balancing act of trying to motivate the local provider to reduce waiting times, while at the same time wishing to support the very same hospital. If they still sent the large majority of their patients to the local provider, this may well satisfy their longing to consider themselves loyal. It was the competition for those sent elsewhere that shook the hospital up, shortened waits, and lowered the number of complaints received from patients. Yet this minority might not have been a sufficient quota to trouble the conscience of GPs in the context of the provider's viability. As a small purchaser, they may have realised that on their own they could not close a hospital, certainly with a relatively small proportion of their list size being referred to a competitor. So they could have found themselves in a position to use the exit option whilst also supporting the nearest trust.

This led five out of the twelve GP fund-holders interviewed for the study to say their purchasing leverage was raised by their smaller budgets, although opinion was divided on this issue. Six felt their relatively small budgets reduced their negotiating strength and the other was uncertain, saying it could go "either way". The forthcoming development of larger primary care groups will test the validity of each view and the discussion of the policy implications of the research will address how a degree of purchasing leverage might be maintained for such bodies in the future.

Allied to ideas about the enhanced leverage of fund-holders, it may also be reinforced by a common perception of the financial environment of the NHS. There has been a tendency for the service to be seen as permanently under funded (see Kember and Macpherson, 1994). In this climate, more priority could have been attached to the potential income from fund-holders than if the finances of providers were considered comfortable. Although individual fund-holding practices may not have had the budgets to close a trust down, in an environment that many could see as 'short-changed' their money was made critical because it was not safe, and it followed patients to a greater extent than income from health authorities.

In brief, the case put forward is that the key to purchasing leverage in the NHS quasi-market was for a single commissioner to have held a small enough budget to free them from a primary obligation to maintain a hospital's financial stability. Health authorities had this responsibility far more than fund-holders, so suffered an obstacle to their flexibility. Any such advantage for fund-holders could have been amplified by a belief that the NHS is under funded. This means the potential income from such practices, which was more attributable to the number of patients treated than was the case with health authority finance, could not be written-off by providers as peripheral. Therefore, the way the internal market was structured has given support to the theory that smaller purchasers will be more effective in gaining benefits for patients than large commissioners because of their flexibility (discussed in the second chapter). The relevance of this to the way primary care groups function will be addressed later.

HOSPITAL BEHAVIOUR

This section moves the theoretical focus of the chapter onto the evolution in models of hospital behaviour. McGuire *et al.* (1988) maintained that much of the literature on this subject comes from the US. They suggested that there are only a few such models, mainly because there is no firm idea of what a typical hospital looks like and it is difficult to identify the chief decision-makers within them. Nevertheless, they outlined models of hospital behaviour that had been formulated. For example, hospitals could attempt to maximise output alongside a consideration of service quality. Another model sees the maximisation of a hospital's status as an important goal. Others focused on the varying internal structures of different hospitals, with there being a balance between the relative strength of doctors and managers in the decision-making process. Although there was often a failure to define the impact of this on conduct, the medical and ethical motives of doctors can still be seen as having a material impact on hospital behaviour.

Eastaugh (1992) also wrote that most of the existing literature on hospital behaviour, incorporating physician behaviour, originates from America and has been characterised by two approaches, each trying to identify the primary motives which drive conduct. Utility maximisation covers such issues as profit, professional status, leisure time, ethics, study time, the number of support staff, plus the complexity and interest of case mixes. Profit maximisation grants a higher status to one of these factors, the role of profit as an incentive, defining this as the most important motive determining behaviour patterns. Yet both sets of theorists accept that behaviour is too complex to be explained solely by profit motives, and the general vagueness of such findings may endorse Donaldson and Gerard's (1993) claim that the literature lacks a satisfactory theory of hospital behaviour.

The non-profit sector

It is noteworthy that Bartlett *et al.* (1994) referred to public providers in the NHS quasi-market as 'not-for-profit' organisations. In using this term they were evidently referring to financial profit and, considering that a primary goal of private firms is to make one (see Oleck, 1956; Cyert, 1988), such hospitals were being distinguished from commercial enterprises. Whilst NHS trusts are empowered to make operating surpluses and are also required to meet financial targets (Propper and Bartlett, 1997), the term 'not-for-profit' means that surpluses must be ploughed back into the corporation rather than provide additional monetary rewards to its managers (Bartlett, 1995). This definition matches the opinion of Weisbrod (1988) that 'non-profit' institutions are designed to prevent entrepreneurs reaping monetary benefits through increasing the organisation's surplus. Consequently, the phrase 'not-for-profit' appears to overlap closely with the expression 'non-profit'.

Most of the literature on the non-profit sector also originates from the US, leading Young (1993) to his judgement that the subject was discovered there. Some work on this topic loses relevance to the NHS by focusing on charitable and private bodies rather than the public domain (for example, see Dobkin Hall, 1987; Douglas, 1987; Young, 1987). Notwithstanding this, studies of the motives underlying the sector can be found in the non-profit literature (see McLaughlin, 1986; Young, 1983). Indeed, Hansmann (1987) divided the economic theories on non-profit bodies into two groups. Some deal with the role of such institutions, including public goods theory and contract failure theory, while others focus on organisational behaviour, like the optimising models.

With regard to the optimising models, it has been alleged that non-profit organisations have strong incentives to accumulate financial surpluses (Tuckman, 1993; Tuckman and Chang, 1993). Linked to this point, Starkweather (1993) addressed the issue of non-profit hospitals making profits and argued that the word 'profit' was often used loosely in relation to the sector, applied interchangeably with terms like 'earnings' and 'net income'. This was seen as narrowing the distinction between for-profit and non-profit hospitals beyond recognition.

Hospital behaviour in the quasi-market

The idea about a narrowing distinction between for-profit and non-profit hospitals makes it easier to understand the behaviour patterns of public providers in the internal market. Regardless of staff at NHS providers not being allowed to procure their organisations' surpluses for themselves (outside of factors like performance bonuses), the incentives to secure income might be almost as strong as in the for-profit private sector. Trusts have to meet financial targets (Propper and Bartlett, 1997) and if performance falls short of reaching them, career prospects could be undermined. The survival of careers, jobs and organisations is a powerful motive and in a climate where employment security in the public sector has been squeezed (see Baker and Perkins, 1995; West, 1997), it seems reasonable to infer that this will be the case in the NHS.

From this, by introducing a greater set of competitive pressures into a service that many may see as under funded, the internal market drove providers into unwritten admission policies that differentiated between fund-holding and other patients for non-urgent elective surgery. The rationale for this was to safeguard the element of their potential income that was most 'at risk', the resources held by fund-holders. The financial priorities of NHS hospitals was the catalyst for competition between them, and this occurred over what was proportionately a fairly marginal number of patients. Those considered by their fund-holding GPs to be mobile, even though this did benefit a much wider group, the non-urgent fund-holding population as a whole.

Also, both hospital managers and most consultants identified with the broad financial interests of their organisation. Hence the survival of trusts can be seen as relevant to the utility of non-clinicians and doctors alike. For most consultants this appeared to have a higher standing in the hierarchy of priorities than issues that might be seen as ethical considerations like the equality of access to services. The importance given by clinicians to the broad financial security of their hospitals can be seen as verified by the remarks of every consultant that was interviewed for the research. While three of the twelve felt that attracting fund-holding work helped their departments' prestige, they all said that the income derived from admitting fund-holding patients earlier went to the trust as a whole, not specifically to them or their individual specialties. So how does this finding relate to the previously mentioned balancing act that may have seen surgeons weigh the interests of their NHS provider against the profitability of their own private practices, a concept that led Paton (1995) to propose that consultants may have competed with themselves?

The answer to this question could be that whilst welcoming fund-holding referrals to their private practices, they might have continued to arrange the work they received at NHS hospitals in a way that benefited the financial status of that provider. This meant calling in routine status fund-holding patients sooner than their non fund-holding counterparts. As such, the interests of both the consultants and their NHS hospital might have been met, at least to an extent. Whilst raising their non-NHS income by accepting fund-holding referrals to their private practice, the work that was left for them at public hospitals was performed, or at least arranged, in a way that helped the financial status of that provider. Consultants also considered the financial well being of their NHS hospital to be in their personal interests. From this, the evidence as it relates to NHS providers seems to correlate with the profit maximising models of hospital and physician behaviour, even though this is an example where the word 'profit' has been used interchangeably with the term 'income'.

EFFICIENCY

Three aspects of efficiency were described in the first chapter of this book, productive and allocative efficiency, plus X-efficiency. The effect of the quasi-market on allocative efficiency, the distribution of resources in a way that produced the closest possible match between what could be produced and what consumers wanted, is at best unclear and at worst unknown. If, as seems very likely, patients wanted shorter waiting times, fund-holding was effective at facilitating this than health authority purchasing.

However, this may have benefited just those non-urgent patients registered with fund-holding practices, not the whole clinically routine population. The internal market might have been efficient on an allocative basis for some, but not others. There is also some doubt as to whether or not the shorter waits of fund-holders were gained at the expense of non fund-holders having longer waiting times. The zero-sum effect was addressed in the fourth chapter. The data from figures 4.4 to 4.7 does not show the actual trends in waiting times were the same as would have been expected if fund-holders had shorter waits due to the longer waits of non fund-holders. Nevertheless, it would be sensible to temper any rejection of the zero-sum effect with caution. The evidence falls short of being truly conclusive.

Regarding X-efficiency, no claims are made that this study addressed the relative costs of health authority and GP fund-holder commissioning, though it seems reasonable to accept that fund-holding was the more expensive of the two systems (see Davies, 1995; Goodwin, 1998). Therefore, if the outcomes from fund-holder and health authority commissioning had been similar, the former might not score very well if X-efficiency were the sole criterion for measuring the success of the two systems. The higher transaction costs caused by the fund-holding scheme could have made it more X-inefficient than health authority purchasing, without bringing any added benefits for patients. But as was implied when Glennerster (1996) reported a small cost-benefit study that suggested the advantages of fund-holding might have outweighed the costs, reality is not so straightforward.

This is because the efficiency goals of the 1991 reforms were not just about X-efficiency, and for non-urgent patients needing operations the outcomes from the two systems were not the same. Those registered with

GP fund-holders tended to benefit from significantly shorter waiting times, and this was shown not to have been derived from factors that would have made the performance of such practices spurious, like receiving overgenerous budgets or chance case mix contrasts. Moreover, if productive efficiency is explicitly connected to expanding patient throughput, this is an area where fund-holding scored well, certainly far better than health authority purchasing. And at the level of patients, where the preference for quick treatment is indicated by people paying for private health care (see Calnan *et al.*, 1993), that higher output by hospitals seems an unambiguous gain in quality for the NHS. For patients may have enjoyed benefits like suffering less inconvenience, pain, or returning to work earlier (as discussed beforehand).

From this, in the context of productive efficiency, commissioning health care services could be a function where the cheap option is not necessarily cheerful, in that you get what you pay for. There may well be an element of truth in that argument, but evidence produced for this book appears to indicate that fund-holding could have been made less expensive without losing effectiveness. For example, NHS trusts had contracts with all the fund-holding practices in its catchment area. These were large documents, often more than thirty pages. Discussions with hospital and practice managers suggested that many hours were spent negotiating these over the years, outside the topic of waiting time standards. To an extent this might have been more necessary in the past. For instance, perhaps better information became given in referral letters and discharge notices.

Yet the evidence from the seventh chapter suggests that contracts had little or no influence on patients' waiting times, and this does beg the question on how much notice was actually paid to the rest of the agreements, whatever they might have said. The opinion of hospital and practice managers was that time and money could have been saved by cutting down on the work attached to contract negotiation. Indeed, this must have been done in some areas of the country as sample provider contracts from outside the county were produced that comprise just a very few pages.[22] As one manager at a practice said, "the only important page is the one itemising our financial commitment. The contracting process, like many aspects of the scheme, has been made unnecessarily bureaucratic by a health authority who say a whole host of worthless jobs must be performed to keep the auditors happy".

---

22. The best examples of this were the contracts produced by both the Guy's and St Thomas' Hospital Trust in London, plus the Southampton University Hospitals NHS Trust.

When speaking of the bureaucratic nature of some elements of fund-holding other than the contracting process, the above manager expanded on the point by confirming he was talking about practices recording every item of care covered by the scheme on their own computer systems. He argued that providers' printouts became accurate enough to make this a "futile exercise", although spot checks would still have been necessary to identify any drop in standards relating to the correctness of the hospital data. As such, it may have been possible to retain the benefits of GP purchasing, if that is what shorter waiting times are considered to be, and limit the costs of fund-holding. Moreover, in accordance with the setting of combined management cost envelopes for health authorities and primary care groups in each area (see Department of Health, 1997), the government is obviously intending to pin down future transaction costs. Nonetheless, this might have been possible under the fund-holding scheme.

In sum, it seems that fund-holding was successful in raising the responsiveness of NHS hospitals to extend the rate of patient throughput, relative to the outcomes from health authority commissioning. Yet it was probably quite expensive to run, even though some of the costs of the system might have been avoidable. As the scheme stood, therefore, the cost of a greater degree of productive efficiency could have been a lower level of X-efficiency. This judgement falls into place with a point made in the first chapter, that the quasi-market reforms should be seen as concerned with enhancing productive efficiency as much, or perhaps even more so, than with cost containment. However, if one part of a dual-purchasing configuration was more effective than the other was in extending hospital responsiveness, only one group of patients was likely to reap the accrued benefits of this. Equity is therefore an important consideration in any review of the policy implications of this study.

EQUITY

One place from which to start a discussion about the implications for equity of any future NHS reforms is to address how equitable, or inequitable, the quasi-market actually was. On the face of it, that may seem a strange starting point. There was a two-tier service for patients awaiting non-urgent elective surgery, so at first glance it is understandable why some would write the internal market and fund-holding experiments off as a blight in the history of a service initiated to reduce inequity. Moreover, such attitudes connect to Mooney and McGuire's (1987) observation that equity and equality are often coupled in the health care literature. Yet the two concepts are not the same. The argument may therefore rely on either a mistaken definition of equity, confusing it with equality, or ignore the fact that equity can work at more than a single level, such as between separate purchasers and also different groups of patients.

The basis for this judgement relates to the point that inequality does not necessarily imply inequity. As Le Grand (1991b, p. 11) wrote, debates are often confused by a failure to distinguish properly between equity and equality, and 'the two concepts are in fact quite distinct'. A foundation for this idea was that equity is compatible with an equality of choice. For a fictitious example of this, say that under some form of enterprise start-up scheme the state gave a couple of its citizens in identical circumstances £5,000 each, this could be seen as equitable (at least between the two of them). One started a legitimate business with the money and through hard work made it a success, soon becoming a millionaire. Meanwhile, the other started experimenting with drugs and used the entire handout to feed a cocaine habit that he or she developed, and as a result ended up destitute. The financial outcome is that these two individuals are not equal, but the inequality was not caused by inequity. They each chose to use the money in different ways.

This notion can be applied to the West Sussex internal market as follows. For operations covered by the fund-holding scheme performed on people from the elective waiting list, patients registered with GP fund-holders generally had shorter waiting times than their non fund-holding counterparts. In that respect the system was unequal. If this inequality had arisen because fund-holding practices had constantly received overgenerous budgets, the system would also have been inequitable. Yet the fifth chapter of this book showed that fund-holding practices in West Sussex had not been systematically over funded for operations. The inequality in waiting times was not a result of financial inequity between the commissioners. Rather, it was a consequence of differences in the way GP fund-holders and the health authority performed as purchasers of elective surgery. Like the cocaine addict and the aspiring entrepreneur above, they used their money differently. Hence at the level of the purchasers, this may have made the system equitable.

Nevertheless, equity theory suggests this should not be taken as the end of the matter. Whilst the system may have been equitable at the level of the purchasers, at the level of patients the inequality of waiting times cannot so easily be dismissed as equitable and thus tolerable. The reason for this is the previously mentioned issue, equality of choice. Le Grand (1991b) argued that it is inequitable if an inequality between individuals occurs through factors outside their control. To apply this idea to the internal market, unequal waiting times might have been inequitable if patients had no choice over who commissioned their health care services, even if the funding levels of the purchasers were equitable. In other words, equity between commissioners can coexist with inequity among patients.

A critical factor in the equity debate is thus the level of choice patients had over which purchaser commissioned their surgery. Obviously people do have a right to change GPs, so as long as there was a mix of fund-holding and non fund-holding practices in a locality, they could in theory exert some control over who commissioned their elective surgery. Someone who considered the health authority to be ineffective in this function could have registered with a fund-holding GP, and vice versa. Yet this opportunity for choice might have been more theoretical than actual. It presumes a level of knowledge in the population about the relative effectiveness of purchasers that may not have been credible, for the following reasons.

Up to the point where the preliminary results of the statistics shown in chapter four of this book were reported (see Dowling, 1997), there was a reliance in academic circles on anecdotal evidence for gauging the relative waiting times of non fund-holding and fund-holding patients. This makes it difficult to see how the general population could have had the chance to make informed choices on which agency was likely to have done the best job in purchasing elective surgery, or any other form of health care. Anyway, even if such information was available, choosing a GP is unlikely to be shaped just by commissioning effectiveness. There could be many other factors that sway a person's choice of practice, including the kindness of doctors, the politeness of receptionists, the availability of car parking spaces, or the courtesy shown by practice nurses. Additionally, these potential influences should not be seen as an exhaustive list. Taken together, it does not seem very realistic to expect patients to react instinctively to purchasing effectiveness in their choice of GP.

Perhaps a legitimate response to this might be that patients who choose not to change GPs to seek the best commissioner should not complain if they have to wait longer for their operations. This idea opens up a complex issue about the responsibilities of individuals in seeking out effective welfare services, and the government in ensuring they are available to the wide population. Finding an answer to that debate is not an aim of this book. Yet there might still be a bottom line at which the state takes responsibility for making sure the services on offer are as uniformly efficient as possible. Extending the uniformity of waiting times is thus a consideration in the context of policy options, and if one system had performed better than the other, perhaps the superior one should have been made available to all? This could expand equity if it provides more of a 'level playing field', so that some patients do not remain disadvantaged by the decision of their general practices to stay outside the commissioning process. Moreover, the general point about inequity, and equity, at the separate levels of patients and purchasers overlaps with a debate covered by Bevan (1998). He put forward a case that there are two types of equity applicable to the NHS, equitable funding between patients of all practices and common waiting times. Fund-holding was criticised for undermining equity on both counts because patients registered with GPs in the scheme allegedly may have benefited from shorter waits because such practices were budgeted over generously. The abolition of the scheme complied with the government's wish to remedy both types of inequity. However, Bevan (1998) also claimed that variations in medical practice make the simultaneous achievement of each sort of equity across general practice populations impossible, and suggested a choice has to be made between them.

Yet the reason why Bevan's (1998) argument overlaps with the points made earlier in this section has nothing directly to do with variation in medical practice. Rather, if more than one purchaser type exists, differences in commissioning practice can impair the chance of achieving both types of equity. In addition to the statistical evidence given in the fifth chapter, senior staff from the West Sussex Health Authority admitted that fund-holders in the county were not over funded. This leads to the following judgement. In West Sussex, differences in waiting times were not a result of an unjust, meaning an inequitable, funding of local fund-holding practices.

From this, if funding in West Sussex had not unfairly advantaged fund-holders, equitable waiting times do not appear consistent with financial equity. To achieve common waits for patients of all practices,[23] fund-holders would presumably have had to be under funded. Therefore, Bevan's (1998) case holds but not only for the reasons he gave. Differences in purchasing effectiveness could be just as important a factor in making the two types of equity incompatible as variations in medical practice. A question that arises from this prospect is what might be the best way to try and achieve both efficiency and equity in the NHS? The following discussion considers that issue, and in doing so also uses the

---

23. This issue was not quite so straightforward as a simple distinction between fund-holding and non fund-holding patients. The average waits over the entire waiting list of patients from either group could differ greatly at separate hospitals. One example showing this is the mean waiting time of 104.7 days for non fund-holding patients at the Mid Sussex provider in 1993/94 (table 4.10), whilst non fund-holders at Crawley Horsham that same year had a mean wait of twice that length, 209.4 days (table 4.9).

points made earlier about purchasing leverage and hospital behaviour in the quasi-market.

POLICY IMPLICATIONS

The policy implications of this research are important because what happens to the NHS in the future will automatically build upon what has gone before. In social policy reform the past inevitably shapes the future to some extent and it is now too late to manufacture the NHS from scratch. Key lessons can thus be learnt from this comparative study of health authorities and GP fund-holders as purchasers with regard to the development of primary care groups and primary care trusts. In particular, what does the study imply about efficiency and equity in the health service, both of which the Labour Government wishes to extend (see Department of Health, 1997), and the levels from which services are best purchased? In the light of this debate, it is perhaps judicious to briefly reflect on GP fund-holding in particular, for the reasons that will be explained next.

GP fund-holding: a post-mortem

It is conceivable that social historians of the future will define GP fund-holding as more than just the forerunner of primary care groups and primary care trusts. The scheme may come to be seen as the genesis of them. After all, the planned involvement of GPs in primary care groups appears to make them a more obvious development of fund-holding than of health authority commissioning. This makes it appropriate to conduct a brief 'post-mortem' on fund-holding.

This study has shown that when patients' waiting times are used as the basic measure of a purchaser's effectiveness, GP fund-holders should be seen as better commissioners of elective surgery than health authorities. Yet despite this and any other successes or failures of the scheme, opinion was so sharply divided (see Robinson and Steiner, 1998) that fund-holding might well be more remembered as the aspect of the 1991 reforms that produced the most controversy and confrontation (see Keeley, 1997b; Millard, 1997). This produced an environment that had allegedly allowed some commentators to disguise their personal and even hostile bias towards fund-holding with an image of informed opinion (see Marum, 1997).

Considering this climate, here is the rub. Could the major problem for fund-holding have been that it was unable to win either way? If it shortened waits or induced other benefits not enjoyed by patients represented by health authorities, it faced the prospect of being blamed for driving a two-tier NHS. Otherwise, if it had not made such differences, what was the point of it? Therefore, without (or short of) firm proof that any advantages of fund-holding were definitely filtering through to all patients (which may be difficult to verify), either success or failure was likely to spell fervent criticism. In short, both ways the grounds were ready made for those who wished to argue in favour of its abolition.

As such, it is probably not too surprising that the format of the internal market was due for a change. However, it would seem that the government was faced with a dilemma. On the one hand, the Labour Party in opposition had formally announced its hostility to the fund-holding scheme, whether or not the tone of its criticism had perhaps calmed over the years. A reason for this was the suspicions of queue jumping (getting shorter waiting times) by fund-holding patients for hospital treatments (see Bevan, 1998). On the other hand, for the 1997 election campaign it had also made a firm manifesto pledge to reduce waiting lists by 100,000 (Warden, 1997).

Yet if fund-holders were getting shorter waiting times, there was always the chance (along with other possibilities) that this might have been because fund-holders were better purchasers of elective surgery than health authorities, even prior to the results of this research being published. As shorter waiting times equate to shorter waiting lists (Yates, 1987) the Labour Party may have been worried, or at least concerned, that it could have imposed upon itself an agenda of objecting to the very policy device that might best have aided the achievement of its manifesto pledge.

Indeed, waiting lists did grow rapidly after the new Labour Government came to power (Warden, 1998b; 1998c), and it also announced that there must be common waiting times for fund-holding and other patients. This trend of growing waiting lists led to the government giving a large cash boost to the NHS of some £320 million to subsequently lower them again (Warden, 1998d). But needing to pump extra funds into the system would not be a favoured policy for many governments, and in part this might have been a self-induced problem for the Blair administration by making the fund-holding scheme redundant (in the context of controlling waiting times) prior to its formal abolition. To get around this problem, if the Labour Government were going to abolish fund-holding, it would hence seem logical to replace it with something that extended the role of GPs in commissioning, rather than abandon the development of this policy.

It is also feasible that fund-holding created a momentum that could not be ignored by the new government. The rapid growth of the scheme in the context of participating practices and patients covered made it difficult to ignore the potential of GPs to play a central role in any future purchasing configuration, despite many people's opposition to the fund-holding experiment. The scheme might have made it very hard, if not impossible, to 'turn the clock back' and relegate GPs to their pre-1991 status. It is likely that many GPs became very committed to the scheme (Ham, 1996b), and antagonising a substantial section of the medical profession is not something many governments would choose to do unless they felt there was an extremely good reason to do so.

This was the climate in which the new administration formulated its plans for the NHS. In short, establishing primary care groups would presumably not have been part of the Labour Government's White Paper if fund-holding had never been introduced.

Beyond the 1991 reforms: primary care groups

Beyond these points, it is necessary to place any discussion of the policy implications of this study into its proper context by highlighting the forthcoming changes that the Labour Government is making to the NHS. In line with this, recommendations can be made that, if adopted, would fashion the structure of the service according to general policy intentions. It seems more logical to do this than completely contradict the government's plans. Hence it is important to briefly describe the main proposals concerning the commissioning function – as outlined in the White Paper (Department of Health, 1997).

There will be four models of primary care groups (with the upper two becoming trusts) formally encompassing all general practices and their patients. They will typically cover around 100,000 people each, but this can vary according to local circumstances and any new evidence on what might be the optimum population size for a group. At the lowest level they will be bodies acting in an advisory capacity to its local health authority. At the highest level, though still accountable to the health authority, the groups will be free standing trusts which will not only commission care from providers but take responsibility for the provision of community services to its population.

The depth of GPs' involvement in the commissioning function should therefore expand as groups move up the levels, although other interests will also be represented in the structure of such bodies – including the nursing profession. Those beginning at the lowest stage of the primary care group ladder will be expected to progress over time to a higher trust level, so that health authorities will eventually relinquish their commissioning function.

Efficiency and equity: where next for the NHS?

The first point to be considered is the type of equity that should be seen as the main goal, financial evenness or common waiting times. The trouble with basing equity on common waits is that it may compromise efficient commissioning. Purchasers that are good at shortening waits will see resources slip away to those who are not, because ineffective commissioners will presumably require additional finance. Although some may see the following sentence as provocative language, it forcefully puts across the point that is being made. Efficiency incentives could feasibly become smothered by an addiction to universal outcomes. To accept this view as valid means that financial equity is the base from which policy must originate, and that would appear to support the use of formula funding.

Though the mechanics of setting a fair formula attracts deliberation and debate, the work towards effective formula funding has resulted in a capitation methodology that was designed for use at the level of individual general practice populations (see NHS Executive, 1997a). This should presumably go some way to nullifying the objections to the aim that could previously have been made: that a robust capitation formula for such small populations was too difficult to achieve. Furthermore, for commissioners covering bigger communities like the average number of people that are likely to be represented by primary care groups, the suitability of formula funding looks even more convincing (see Martin *et al.*, 1997). However, not everybody shares this optimism, as was shown by Baker's (1998) claim that funding primary care groups by capitation methods could lead to chaos.

Nevertheless, allocating funds by way of a capitation formula might provide the best hope of alleviating the other cause of inequity identified by Bevan (1998), variation in medical practice. If the expenditure limits implied by the budgets are vigorously applied, when GPs are purchasers and have incentives to avoid over spends against the allotted sum, this might have more effect than most other policy options on tempering differences in medical practice between GPs. Furthermore, it should still be remembered that the most expensive items of health care, including things like major surgery, renal dialysis and oncology services, will only be provided when a hospital doctor – not a GP, define them as necessary. Consequently, many contrasts in the costs of secondary services for patients of individual general practices may have more to do with genuine need than differences in medical practice between GPs.

However, regardless of differences in medical practice, it has already been discussed at some length how the inequitable waiting times at four West Sussex providers did not seem to be a consequence of fund-holders having overgenerous budgets. Yet something must still be done to match the financial equity that may derive from capitation funding with a better chance of an equitable access for all patients requiring non-urgent elective surgery. One option could be to remove purchasing responsibilities from the practices that already have it. Yet this would mean passing it back to the purchaser who generally obtained longer waits for the patients of non fund-holding GPs, the health authorities. It seems feasible that doing this might equalise patients' waiting times at a higher level than may otherwise be possible, perhaps gaining uniformity at the expense of reducing all to the level of the least effective. If this was to be the case it seems a somewhat bizarre, if not a perverse way, of achieving greater equality in patients' access to hospital services.

Returning to a point made earlier, perhaps the most obvious potential solution to this dilemma is to extend the benefits of GP purchasing (like shorter waits) to all patients, rather than just the population registered with fund-holding practices.[24] And considering the likely balance in the influence of health authorities and GPs between the four levels of primary care groups and trusts, it would appear to be important for such groups to move up the four stages as quickly as is possible. From this, if the outcome of primary care groups is to pass the commissioning function to GPs, the government could be moving the NHS in the right direction. Particularly as their White Paper said a national schedule of reference costs will itemise what individual treatments cost across the NHS, and providers will publish and benchmark their charges on the same basis (see Department of Health, 1997).

Carrying this idea forward to cover services that were outside the standard fund-holding scheme could well be vital to the eventual success of the changes. For an implication from the fifth chapter of this book was the potential for money to be wasted due to the health authority not knowing what it was paying for which procedures. While this is not an argument for blanket cost-per-case arrangements, the block agreements of the future should be more like fund-holders' block contracts than the less specific type used by some health authorities. Identifiable costs must be attributed to each identified treatment, and providers should be penalised if there are wide discrepancies between the contracted and actual volume of activity.

But in the context of shortening waits, a success of fund-holding was its ability to make hospitals responsive to commissioners. An idea put forward earlier in this chapter was that the limited budgets of fund-holders

---

24. While this may reduce differences in the services received by patients that were driven by arbitrary policy rules (the opportunities for practices to choose between fund-holding and non fund-holding status) it is unlikely to reduce disparities in other aspects of care. This point is reinforced by the way Glennerster *et al.* (1994a) emphasised stark contrasts in the standards of separate general practices even before the fund-holding era.

might have give them extra purchasing leverage because it freed them from the worries associated with the potential to close a hospital down. Yet primary care groups and primary care trusts, if they typically cover populations of about 100,000, may adopt a responsibility for keeping their local providers open. However, if the block payments are attributed to individual items of service, the leverage may still be retained. The feature which created leverage, the capacity to transfer a relatively small proportion of referrals to other providers when money for the treatments follows the patient, could become spread around all practices rather than concentrated in the hands of fund-holders (as it was during the internal market era). As such, the flexibility that gave strength to the small purchasers (GP fund-holders) in the quasi-market could thus be carried over to larger primary care groups.

Further, because the moveable patients may well be a relatively minor proportion of the population, much of the fixed costs of providers should be covered by the payments for the services supplied to the majority of patients who are not going to be referred elsewhere. In general, a cautious optimism about the proposed reforms therefore seems justified, although there are a number of factors that seem critical. For example, GPs would need the freedom to refer patients to where they want and the money for all treatments should explicitly follow the patient to the provider supplying the service. Most episodes of care can be supplied under block contracts (to be called service agreements) similar to the types used by fund-holders, with payments being measurable against precise levels of service utilisation. Yet the system should be flexible enough to allow specific payments for individual treatments at rarely used providers. Hence there should still be room for some payments to be made on a cost-per-case basis.

However, there is a danger that budgets covering populations of about 100,000 might be so vague and intangible to GPs that any incentives for individual practices to stay within the allotted sum are negated. This could undermine budget discipline at a level where professional self-regulation can work. If the administrative costs are not too excessive, budgets should thus be devolved for some services to smaller levels within primary care groups, like individual practices. Hence the extent to which each practice was over or under running against its budget could be monitored and both the potential problems in providing incentives to innovate for larger groups of GPs, plus the difficulties in managing them, could be addressed. This may also comply with more GPs being involved in the management of groups and also with an observation of a health authority manager, quoted in the last chapter, that distinct services are best purchased at varying levels. For example, if the purchase of bone marrow transplants is performed better for wide populations, this should occur. If elective surgery is best commissioned by individual practices, primary care groups must be flexible enough to permit this.

From this, a key task for the future must therefore be to distinguish what should be commissioned at any level, and to allow purchasing decisions to be taken in line with such evidence, a question that was addressed by Le Grand *et al.* (1998). Indeed, the need for primary care groups to do some things at devolved levels may find support from the evaluative work on total purchasing projects by Goodwin *et al.* (1998). They wrote that single practice and small multi-practice pilots were more likely than large projects to report meeting their objectives.

Moreover, the outcomes from primary care groups will doubtless offer opportunities for future research. For instance, it may be interesting to investigate the effectiveness of such groups at varying levels, and their commissioning of different kinds of service. The success of groups in purchasing treatments where the prospect for leverage is more explicitly to do with the exit option, like elective surgery, could be evaluated against their performance in commissioning procedures less open to market mechanisms, like accident and emergency or maternity services. This may inform the debate on how the engagement of GPs in the planning process behind secondary care compares to their capacity to exercise the exit option.

CONCLUSION

It is noticeable that some of the ideas put forward in the previous section on policy implications are dependent on continuing the right of GPs to switch referrals between providers. If this reflects the true nature of primary care groups, a degree of competition should be induced between hospitals. Yet although the new government's White Paper does include the point that the internal market will be abolished (see Department of Health, 1997), such competition does not contradict any of the details in that document. For instance, the White Paper indicates that both the separation between providers and commissioners plus the right of purchasers to redirect work between hospitals is to be maintained.

Accordingly, it would seem that the potential success of primary care groups rely on some of the language used in the White Paper, most obviously the point about abolishing the internal market, having more to do with political rhetoric than firm intentions. The evidence that market mechanisms gave some patients shorter waiting times can perhaps be seen as confirming that the quasi-market, far from being all bad, did have some very positive features. As a result, the argument being made is that if the internal market in its present guise is to be abolished, it should be replaced with another form of quasi-market.

There is no reason why this proposal should be seen as contrary to the ideology of the present government. If there is a baseline doctrine behind the concept that has become known as 'new Labour', it is likely to correspond in some way with the philosophy of market socialism. A fundamental idea behind this notion is that under certain conditions markets can produce virtuous outcomes (Estrin and Le Grand, 1989; Le Grand, 1989). Correspondingly, if ends are seen as more important than means, claims to the beneficial outcomes of markets should not be seen as a prerogative of the new right (see Miller, 1989).

From this, markets do not inevitably have to contradict the principles of equity. If the opportunity to switch referrals encapsulates all GPs and the money for NHS treatments follows patients, the prospects for both equitable and shorter waiting times, plus lower waiting lists, should theoretically be improved. Le Grand (1991b, p. 20) wrote that it is 'commonly asserted that there is, or that in most situations there is likely to be, a trade-off between equity and efficiency', an assertion also made by Williams (1993). In the context of productive efficiency, perhaps this is one of the occasions where a trade-off is not necessary. For a government that once found itself embarrassed by growing NHS waiting lists (Warden, 1998b; 1998c) as well as seeing them become the main test of its political virility (Warden, 1998e), it should be a tempting proposition to follow a policy that could both reduce waits and extend equity.

Allied to this point, what is the alternative to GPs taking on the wide commissioning function within the NHS? It would appear to be the health authority doing this. Primary care groups would remain at level one. If their block contracts were changed to mirror those used by fund-holders, where payments are compared to the actual activity that has taken place and modified to reflect it on a global basis, GPs may still have the exit option backed by money following the patients. Yet considering that the financial responsibility of GPs grow as primary care groups move up the stages, at the lowest level questions could be asked as to whether it would be wrong for GPs not to hold the budget for the secondary care received by their patients. After all, it was an interviewee from the health authority who argued that GPs should hold responsibility for elective care plus accident and emergency services, for they also arrange many of the admissions for the latter (see the seventh chapter).

The rationale for this argument is that the growth in the demand for emergency services may not necessarily be down to the same expansion in the need for such services. People can be admitted as emergencies for a large number of reasons and in a wide variety of conditions. It could be that some patients are admitted now who would not have been in the past. While this could mean that some patients who should have been admitted in the past were not, it might also be that some people are taken in now who do not need to be admitted as emergencies. Of course, not all such admissions are arranged by GPs. For example, they have no control over self-referrals by patients. But GPs do arrange many emergency admissions themselves, and in such cases this is a service where the costs of hospital services are directly driven by practices.

As such, if GPs are the gatekeepers to such services, it seems logical that they should hold the funding as well. Considering the alleged rise in the costs of emergency services (discussed in the fifth chapter), perhaps a major fault of the standard fund-holding scheme was that it excluded GPs from any financial responsibility for too many services? It left the agents with influence on the rate of such admissions with little incentive to check any unnecessary costs, outside a moral obligation to curb NHS spending. That is not a claim that fund-holders were more likely than other GPs to show little interest in controlling the costs for services outside the scheme. The results of research into the emergency services fails to support this idea, despite the fact that such expenditure fell outside the remit of fund-holders (see Toth *et al.*, 1997). But fund-holders still had little personal reason to try and check unnecessary emergency admissions, apart from being taxpayers, and neither did non fund-holders. Perhaps it is small wonder that the costs grew.

It may therefore be a good thing that primary care trusts should extend the purchasing responsibility of GPs beyond the remit of the current standard fund-holding scheme. Linked to this, it would seem sensible for primary care groups to be encouraged to move up the four levels, or join at the highest feasible level to start with, as soon as possible. Perhaps hesitancy over this could result from the financial skills required to manage the budgets for services outside the fund-holding scheme. Yet primary care trusts will have staffing structures, and accountants can be part of this. Anyway, the financial performance of GPs within the fund-holding scheme does not seem to give cause for concern. A senior finance manager from the local health authority confirmed that West Sussex fund-holders had a net under spend against their aggregate hospital and community health services budgets in the years relevant to this research, similar to a national trend identified by Goodwin (1998).

Furthermore, Mulligan (1998b) made the point that although health authorities had initially under spent by less than fund-holders and on an aggregate basis had then moved into deficit, the reasons for this were unclear. However, with regard to the prospect that fund-holders may have been over funded, this research has shown that does not appear to have been the case in West Sussex. Although managing the budget for care covered by the standard fund-holding scheme will be easier than the funds for all services, the situation in West Sussex suggests there is little reason to immediately write-off primary care trusts as being unable to carry out this function to acceptable standards.

In sum, the evidence from this study suggests elective surgery (and from this perhaps most health care services) should be purchased by general practices. So that purchasing leverage and hospital behaviour can contribute to efficiency and equity in the context of waiting times, the following format for the new NHS is implied. Trusts give priority to income maximisation. This can be made to work for patients by giving all GPs, through their primary care groups, the freedom to switch referrals between different providers. This is likely to happen with a minority of a hospital's caseload, so that much of its fixed costs should remain covered. But as long as money follows the patients through making payments attributable to the number treated, trusts should be responsive and try to cut waiting times to attract referrals. Hence the efficiency of providers might be advanced, with purchasing leverage spread around all GPs. With primary care groups funded by a capitation methodology, this could create equal access for patients.

Moreover, incentives for GPs to act as efficient commissioners, beyond improving the lot of their patients, should be maintained. Devolving budgets within primary care groups for some services may open up the potential for under spends to be used by practices in similar ways to fund-holding savings. There should also be room to cut the transaction costs incurred with fund-holding by decreasing the volume of data recorded at general practices. Cutting the detail in contracts and making the contracting process less time consuming could reduce transaction costs as well – a result that is intended from the move towards three-year and in some cases five-year service agreements (see Department of Health, 1997). Taking these points into account, it seems equity can be achieved at the levels of purchasers and patients, alongside hospital efficiency and lower transaction costs. While this seems a realistic proposition in theory, further research will be required in the future to ascertain whether events actually turn out that way.

Appendix

Listed below are the groups of procedures used for the case mix comparison in the sixth chapter. The groups are characterised by having procedures within them that at some point were covered by the standard fund-holding scheme up to and including the 1995/96 financial year. This does not mean every separate operation code in a group was always covered by the scheme, and some may never have been. For example, in 1995/96, of the cranial nerve procedures running from A24 to A36, only operations within the A27 code were included in the standard fund-holding scheme. The codes not covered by the scheme in a particular year will not be included in the applicable tables of the sixth chapter. Moreover, to appear as a distinct group in those tables, the number of operations that were relevant to it would have made it one of the ten most common of all the procedure groups below at a provider in a specific year.

Nervous system
A24-A36   Cranial nerves
A44-A57   Spinal cord and other contents of spinal canal
A59-A73   Peripheral nerves

Endocrine system and breast
B08-B16   Thyroid and parathyroid glands
B27-B37   Breast

Eye
C10-C22   Eyebrow and eyelid
C24-C29   Lacrimal apparatus
C31-C37   Muscles of eye
C39-C51   Conjunctiva and cornea
C53-C64   Sclera and iris
C66-C77   Anterior chamber of eye and lens
C79-C86   Retina and other parts of eye

Ear
D10-D20   Mastoid and middle ear
D22-D28   Inner ear and eustachian canal

Respiratory tract
E01-E10   Nose
E12-E17   Nasal sinuses
E19-E27   Pharynx
E29-E38   Larynx
E39-E52   Trachea and bronchus
E53-E63   Lung and mediastinum

Mouth
F34-F42   Tonsil and other parts of mouth
F44-F58   Salivary apparatus

Upper digestive tract
G01-G25   Oesophagus including hiatus hernia
G27-G48   Stomach pylorus and general upper gastrointestinal tract
          endoscopy
G49-G57   Duodenum
G58-G67   Jejunum
G69-G82   Ileum

Lower digestive tract
H04-H30   Colon
H33-H46   Rectum
H47-H62   Anus and perianal region

Other abdominal organs – principally digestive
J18-J26   Gall bladder
J27-J52   Bile duct

Heart
K25-K38   Valves of heart and adjacent structures
K40-K51   Coronary artery

Arteries and veins
L74-L97   Veins and other blood vessels

Urinary

M01-M16 Kidney
M18-M32 Ureter
M34-M49 Bladder
M51-M70 Outlet of bladder and prostate
M72-M83 Urethra and other part of urinary tract

Male genital organs

N01-N13 Scrotum and testes
N15-N24 Spermatic cord and male perineum
N26-N34 Penis and other male genital organs

Lower female genital tract

P01-P13 Vulva and female perineum
P14-P31 Vagina

Upper female genital tract

Q01-Q20 Uterus
Q22-Q41 Fallopian tube
Q43-Q56 Ovary and broad ligament

Skin

S01-S62 Skin or subcutaneous tissue
S64-S70 Nail

Soft tissue

T19-T31 Abdominal wall
T33-T48 Peritoneum
T50-T62 Fascia ganglion and bursa
T64-T74 Tendon
T85-T96 Lymphatic tissue

Bones and joints of skull and spine

V22-V54 Bones and joints of spine

Other bones and joints

W05-W36 Bone
W37-W92 Joint

Bibliography

Akehurst, R. and Ferguson, B. (1993) 'The purchasing authority', in Drummond, M. and Maynard, A. (eds) *Purchasing and Providing Cost-effective Health Care*, London: Longman.

Allsop, J. (1989) 'Health', in McCarthy, M. (ed.) *The New Politics of Welfare: An Agenda for the 1990s?*, London: Macmillan.

Allsop, J. (1995) *Health Policy and the NHS Towards 2000*, Harlow: Longman.

Appleby, J. (1992) *Financing Health Care in the 1990s*, Buckingham: Open University Press.

Appleby, J., Smith, P., Ranade, W., Little, V. and Robinson, R. (1993) 'Competition and the NHS: monitoring the market', in Tilley, I. (ed.) *Managing the Internal Market*, London: Paul Chapman.

Appleby, J., Smith, P., Ranade, W., Little, V. and Robinson, R. (1994) 'Monitoring managed competition', in Robinson, R. and Le Grand, J. (eds) *Evaluating the NHS Reforms*, London: King's Fund Institute.

Arblaster, L., Lambert, M., Entwistle, V., Forster, M., Fullerton, D., Sheldon, T. and Watt, I. (1996) 'A systematic review of the effectiveness of health service interventions aimed at reducing inequalities in health', *Journal of Health Services Research and Policy*, vol. 1, pp. 93-103.

Arvidsson, G. (1995) 'Regulation of planned markets in health care', in Saltman, R. and von Otter, C. (eds) *Implementing Planned Markets in Health Care*, Buckingham: Open University Press.

Ashburner, L. (1993) 'The composition of NHS trust boards: a national perspective', in Peck, E. and Spurgeon, P. (eds) *NHS Trusts in Practice*, Harlow: Longman.

Audit Commission (1993) *Their Health, Your Business: The New Role of the District Health Authority*, London: HMSO.

Audit Commission (1995) *Briefing on GP Fundholding*, London: HMSO.

Audit Commission (1996a) *What the Doctor Ordered: A Study of GP Fundholders in England and Wales*, London: HMSO.

Audit Commission (1996b) *Fundholding Facts*, London: HMSO.

Baeza, J., Salt, D. and Tilley, I. (1993) 'Four providers' strategic responses and the internal market', in Tilley, I. (ed.) *Managing the Internal Market*, London: Paul Chapman.

Baggott, R. (1994) *Health and Health Care in Britain*, London: Macmillan.

Bailey, J., Black, M. and Wilkin, D. (1994) 'Specialist outreach clinics in general practice', *British Medical Journal*, vol. 308, pp. 1083-1086.

Bain, J. (1992) 'Budget holding in Calverton: one year on', *British Medical Journal*, vol. 304, pp. 971-973.

Bain, J. (1994) 'Fundholding: a two tier system', *British Medical Journal*, vol. 309, pp. 396-399.

Baines, D. and Whynes, D. (1996) 'Selection bias in GP fundholding', Health Economics, vol. 5, pp. 129-140.

Baker, A. and Perkins, D. (1995) 'Managing people and teams', in Glynn, J. and Perkins, D. (eds) *Managing Health Care: Challenges for the 90s*, London: Saunders.

Baker, J. and van der Gaag, J. (1993) 'Equity in health care and health care financing: evidence from five developing countries', in Van Doorslaer, E., Wagstaff, A. and Rutten, F. (eds) *Equity in the Finance and Delivery of Health Care: An International Perspective*, Oxford: Oxford University Press.

Baker, Y. (1998) 'Use of capitation formulas for primary care groups could result in chaos', *British Medical Journal*, vol. 317, pp. 210-211.

Baldock, J. (1993) 'Patterns of change in the delivery of welfare in Europe', in Taylor-Gooby, P. and Lawson, R. (eds) *Markets and Managers: New Issues in the Delivery of Welfare*, Buckingham: Open University Press.

Ball, S., Bowe, R. and Gewirtz, S. (1994) 'Schools in the market place: an analysis of local market relations', in Bartlett, W., Propper, C., Wilson, D. and Le Grand, J. (eds) *Quasi-markets in the Welfare State*, Bristol: SAUS.

Balogh, R. (1996) 'Exploring the role of localities in health commissioning: a review of the literature', *Social Policy and Administration*, vol. 30, pp. 99-113.

Barker, K., Chalkley, M., Malcomson, J. and Montgomery, J. (1997) 'Contracting in the National Health Service: legal and economic issues', in Flynn, R. and Williams, G. (eds) *Contracting for Health*, New York: Oxford University Press.

Barr, N. (1993) *The Economics of the Welfare State*, London: Orion.

Barr, N., Glennerster, H. and Le Grand, J. (1988) *Reform and the National Health Service*, STICERD Welfare State Discussion Paper WSP/32, London: London School of Economics.

Barrowcliffe, M. (1996) 'Labour lends an ear to industry's concerns', *Pharmaceutical Marketing*, vol. 7, pp. 38-40.

Barry, N. (1987) 'Understanding the market', in Loney, M. with Bocock, R., Clarke, J., Cochrane, A., Graham, P. and Wilson, M. (eds) *The State or the Market: Politics and Welfare in Contemporary Britain*, London: Sage.

Bartlett, W. (1991a) *Privatisation and Quasi-markets*, Studies in Decentralisation and Quasi-markets No. 7, Bristol: SAUS.

Bartlett, W. (1991b) 'Quasi-markets and contracts: a markets and hierarchies perspective on NHS reform', *Public Money & Management*, vol. 11, pp. 53-61.

Bartlett, W. (1995) *Privatisation, Non-profit Trusts and Contracts*, Studies in Decentralisation and Quasi-markets No. 20, Bristol: SAUS.

Bartlett, W. and Harrison, L. (1993) 'Quasi-markets and the National Health Service reforms', in Le Grand J. and Bartlett, W. (eds) *Quasi-markets and Social Policy*, London: Macmillan.

Bartlett, W. and Le Grand, J. (1993) 'The theory of quasi-markets', in Le Grand, J. and Bartlett, W. (eds) *Quasi-markets and Social Policy*, London: Macmillan.

Bartlett, W. and Le Grand, J. (1994a) 'The performance of trusts', in Robinson, R. and Le Grand, J. (eds) *Evaluating the NHS Reforms*, London: King's Fund Institute.

Bartlett, W. and Le Grand, J. (1994b) *Costs and Trusts*, Studies in Decentralisation and Quasi-markets No. 18, Bristol: SAUS.

Bartlett, W., Le Grand, J. and Propper, C. (1994) 'Where next', in Bartlett, W., Propper, C., Wilson, D. and Le Grand, J. (eds) *Quasi-markets in the Welfare State*, Bristol: SAUS.

Besley, T., Hall, J. and Preston, I. (1996) *Private Health Insurance and the State of the NHS*, London: Institute for Fiscal Studies.

Bevan, G. (1998) 'Taking equity seriously: a dilemma for government from allocating resources to primary care groups', *British Medical Journal*, vol. 316, pp. 39-42.

Bevan, G., Copeman, H., Perrin, J. and Rosser, R. (1980) *Health Care Priorities and Management*, London: Croom Helm.

Bevan, G., Holland, W. and Mays, N. (1989) 'Working for which patients and at what cost?', *The Lancet*, vol. 1, pp. 947-949.

Black, D., Birchall, A. and Trimble, I. (1994) 'Non-fundholding in Nottingham: a vision of the future', *British Medical Journal*, vol. 309, pp. 930-932.

Black, D., Morris, J., Smith, C. and Townsend, P. (1988) 'The Black Report', in Townsend, P. and Davidson, N. (eds) *Inequalities in Health*, London: Penguin.

Black, N. (1998) 'Potential biases were not taken into account in study of waiting times', *British Medical Journal*, vol. 316, p. 149.

Bloor, K. and Maynard, A. (1997) 'An outsider's view of the NHS reforms: enthusiasts at the OECD should not induce complacency', *British Medical Journal*, vol. 309, pp. 352-353.

Boaden, N. (1997) *Primary Care: Making Connections*, Buckingham: Open University Press.

Bobrow, D. and Dryzek, J. (1987) *Policy Analysis by Design*, Pittsburgh: University of Pittsburgh Press.

Bosanquet, N. (1996) 'Fundholding: the real gains are still to come', *The NHS Fundholding and Commissioning Guide 1996/97*, London: Medical Information Systems.

Bowie, C. and Spurgeon, R. (1994) 'Better data needed for analysis', *British Medical Journal*, vol. 309, p. 34.

Bradlow, J. and Coulter, A. (1993) 'Effect of fundholding and indicative prescribing schemes on general practitioners' prescribing costs', *British Medical Journal*, vol. 307, pp. 1186-1189.

Brazier, J., Hutton, J. and Jeavons, R. (1990) 'Evaluating the reform of the NHS', in Culyer, A., Maynard, A. and Posnett, J. (eds) *Competition in Health Care: Reforming the NHS*, London: Macmillan.

Brogan, S. (1993) 'Who says fundholders are loaded?', *The Health Service Journal*, vol. 103: no. 5342, p. 22.

Brommels, M. (1995) 'Contracting and political boards in planned markets', in Saltman, R. and von Otter, C. (eds) *Implementing Planned Markets in Health Care*, Buckingham: Open University Press.

Brown, C. (1997) 'Dobson to go slow on GP funds', *Doctor*, 15 May, p. 1.

Bryden, P. (1992) 'The future of primary care', in Loveridge, R. and Starkey, K. (eds) *Continuity and Crisis in the NHS*, Buckingham: Open University Press.

Butler, J. (1992) *Patients, Policies and Politics: Before and After Working for Patients*, Buckingham: Open University Press.

Butler, J. (1993) 'A case study in the National Health Service: working for patients', in Taylor-Gooby, P. and Lawson, R. (eds) *Markets and Managers: New Issues in the Delivery of Welfare*, Buckingham: Open University Press.

Butler, J. (1994) 'Origins and early development', in Robinson, R. and Le Grand, J. (eds) *Evaluating the NHS Reforms*, London: King's Fund Institute.

Caines, E. (1993) 'The impact of trusts in the management of the NHS', in Peck, E. and Spurgeon, P. (eds) *NHS Trusts in Practice*, Harlow: Longman.

Calnan, M., Cant, S. and Gabe, J. (1993) *Going Private: Why People Pay for their Health Care*, Buckingham: Open University Press.

Carr-Hill, R., Sheldon, T., Smith, P., Martin, S., Peacock, S. and Hardman, G. (1994) 'Allocating resources to health authorities: development of method for small area analysis of use of inpatient services', *British Medical Journal*, vol. 309, pp. 1046-1049.

Challis, L., Day, P., Klein, R. and Scrivens, E. (1994) 'Managing quasi-markets: institutions of regulation', in Bartlett, W., Propper, C., Wilson, D. and Le Grand, J. (eds) *Quasi-markets in the Welfare State*, Bristol: SAUS.

Checkland, P. (1997) 'Rhetoric and reality in contracting: research in and on the national health service', in Flynn, R. and Williams, G. (eds) *Contracting for Health*, New York: Oxford University Press.

Chinegwundoh, F. (1997) 'Doctors should not be penalised for doing private work in spare time', *British Medical Journal*, vol. 315, p. 1231.

Cook, T. (1993) 'The NHS reforms and the finance function', in Spurgeon, P. (ed.) *The New Face of the NHS*, Harlow: Longman.

Corney, R. (1994) 'Experiences of first wave general practice fundholders in South East Thames Regional Health Authority', *British Journal of General Practice*, vol. 44, pp. 34-37.

Coulter, A. (1992a) 'The patient's perspective', in Roland, M. and Coulter, A. (eds) *Hospital Referrals*, Oxford: Oxford University Press.

Coulter, A. (1992b) 'The interface between primary and secondary care', in Roland, M. and Coulter, A. (eds) *Hospital Referrals*, Oxford: Oxford University Press.

Coulter, A. (1992c) 'Fundholding general practices: early successes – but will they last?', *British Medical Journal*, vol. 304, pp. 397-398.

Coulter, A. (1992d) 'Auditing referrals', in Roland, M. and Coulter, A. (eds) *Hospital Referrals*, Oxford: Oxford University Press.

Coulter, A. (1995a) 'Evaluating general practice fundholding in the United Kingdom', *European Journal of Public Health*, vol. 5, pp. 233-239.

Coulter, A. (1995b) 'General practice fundholding: time for a cool appraisal', *British Journal of General Practice*, vol. 45, pp. 119-120.

Coulter, A. (1996) 'Why should health services be primary care-led?', *Journal of Health Services Research and Policy*, vol. 1, pp. 122-124.

Coulter, A. (1998) 'Managing demand at the interface between primary and secondary care', *British Medical Journal*, vol. 316, pp. 1974-1976.

Coulter, A. and Bradlow, J. (1993) 'Effect of NHS reforms on general practitioners' referral patterns', *British Medical Journal*, vol. 306, pp. 433-437.

Coulter, A., Seagroatt, V. and McPherson, K. (1990) 'Relation between general practices' outpatient referral rates and rates of elective admission to hospital', *British Medical Journal*, vol. 301, pp. 273-276.

Cowen, T. (1988) 'Public goods and externalities: old and new perspectives', in Cowen, T. (ed.) *The Theory of Market Failure*, Fairfax: George Mason University Press.

Cox, D. (1992) 'Crisis and opportunity in health service management', in Loveridge, R. and Starkey, K. (eds) *Continuity and Crisis in the NHS*, Buckingham: Open University Press.

Crump, B., Cubbon, J., Drummond, M., Hawkes, R. and Marchment, M. (1991) 'Fundholding in general practice and financial risk', *British Medical Journal*, vol. 302, pp. 1582-1584.

Crump, B. and Griffiths, R. (1993) 'Working for patients...a public health perspective', in Spurgeon, P. (ed.) *The New Face of the NHS*, Harlow: Longman.

Cullis, J. (1993) 'Waiting lists and health policy', in Frankel, S. and West, R. (eds) *Rationing and Rationality in the National Health Service: The Persistence of Waiting Lists*, London: Macmillan.

Culyer, A. (1993a) 'Health, health expenditures, and equity', in Van Doorslaer, E., Wagstaff, A. and Rutten, F. (eds) *Equity in the Finance and Delivery of Health Care: An International Perspective*, Oxford: Oxford University Press.

Culyer, A. (1993b) 'Health care insurance and provision', in Barr, N. and Whynes, D. (eds) *Current Issues in the Economics of Welfare*, London: Macmillan.

Culyer, A. and Cullis, J. (1976) 'Some economics of hospital waiting lists in the NHS', *Journal of Social Policy*, vol. 5, pp. 239-264.

Culyer, A., Maynard, A. and Posnett, J. (1990) 'Reforming health care: an introduction to the economic issues', in Culyer, A., Maynard, A. and Posnett, J. (eds) *Competition in Health Care: Reforming the NHS*, London: Macmillan.

Culyer, A. and Posnett, J. (1990) 'Hospital behaviour and competition', in Culyer, A., Maynard, A. and Posnett, J. (eds) *Competition in Health Care: Reforming the NHS*, London: Macmillan.

Culyer, A. and Wagstaff, A. (1992) *Need, Equity and Equality in Health and Health Care*, Centre for Health Economics Discussion Paper 95, York: University of York.

Cyert, R. (1988) *The Economic Theory of Organization and the Firm*, Hemel Hempstead: Harvester Wheatsheaf.

Davies, J. (1995) 'How much does the scheme cost?', *Fundholding*, vol. 4, pp. 22-24.

Davis, A. (1993) 'Community care', in Spurgeon, P. (ed.) *The New Face of the NHS*, Harlow: Longman.

Dawson, D. (1994) *Costs and Prices in the Internal Market: Market vs the NHS Management Executive Guidelines*, Centre for Health Economics Discussion Paper 115, York: University of York.

Day, P. and Klein, R. (1991) 'Variations in budgets of fundholding practices', *British Medical Journal*, vol. 303, pp. 168-170.

Dennis, J. (1993a) 'NHS trusts – purchaser perspectives', in Peck, E. and Spurgeon, P. (eds) *NHS Trusts in Practice*, Harlow: Longman.

Dennis, J. (1993b) 'How does it really feel?', in Spurgeon, P. (ed.) *The New Face of the NHS*, Harlow: Longman.

Department of Health (1989a) *Working for Patients*, London: HMSO.

Department of Health (1989b) *Self-governing Hospitals*, London: HMSO.

Department of Health (1989c) *Practice Budgets for General Medical Practitioners*, London: HMSO.

Department of Health (1990) *Developing Districts*, London: HMSO.

Department of Health (1991) *The Patient's Charter*, London: HMSO.

Department of Health (1995a) *Variations in Health: What can the Department of Health and the NHS do?*, London: HMSO.

Department of Health (1995b) *The Patient's Charter & You*, London: Department of Health.

Department of Health (1997) *The New NHS: Modern · Dependable*, London: The Stationery Office Limited.

Department of Health and the Welsh Office (1989) *General Practice in the National Health Service: A New Contract*, London: Department of Health.

Dixon, J. (1994) 'Can there be fair funding for fundholding practices?', *British Medical Journal*, vol. 308, pp. 772-775.

Dixon, J. (1998) 'The context', in Le Grand, J., Mays, N. and Mulligan, J. (eds) *Learning from the NHS Internal Market: A Review of the Evidence*, London: King's Fund.

Dixon, J., Dinwoodie, M., Hodson, D., Dodd, S., Poltorak, T., Garrett, C., Rice, P., Doncaster, I. and Williams, M. (1994) 'Distribution of NHS funds between fundholding and non-fundholding practices', *British Medical Journal*, vol. 309, pp. 30-34.

Dixon, J. and Glennerster, H. (1995) 'What do we know about fundholding in general practice?', *British Medical Journal*, vol. 311, pp. 727-730.

Dixon, J., Holland, P. and Mays, N. (1998) 'Developing primary care: gatekeeping, commissioning, and managed care', *British Medical Journal*, vol. 317, pp. 125-128.

Dixon, J. and Mays, N. (1997) 'New labour, new NHS? The white paper spells evolution not revolution', *British Medical Journal*, vol. 315, pp. 1639-1640.

Dobkin Hall, P. (1987) 'A historical overview of the private nonprofit sector', in Powell, W. (ed.) *The Nonprofit Sector: A Research Handbook*, New Haven: Yale University Press.

Dobson, J. (1993) 'DoH rethinks GP freedoms as two tier service emerges', *The Health Service Journal*, vol. 103: no. 5336, p. 3.

Donaldson, C. and Gerard, K. (1993) *Economics of Health Care Financing: The Invisible Hand*, London: Macmillan.

Douglas, J. (1987) 'Political theories of nonprofit organization', in Powell, W. (ed.) *The Nonprofit Sector: A Research Handbook*, New Haven: Yale University Press.

Dowell, J., Snadden, D. and Dunbar, J. (1995) 'Changing to generic formulary: how one fundholding practice reduced prescribing costs', *British Medical Journal*, vol. 310, pp. 505-508.

Dowling, B. (1997) 'Effect of fundholding on waiting times: database study', *British Medical Journal*, vol. 315, pp. 290-292.

Dowling, B. (1998) 'Potential biases do not affect results of waiting time study', *British Medical Journal*, vol. 317, p. 79.

Dowling, B. and Richardson, R. (1997) 'Evaluating performance-related pay for managers in the National Health Service', *The International Journal of Human Resource Management*, vol. 8, pp. 348-366.

Drummond, M. (1993) 'Assessing efficiency in the new NHS', in Spurgeon, P. (ed.) *The New Face of the NHS*, Harlow: Longman.

Dunleavy, P. (1991) *Democracy, Bureaucracy and Public Choice: Economic Explanations in Political Science*, Hemel Hempstead: Harvester Wheatsheaf.

Eastaugh, S. (1992) *Health Economics: Efficiency, Quality and Equity*, Westport: Auburn House.

Ebrahim, S. (1993) 'Health care of the elderly and the internal market', in Tilley, I. (ed.) *Managing the Internal Market*, London: Paul Chapman.

Eckel, C. and Steinberg, R. (1993) 'Competition, performance, and public policy towards nonprofits', in Hammack, D. and Young, D. (eds) *Nonprofit Organizations in a Market Economy*, San Francisco: Jossey-Bass.

Edwards, R. and Barlow, J. (1994) *Rationing Health Care by Waiting List: An Extra-welfarist Perspective*, Centre for Health Economics Discussion Paper 114, York: University of York.

Ellwood, S. (1993) 'Pricing acute health care in the NHS internal market', in Malek, M., Vacani, P., Rasquinna, J. and Davey, P. (eds) *Managerial Issues in the Reformed NHS*, Chichester: Wiley.

Enthoven, A. (1985) *Reflections on the Management of the National Health Service*, London: Nuffield Provincial Hospitals Trust.

Estrin, S. and Le Grand, J. (1989) 'Market socialism', in Le Grand, J. and Estrin, S. (eds) *Market Socialism*, Oxford: Oxford University Press.

Evandrou, M., Falkingham, J., Le Grand, J. and Winter, D. (1992) 'Equity in health and social care', *Journal of Social Policy*, vol. 21, pp. 489-523.

Farrow, S. and Jewell, D. (1993) 'Opening the gate: referrals from primary to secondary care', in Frankel, S. and West, R. (eds) *Rationing and Rationality in the National Health Service: The Persistence of Waiting Lists*, London: Macmillan.

Ferlie, E. (1994) 'The evolution of quasi-markets in the NHS: early evidence', in Bartlett, W., Propper, C., Wilson, D. and Le Grand, J. (eds) *Quasi-markets in the Welfare State*, Bristol: SAUS.

Ferlie, E., Cairncross, L. and Pettigrew, A. (1993) 'Understanding internal markets in the NHS', in Tilley, I. (ed.) *Managing the Internal Market*, London: Paul Chapman.

Figueras, J., Roberts, J. and Sanderson, C. (1993) 'Contracting, planning, competition and efficiency', in Malek, M., Vacani, P., Rasquinna, J. and Davey, P. (eds) *Managerial Issues in the Reformed NHS*, Chichester: Wiley.

Fisher, A. (1993) 'Fundholding', *British Medical Journal*, vol. 306, p. 1003.

Fisher, P. (1993) 'Fundholding practices get preference', *British Medical Journal*, vol. 306, p. 141.

Flannery, N. (1996) 'Political footballers' own-goals', *The Health Service Journal*, vol. 106: no. 5489, p. 23.

Fleming, D. (1992) 'The interface between general practice and secondary care in Europe and North America', in Roland, M. and Coulter, A. (eds) *Hospital Referrals*, Oxford: Oxford University Press.

Fleming, M. and Nellis, J. (1994) *Principles of Applied Statistics*, London: Routledge.

Fletcher, D. (1997) 'Dobson to freeze 'unfair' GP fundholding', *The Daily Telegraph*, 21 May, p. 11.

Flynn, R. and Williams, G. (1997) 'Contracting for health', in Flynn, R. and Williams, G. (eds) *Contracting for Health*, New York: Oxford University Press.

Frankel, S. (1993) 'The origins of waiting lists', in Frankel, S. and West, R. (eds) *Rationing and Rationality in the National Health Service: The Persistence of Waiting Lists*, London: Macmillan.

Frankel, S. and Robbins, M. (1993) 'Entering the lobby: access to outpatient assessment', in Frankel, S. and West, R. (eds) *Rationing and Rationality in the National Health Service: The Persistence of Waiting Lists*, London: Macmillan.

Frankel, S. and West, R. (1993) 'What is to be done?', in Frankel, S. and West, R. (eds) *Rationing and Rationality in the National Health Service: The Persistence of Waiting Lists*, London: Macmillan.

Freudenstein, U. (1993) 'Fundholding from the inside', *Medical World*, vol. 13, pp. 10-11.

Frostick, S. and Wallace, W. (1993) 'Mainstream specialisms and the NHS market: the case of surgery', in Tilley, I. (ed.) *Managing the Internal Market*, London: Paul Chapman.

Gambrill, E. (1990) *Critical Thinking in Clinical Practice: Improving the Accuracy of Judgements and Decisions About Clients*, San Francisco: Jossey-Bass.

Glatter, R. and Woods, P. (1994) 'The impact of competition and choice on parents and schools', in Bartlett, W., Propper, C., Wilson, D. and Le Grand, J. (eds) *Quasi-markets in the Welfare State*, Bristol: SAUS.

Glennerster, H. (1992) *Paying for Welfare: The 1990s*, Hemel Hempstead: Prentice Hall.

Glennerster, H. (1995) *British Social Policy Since 1945*, Oxford: Blackwell.

Glennerster, H. (1996) 'Fixed budgets for fundholding general practitioners in the UK', in Schwartz, F., Glennerster, H. and Saltman, R. (eds) *Fixing Health Budgets: Experience From Europe and North America*, Chichester: Wiley.

Glennerster, H. (1997) *Paying for Welfare: Towards 2000*, Hemel Hempstead: Harvester Wheatsheaf.

Glennerster, H. (1998) 'Competition and quality in health care: the UK experience', *International Journal for Quality in Health Care*, vol. 10, pp. 403-410.

Glennerster, H., Cohen, A. and Bovell, V. (1998) 'Alternatives to fundholding', *International Journal of Health Services*, vol. 28, pp. 47-66.

Glennerster, H. and Le Grand, J. (1995) 'The development of quasi-markets in welfare provision in the United Kingdom', *International Journal of Health Services*, vol. 25, pp. 203-218.

Glennerster, H. and Matsaganis, M. (1994) 'The English and Swedish health care reforms', *International Journal of Health Services*, vol. 24, pp. 231-251.

Glennerster, H., Matsaganis, M. and Owens, P. (1992) *A Foothold for Fundholding: A Preliminary Report on the Introduction of GP Fundholding*, Research Report 12, London: King's Fund Institute.

Glennerster, H., Matsaganis, M. and Owens, P. with Hancock, S. (1994a) *Implementing GP Fundholding: Wild Card or Winning Hand?*, Buckingham: Open University Press.

Glennerster, H., Matsaganis, M., Owens, P. with Hancock, S. (1994b) 'GP fundholding: wild card or winning hand?', in Robinson, R. and Le Grand, J. (eds) *Evaluating the NHS Reforms*, London: King's Fund Institute.

Goodwin, N. (1994) 'Making the internal market work', *British Medical Journal*, vol. 308, p. 206.

Goodwin, N. (1998) 'GP fundholding', in Le Grand, J., Mays, N. and Mulligan, J. (eds) *Learning from the NHS Internal Market: A Review of the Evidence*, London: King's Fund.

Goodwin, N., Mays, N., McLeod, H., Malbon, G. and Raftery, J. (1998) 'Evaluation of total purchasing pilots in England and Scotland and implications for primary care groups in England: personal interviews and analysis of routine data', *British Medical Journal*, vol. 317, pp. 256-259.

Gosden, T., Torgerson, D. and Maynard, A. (1997) 'What is to be done about fundholding', *British Medical Journal*, vol. 315, pp. 170-171.

Graffy, J. and Williams, J. (1994) 'Purchasing for all: an alternative to GP fundholding', *British Medical Journal*, vol. 308, pp. 391-394.

Graham, C. (1993) 'NHS trusts: continuity or discontinuity', in Peck, E. and Spurgeon, P. (eds) *NHS Trusts in Practice*, Harlow: Longman.

Gray, A. and Jenkins, B. (1993) 'Markets, managers and the public service: the changing of a culture', in Taylor-Gooby, P. and Lawson, R. (eds) *Markets and Managers: New Issues in the Delivery of Welfare*, Buckingham: Open University Press.

Gray, J. (1992) *The Moral Foundations of Market Institutions*, London: IEA Health and Welfare Unit.

Gregory, W. and Walsh, M. (1993) 'Quality, ideology and consumer choice – health care standards and stakeholder participation', in Malek, M., Vacani, P., Rasquinna, J. and Davey, P. (eds) *Managerial Issues in the Reformed NHS*, Chichester: Wiley.

Haines, A. and Armstrong, D. (1992) 'Developing referral guidelines', in Roland, M. and Coulter, A. (eds) *Hospital Referrals*, Oxford: Oxford University Press.

Ham, C. (1992) *Health Policy in Britain: The Politics and Organisation of the National Health Service*, London: Macmillan.

Ham, C. (1994) 'Where now for the NHS reforms? Making them up as they go along', *British Medical Journal*, vol. 309, pp. 351-352.

Ham, C. (1996a) 'Priority setting: political issues', in Schwartz, F., Glennerster, H. and Saltman, R. (eds) *Fixing Health Budgets: Experience From Europe and North America*, Chichester: Wiley.

Ham, C. (1996b) 'Primary care led purchasing in the NHS: fundholding and other models', in Griffin, J. (ed.) *The Future of Primary Care*, London: Office of Health Economics.

Ham, C. (1997a) 'Lessons and conclusions', in Ham, C. (ed.) *Health Care Reform*, Buckingham: Open University Press.

Ham, C. (1997b) 'Replacing the NHS internal market: the white paper should focus on incentives as well as directives', *British Medical Journal*, vol. 315, pp. 1175-1176.

Ham, C. (1997c) *Management and Competition in the NHS*, Abingdon: Radcliffe.

Ham, C. and Hunter, D. (1988) *Managing Clinical Activity in the NHS*, London: King's Fund Institute.

Ham, C., Hunter, D. and Robinson, R. (1995) 'Evidence based policymaking: research must inform health policy as well as medical care', *British Medical Journal*, vol. 310, pp. 71-72.

Ham, C., Robinson, R. and Benzeval, M. (1990) *Health Check: Health Care Reforms in an International Context*, London: King's Fund Institute.

Ham, C. and Shapiro, J. (1995) 'The future of fundholding', *British Medical Journal*, vol. 310, pp. 1150-1151.

Ham, C. and Spurgeon, P. (1993) 'The development of the purchasing function', in Spurgeon, P. (ed.) *The New Face of the NHS*, Harlow: Longman.

Hamblin, R. (1998) 'Trusts', in Le Grand, J., Mays, N. and Mulligan, J. (eds) *Learning from the NHS Internal Market: A Review of the Evidence*, London: King's Fund.

Hamilton, J. (1997) 'Purchasers, not surgeons, control waiting lists', *British Medical Journal*, vol. 315, p. 1231.

Handysides, S. (1994a) 'Morale in general practice: is change the problem or the solution', *British Medical Journal*, vol. 308, pp. 32-34.

Handysides, S. (1994b) 'Building an efficient and healthy practice', *British Medical Journal*, vol. 308, pp. 179-182.

Hansmann, H. (1987) 'Economic theories of nonprofit organization', in Powell, W. (ed.) *The Nonprofit Sector: A Research Handbook*, New Haven: Yale University Press.

Hargadon, J. (1993) 'NHS trusts – two provider perspectives: views from the bridge', in Peck, E. and Spurgeon, P. (eds) *NHS Trusts in Practice*, Harlow: Longman.

Harris, A. (1994) 'Specialist outreach clinics: more questions than answers until they have been properly evaluated', *British Medical Journal*, vol. 308, p. 1053.

Harris, C. and Scrivener, G. (1996) 'Fundholders' prescribing costs: the first five years', *British Medical Journal*, vol. 313, pp. 1531-1534.

Harrison, A., Dixon, J., New, B. and Judge, K. (1997) 'Funding the NHS: is the NHS sustainable?', *British Medical Journal*, vol. 314, pp. 296-298.

Harrison, J. and Nutley, S. (1993) 'Whither health service management?', in Malek, M., Vacani, P., Rasquinna, J. and Davey, P. (eds) *Managerial Issues in the Reformed NHS*, Chichester: Wiley.

Harrison, S. (1995) 'Clinical autonomy and planned markets: the British case', in Saltman, R. and von Otter, C. (eds) *Implementing Planned Markets in Health Care*, Buckingham: Open University Press.

Harrison, S. and Hunter, D. (1994) *Rationing Health Care*, London: Institute for Public Policy Research.

Harrison, S., Hunter, D. and Pollitt, C. (1990) *The Dynamics of British Health Policy*, London: Routledge.

Harrison, S. and Pollitt, C. (1994) *Controlling Health Professionals*, Buckingham: Open University Press.

Hart, J. (1994) 'NHS reforms: a conspiracy exists', *British Medical Journal*, vol. 309, p. 739.

Harvey, I. (1993) 'And so to bed: access to inpatient services', in Frankel, S. and West, R. (eds) *Rationing and Rationality in the National Health Service: The Persistence of Waiting Lists*, London: Macmillan.

Haycox, A. (1993) 'Pharmacy policy and practice – the future', in Malek, M., Vacani, P., Rasquinna, J. and Davey, P. (eds) *Managerial Issues in the Reformed NHS*, Chichester: Wiley.

Healey, J. (1996) *Statistics: A Tool for Social Research*, Belmont: Wadsworth.

Health Departments of Great Britain (1989) *General Practice in the National Health Service: The 1990 Contract*, London: Department of Health.

Hill, M. (1993) *The Welfare State in Britain: A Political History Since 1945*, Aldershot: Edward Elgar.

Hirschman, A. (1970) *Exit, Voice and Loyalty: Responses to Decline in Firms, Organizations and States*, Massachusetts: Harvard University Press.

Hoey, A. (1995) 'GP fundholding: mixing money and medicine', *Consumer Policy Review*, vol. 5, pp. 175-179.

Holstrom, B. and Tirole, J. (1989) 'The theory of the firm', in Schmalensee, R. and Willig, R. (eds) *Handbook of Industrial Organization*, Amsterdam: Elsevier Science.

Honigsbaum, F. (1979) *The Division in British Medicine: A History of the Separation of General Practice from Hospital Care 1911-1968*, London: Kogan Page.

Howie, J., Heaney, D. and Maxwell, M. (1994) 'Evaluating care of patients reporting pain in fundholding practices', *British Medical Journal*, vol. 309, pp. 705-710.

Hunter, D. (1993) 'The internal market: the shifting agenda', in Tilley, I. (ed.) *Managing the Internal Market*, London: Paul Chapman.

Hutton, J. (1993) 'How providers should respond to purchasers' needs', in Drummond, M. and Maynard, A. (eds) *Purchasing and Providing Cost-effective Health Care*, London: Longman.

Iliffe, S. and Freudenstein, U. (1994) 'Fundholding: from solution to problem: rigorous evaluation should precede any further extension of the scheme', *British Medical Journal*, vol. 308, pp. 3-4.

Illsley, R. and Le Grand, J. (1987) 'The measurement of inequality in health', in Williams, A. (ed.) *Health and Economics*, London: Macmillan.

Johnes, G. and Cave, M. (1994) 'The development of competition among higher education institutions', in Bartlett, W., Propper, C., Wilson, D. and Le Grand, J. (eds) *Quasi-markets in the Welfare State*, Bristol: SAUS.

Jones, R. (1992) 'Decision-making and hospital referrals', in Roland, M. and Coulter, A. (eds) *Hospital Referrals*, Oxford: Oxford University Press.

Jordan, K., Ong, B. and Croft, P. (1998) *Mastering Statistics: A Guide for Health Service Professionals and Researchers*, Cheltenham: Stanley Thornes.

Kane, N. (1995) 'Costs, productivity and financial outcomes of managed care', in Saltman, R. and von Otter, C. (eds) *Implementing Planned Markets in Health Care*, Buckingham: Open University Press.

Keeley, D. (1994) 'Prescribing costs: fundholders had a head start', *British Medical Journal*, vol. 308, pp. 206-207.

Keeley, D. (1997a) 'Author's reply', *British Medical Journal*, vol. 315, p. 749.

Keeley, D. (1997b) 'General practice fundholding and health care costs', *British Medical Journal*, vol. 315, p. 139.

Kember, T. and Macpherson, G. (1994) *The NHS – A Kaleidoscope of Care – Conflicts of Service and Business Values*, London: Nuffield Provincial Hospitals Trust.

Kerrison, S. (1993) 'Contracting and the quality of medical care', in Tilley, I. (ed.) *Managing the Internal Market*, London: Paul Chapman.

Kind, P., Leese, B., Cameron, I. and Carpenter, J. (1993) 'Quantifying quality – measuring quality in the provision of health care', in Malek, M., Vacani, P., Rasquinna, J. and Davey, P. (eds) *Managerial Issues in the Reformed NHS*, Chichester: Wiley.

Kirkwood, B. (1988) *Essentials of Medical Statistics*, Oxford: Blackwell.

Klein, R. (1995) *The New Politics of the NHS*, Harlow: Longman.

Klein, R., Day, P. and Redmayne, S. (1996) *Managing Scarcity: Priority Setting and Rationing in the National Health Service*, Buckingham: Open University Press.

Knapp, M., Wistow, G., Forder, J. and Hardy, B. (1994) 'Markets for social care: opportunities, barriers and implications', in Bartlett, W., Propper, C., Wilson, D. and Le Grand, J. (eds) *Quasi-markets in the Welfare State*, Bristol: SAUS.

Koch, H. (1993) 'Buying and selling high-quality health care', in Spurgeon, P. (ed.) *The New Face of the NHS*, Harlow: Longman.

Koeck, C. and Neugaard, B. (1995) 'Competitive hospital markets based on quality: the case of Vienna', in Saltman, R. and von Otter, C. (eds) *Implementing Planned Markets in Health Care*, Buckingham: Open University Press.

Labour Party (1993) *GP Fundholding: Bad for your Health*, London: Campaigns and Communications Directorate.

Langlois, R. and Robertson, P. (1995) *Firms, Markets and Economic Change*, London: Routledge.

Lapsley, I. and Llewellyn, S. (1997) 'Statements of mutual faith: soft contracts in social care', in Flynn, R. and Williams, G. (eds) *Contracting for Health*, New York: Oxford University Press.

Lapsley, I. and Llewellyn, S. with Grant, J. (1997) *GP Fundholders: Agents of Change*, Edinburgh: Institute of Chartered Accountants of Scotland.

Leese, B. and Drummond, M. (1993) 'General practice fundholding: maverick or catalyst', in Drummond, M. and Maynard, A. (eds) *Purchasing and Providing Cost-effective Health Care*, London: Longman.

Le Grand, J. (1982) *The Strategy of Equality: Redistribution and the Social Services*, London: George Allen and Unwin.

Le Grand, J. (1989) 'Markets, welfare, and equality', in Le Grand, J. and Estrin, S. (eds) *Market Socialism*, Oxford: Oxford University Press.

Le Grand, J. (1990) 'The state of welfare', in Hills, J. (ed.) *The State of Welfare: The Welfare State in Britain Since 1974*, Oxford: Oxford University Press.

Le Grand, J. (1991a) 'Quasi-markets and social policy', *The Economic Journal*, vol. 101, pp. 1256-1267.

Le Grand, J. (1991b) *Equity and Choice: An Essay in Economics and Applied Philosophy*, London: Harper Collins.

Le Grand, J. (1991c) 'The distribution of health care revisited: a commentary on Wagstaff, van Doorslaer and Paci, and O'Donnell and Propper', *Journal of Health Economics*, vol. 10, pp. 239-245.

Le Grand, J. (1991d) 'The theory of government failure', *British Journal of Political Science*, vol. 21, pp. 215-239.

Le Grand, J. (1993) 'Equity in the distribution of health care: the British debate', in Van Doorslaer, E., Wagstaff, A. and Rutten, F. (eds) *Equity in the Finance and Delivery of Health Care: An International Perspective*, Oxford: Oxford University Press.

Le Grand, J. (1994a) 'Evaluating the NHS reforms', in Robinson, R. and Le Grand, J. (eds) *Evaluating the NHS Reforms*, London: King's Fund Institute.

Le Grand, J. (1994b) 'Internal market rules OK', *British Medical Journal*, vol. 309, pp. 1596-1597.

Le Grand, J. (1995) 'The strategy of equality revisited: a reply', *Journal of Social Policy*, vol. 24, pp. 187-191.

Le Grand, J. (1997) 'Knights, knaves or pawns? Human behaviour and social policy', *Journal of Social Policy*, vol. 26, pp. 149-169.

Le Grand, J. and Bartlett, W. (1993) 'Quasi-markets and social policy: the way forward', in Le Grand, J. and Bartlett, W. (eds) *Quasi-markets and Social Policy*, London: Macmillan.

Le Grand, J., Mays, N. and Dixon, J. (1998) 'The reforms: success or failure or neither?', in Le Grand, J., Mays, N. and Mulligan, J. (eds) *Learning from the NHS Internal Market: A Review of the Evidence*, London: King's Fund.

Le Grand, J., Propper, C. and Robinson, R. (1992) *The Economics of Social Problems*, London: Macmillan.

Le Grand, J., Winter, D. and Woolley, F. (1990) 'The National Health Service: safe in whose hands?', in Hills, J. (ed.) *The State of Welfare: The Welfare State in Britain since 1974*, Oxford: Oxford University Press.

Leibenstein, H. (1987) *Inside the Firm: The Inefficiencies of Hierarchy*, Massachusetts: Harvard University Press.

Lerner, C. and Claxton, K. (1994) *Modelling the Behaviour of General Practitioners: A Theoretical Foundation for Studies of Fundholding*, Centre for Health Economics Discussion Paper 116, York: University of York.

Levacic, R. (1994) 'Evaluating the performance of quasi-markets in education', in Bartlett, W., Propper, C., Wilson, D. and Le Grand, J. (eds) *Quasi-markets in the Welfare State*, Bristol: SAUS.

Levitt, R. and Wall, A. (1984) *The Reorganised National Health Service*, London: Croom Helm.

Light, D. (1997) 'The real ethics of rationing', *British Medical Journal*, vol. 315, pp. 112-115.

Light, D. (1998) 'Is NHS purchasing serious? An American perspective', *British Medical Journal*, vol. 316, pp. 217-220.

Loveridge, R. (1992) 'The future of health care delivery – markets or hierarchy', in Loveridge, R. and Starkey, K. (eds) *Continuity and Crisis in the NHS*, Buckingham: Open University Press.

Loveridge, R. and Schofield, J. (1993) 'Markets or hierarchies? Top down or bottom up reform of primary care delivery in the NHS?', in Malek, M., Vacani, P., Rasquinna, J. and Davey, P. (eds) *Managerial Issues in the Reformed NHS*, Chichester: Wiley.

Loveridge, R. and Starkey, K. (1992) 'Introduction: innovation and interest in the organization of health care delivery', in Loveridge, R. and Starkey, K. (eds) *Continuity and Crisis in the NHS*, Buckingham: Open University Press.

Luxton, D. (1993) 'Fundholding practices get preference', *British Medical Journal*, vol. 306, pp. 206-207.

MacKerrell, D. (1993) 'Contract pricing: a management opportunity', in Tilley, I. (ed.) *Managing the Internal Market*, London: Paul Chapman.

McAvoy, B. (1993) 'Heartsink hotel revisited', *British Medical Journal*, vol. 306, pp. 694-695.

McCullough, C. (1993) 'Fundholding practices get preference', *British Medical Journal*, vol. 306, p. 141.

McGuire, A., Henderson, J. and Mooney, G. (1988) *The Economics of Health Care: An Introductory Text*, London: Routledge.

McLaughlin, C. (1986) *The Management of Nonprofit Organizations*, New York: Wiley.

Mahon, A., Wilkin, D. and Whitehouse, C. (1994) 'Choice of hospital for elective surgery referral: GPs' and patients' views', in Robinson, R. and Le Grand, J. (eds) *Evaluating the NHS Reforms*, London: King's Fund Institute.

Majeed, A. (1998) 'Commentary: equity in the allocation of resources to general practices will be difficult to achieve', *British Medical Journal*, vol. 316, p. 43.

Malek, M., Vacani, P. and Rasquinha, J. (1993) 'NHS reform – the final frontier?', in Malek, M., Vacani, P., Rasquinna, J. and Davey, P. (eds) *Managerial Issues in the Reformed NHS*, Chichester: Wiley.

Mannion, R. and Smith, P. (1995) *How Providers are Chosen in the Mixed Economy of Community Care*, Paper to the ESRC quasi-markets research seminar on 20-21 March, Bristol: SAUS.

Mant, D. and Towse, A. (1996) 'The future of general practice: an overview', in Griffin, J. (ed.) *The Future of Primary Care*, London: Office of Health Economics.

March, J. and Olsen, J. (1989) *Rediscovering Institutions: The Organizational Basis of Politics*, New York: Free Press.

March, J. and Simon, H. (1993) *Organizations*, Massachusetts: Blackwell.

Martin, S., Rice, N. and Smith, P. (1997) *Risk and the GP Budget Holder*, Centre for Health Economics Discussion Paper 153, York: University of York.

Marum, M. (1997) 'Fundholding has curbed increases in prescribing costs', *British Medical Journal*, vol. 315, pp. 748-749.

Matsaganis, M. and Glennerster, H. (1994a) 'Cream-skimming and fundholding', in Bartlett, W., Propper, C., Wilson, D. and Le Grand, J. (eds) *Quasi-markets in the Welfare State*, Bristol: SAUS.

Matsaganis, M. and Glennerster, H. (1994b) 'The threat of 'cream skimming' in the post-reform NHS', *Journal of Health Economics*, vol. 13, pp. 31-60.

Maxwell, M., Heaney, D., Howie, J. and Noble, S. (1993) 'General practice fundholding: observations on prescribing patterns and costs using the defined daily dose method', *British Medical Journal*, vol. 307, pp. 1190-1194.

Maynard, A. (1986) 'Performance incentives in general practice', in Teeling Smith, G. (ed.) *Health Education and General Practice*, London: Office of Health Economics.

Maynard, A. (1987) 'Markets and health care', in Williams, A. (ed.) *Health and Economics*, London: Macmillan.

Maynard, A. (1993a) 'Creating competition in the NHS: Is it possible? Will it work?', in Tilley, I. (ed.) *Managing the Internal Market*, London: Paul Chapman.

Maynard, A. (1993b) 'The significance of cost-effective purchasing', in Drummond, M. and Maynard, A. (eds) *Purchasing and Providing Cost-effective Health Care*, London: Longman.

Maynard, A. (1996) 'Efficiency of spending under fixed budgets', in Schwartz, F., Glennerster, H. and Saltman, R. (eds) *Fixing Health Budgets: Experience From Europe and North America*, Chichester: Wiley.

Mays, N. (1997) 'Fundholding seems not to be implicated in rise in emergency admissions', *British Medical Journal*, vol. 315, p. 749.

Mays, N. and Bevan G. (1987) *Resource Allocation in the Health Service: A Review of the Methods of the Resource Allocation Working Party (RAWP)*, London: Bedford Square Press.

Mays, N., Goodwin, N., Bevan, G. and Wyke, S. (1997) 'What is total purchasing', *British Medical Journal*, vol. 315, pp. 652-655.

Mays, N. and Mulligan, J. (1998) 'Total purchasing', in Le Grand, J., Mays, N. and Mulligan, J. (eds) *Learning from the NHS Internal Market: A Review of the Evidence*, London: King's Fund.

Means, R., Hoyes, L., Lart, R. and Taylor, M. (1994) 'Quasi-markets and community care: towards user empowerment?', in Bartlett, W., Propper, C., Wilson, D. and Le Grand, J. (eds) *Quasi-markets in the Welfare State*, Bristol: SAUS.

Means, R. and Langan, J. (1996) 'Charging and quasi-markets in community care: implications for elderly people with dementia', *Social Policy and Administration*, vol. 30, pp. 244-262.

Millard, R. (1997) 'Fundholding gives choice of alternatives if local services are poor', *British Medical Journal*, vol. 315, p. 749.

Miller, D. (1989) 'Why markets?', in Le Grand, J. and Estrin, S. (eds) *Market Socialism*, Oxford: Oxford University Press.

Mintzberg, H. (1979) *The Structuring of Organizations*, New Jersey: Prentice-Hall.

Mohan, J. (1987) 'Transforming the geography of health care: spatial inequality and health care in contemporary England', in Williams, A. (ed.) *Health and Economics*, London: Macmillan.

Mohan, J. (1995) *A National Health Service? The Restructuring of Health Care in Britain since 1979*, New York: St. Martin's Press.

Mooney, G. and McGuire, A. (1987) 'Distributive justice with special reference to geographical inequality and health care', in Williams, A. (ed.) *Health and Economics*, London: Macmillan.

Moore, L. and Dalziel, M. (1993) 'Making the internal market work: a case for managed change', *British Medical Journal*, vol. 307, pp. 1270-1272.

Mullen, P. (1990) 'Which internal market? The NHS white paper and internal markets', *Financial Accountability and Management*, vol. 6, pp. 33-50.

Mullen, P. (1993) 'Planning and internal markets', in Spurgeon, P. (ed.) *The New Face of the NHS*, Harlow: Longman.

Mulligan, J. (1998a) 'Locality and GP commissioning', in Le Grand, J., Mays, N. and Mulligan, J. (eds) *Learning from the NHS Internal Market: A Review of the Evidence*, London: King's Fund.

Mulligan, J. (1998b) 'Health authority purchasing', in Le Grand, J., Mays, N. and Mulligan, J. (eds) *Learning from the NHS Internal Market: A Review of the Evidence*, London: King's Fund.

Murray, I. (1997) 'Fundholder patients must join the queue', *The Times*, 17 July, p. 9.

National Audit Office (1994) *General Practitioner Fundholding in England*, London: HMSO.

New, B. and Le Grand, J. (1996) *Rationing in the NHS: Principles and Pragmatism*, London: King's Fund.

Newhouse, J., Manning, W., Keeler, E. and Sloss, E. (1989) 'Adjusting capitation rates using objective health measures and prior utilisation', *Health Care Financing Review*, vol. 10, pp. 41-54.

Newton, J., Fraser, M., Robinson, J. and Wainwright, D. (1993) 'Fundholding in northern region: the first year', *British Medical Journal*, vol. 306, pp. 375-378.

NHS Executive (1992) 'Priorities and planning guidance 1993/94', *Executive Letter EL(92)47*, Leeds: NHSE.

NHS Executive (1994a) 'GP fund-holding: The National Health Service (fund-holding practices) amendment regulations 1994, *Health Service Guidelines HSG(94)26*, Leeds: NHSE.

NHS Executive (1994b) 'Developing NHS purchasing and GP fundholding', *Executive Letter EL(94)79*, Leeds: NHSE.

NHS Executive (1994c) *Hospital and Community Health Services Resource Allocation*, Leeds: NHSE.

NHS Executive (1994d) *Data Manual: Module 1 – Hospital Services – Version 2.0*, Leeds: NHSE.

NHS Executive (1994e) 'Clinical priority on waiting lists', *Executive Letter EL(94)19*, Leeds: NHSE.

NHS Executive (1995a) 'Priorities and planning guidance for the NHS: 1995/96', *Executive Letter EL(95)68*, Leeds: NHSE.

NHS Executive (1995b) 'GP fundholding: revised lists of goods and services', *Health Service Guidelines HSG(95)65*, Leeds: NHSE.

NHS Executive (1995c) *Developing NHS Purchasing and GP Fundholding: Towards a Primary Care-led NHS*, London: Department of Health.

NHS Executive (1995d) *General Practice Fundholding: A Primary Care Led NHS*, London: Department of Health.

NHS Executive (1995e) *GP Fundholding: Focusing on the Facts*, London: Department of Health.

NHS Executive (1996a) *GP Fundholder Budget Setting: The National Framework*, Leeds: NHSE.

NHS Executive (1996b) *NHS Waiting Times: Guidelines for Good Administrative Practice*, London: Department of Health.

NHS Executive (1996c) 'Guidance notes for total purchasing sites', *Health Service Guidelines HSG(96)57*, Leeds: NHSE.

NHS Executive (1996d) *NHS Waiting Times: Good Practice Guide*, London: Department of Health.

NHS Executive (1997a) *Local Budget-setting and Financial Management*, London Department of Health.

NHS Executive (1997b) 'The National Health Service (fund-holding practices) amendment No 2 regulations', *Health Service Guidelines HSG(97)34*, Leeds: NHSE.

NHS Executive (1997c) 'Changing the internal market', *Executive Letter EL(97)33*, Leeds: NHSE.

NHS Executive (1997d) *Community Healthcare Resource Groups: A Report*, Version 1.1, Leeds: NHSE.

NHS Executive Trent (1995) 'A framework for contracting', *The Fund Manager Survival Guide*, Macclesfield: Greenhalgh & Company.

NHS Management Executive (1991) 'General practice fundholding: financial matters', *Executive Letter EL(91)36*, Leeds: NHSME.

Niskanen, W. (1971) *Bureaucracy and Representative Government*, Chicago: Aldine-Atherton.

Niskanen, W. (1973) *Bureaucracy: Servant or Master: Lessons From America*, London: Institute of Economic Affairs.

O'Donnell, O. and Propper, C. (1991) 'Equity and the distribution of U.K. national health service resources', *Journal of Health Economics*, vol. 10, pp. 1-20.

O'Donnell, O. Propper, C. and Upward, R. (1993) 'United Kingdom', in Van Doorslaer, E., Wagstaff, A. and Rutten, F. (eds) *Equity in the Finance and Delivery of Health Care: An International Perspective*, Oxford: Oxford University Press.

Office of Population Censuses and Surveys (1990) *Tabular List of the Classification of Surgical Operations and Procedures*, London: HMSO.

Oleck, H. (1956) *Non-profit Corporations and Associations: Organization, Management, and Dissolution*, Englewood Cliffs: Prentice-Hall.

Opit, L. (1993) 'Commissioning: an appraisal of a new role', in Tilley, I. (ed.) *Managing the Internal Market*, London: Paul Chapman.

O'Reilly, D., Steele, K., Merriman, B., Gilliland, A. and Brown, S. (1998) 'Effect of fundholding on removing patients from general practitioners' lists: retrospective study', *British Medical Journal*, vol. 317, pp. 785-786.

Osborne, D. and Gaebler, T. (1992) *Reinventing Government: How the Entrepreneurial Spirit is Transforming the Public Sector*, New York: Penguin.

Oswald, N. (1992) 'The history and development of the referral system', in Roland, M. and Coulter, A. (eds) *Hospital Referrals*, Oxford: Oxford University Press.

Packwood, T., Keen, J. and Buxton, M. (1991) *Hospitals in Transition*, Buckingham: Open University Press.

Paris, J., Williams, K. and Waterland, M. (1994) 'Incentives help curb prescribing costs', *British Medical Journal*, vol. 308, p. 477.

Paton, C. (1992) *Competition and Planning in the NHS: The Dangers of Unplanned Markets*, London: Chapman and Hall.

Paton, C. (1994) 'Planning and markets in the NHS', in Bartlett, W., Propper, C., Wilson, D. and Le Grand, J. (eds) *Quasi-markets in the Welfare State*, Bristol: SAUS.

Paton, C. (1995) 'Present dangers and future threats: some perverse incentives in the NHS reforms', *British Medical Journal*, vol. 310, pp. 1245-1248.

Paton, C. (1996) *Health Policy and Management: The Healthcare Agenda in a British Political Context*, London: Chapman and Hall.

Paton, C. and Bach, S. (1990) *Case Studies in Health Policy and Management*, London: Nuffield Provincial Hospitals Trust.

Paton, C. with Hunt, K., Birch, K. and Jordan, K. (1998) *Competition and Planning in the NHS: The Consequences of the NHS Reforms*, Cheltenham: Stanley Thornes.

Peck, E. (1993a) 'The prospective roles, selection and characteristics of an NHS trust board', in Peck, E. and Spurgeon, P. (eds) *NHS Trusts in Practice*, Harlow: Longman.

Peck, E. (1993b) 'The roles of an NHS trust board – aspirations, observations and perceptions', in Peck, E. and Spurgeon, P. (eds) *NHS Trusts in Practice*, Harlow: Longman.

Peck, E. and Spurgeon, P. (1993a) 'Introduction', in Peck, E. and Spurgeon, P. (eds) *NHS Trusts in Practice*, Harlow: Longman.

Peck, E. and Spurgeon, P. (1993b) 'Forward from here: future development', in Peck, E. and Spurgeon, P. (eds) *NHS Trusts in Practice*, Harlow: Longman.

Pereira, J. (1993) 'What does equity in health mean?', *Journal of Social Policy*, vol. 22, pp. 19-48.

Petchey, R. (1995) 'General practitioner fundholding: weighing the evidence', *The Lancet*, vol. 346, pp. 1139-1142.

Pietroni, R. (1993) 'General practitioners and the market', in Tilley, I. (ed.) *Managing the Internal Market*, London: Paul Chapman.

Pitelis, C. (1991) *Market and Non-market Hierarchies: Theory of Institutional Failure*, Oxford: Blackwell.

Pollitt, C. (1984) 'The state and health care', in McLennan, G., Held, D. and Hall, S. (eds) *State and Society in Contemporary Britain*, Cambridge: Polity.

Pollitt, C. (1993) *Managerialism and the Public Services*, Oxford: Blackwell.

Powell, M. (1995) 'The strategy of equality revisited', *Journal of Social Policy*, vol. 24, pp. 163-185.

Powell, M. (1998) *Evaluating the National Health Service*, Buckingham: Open University Press.

Propper, C. (1993a) 'Quasi-markets, contracts and quality in health and social care: the US experience', in Le Grand, J. and Bartlett, W. (eds) *Quasi-markets and Social Policy*, London: Macmillan.

Propper, C. (1993b) 'Quasi-markets and regulation', in Le Grand, J. and Bartlett, W. (eds) *Quasi-markets and Social Policy*, London: Macmillan.

Propper, C. and Bartlett, W. (1997) 'The impact of competition on the behaviour of National Health Service trusts', in Flynn, R. and Williams, G. (eds) *Contracting for Health*, New York: Oxford University Press.

Propper, C., Bartlett, W. and Wilson, D. (1994) 'Introduction', in Bartlett, W., Propper, C., Wilson, D. and Le Grand, J. (eds) *Quasi-markets in the Welfare State*, Bristol: SAUS.

Propper, C. and Maynard, A. (1990) 'Whither the private health care sector', in Culyer, A., Maynard, A. and Posnett, J. (eds) *Competition in Health Care: Reforming the NHS*, London: Macmillan.

Propper, C. and Söderlund, N. (1998) Competition in the internal market: an overview of its effects on hospital prices and costs', *Health Economics*, vol. 7, pp. 187-197.

Propper, C., Wilson, D. and Söderlund, N. (1998) 'The effects of regulation and competition in the NHS internal market: the case of general practice fundholder prices', *Journal of Health Economics*, vol. 17, pp. 645-673.

Rafferty, T., Wilson-Davis, K. and McGavock, H. (1997) 'How has fundholding in Northern Ireland affected prescribing patterns? A longitudinal study', *British Medical Journal*, vol. 315, pp. 166-170.

Rees, G. (1969) *St Michael: A History of Marks and Spencer*, London: Weidenfeld and Nicolson.

Riis, P. (1982) 'How therapeutic decisions are motivated', in Tygstrup, N., Lachin, J. and Juhl, E. (eds) *The Randomized Clinical Trial and Therapeutic Decisions*, New York: Marcel Dekker.

Robinson, J., Wainwright, D., Newton, J. and Fraser, M. (1993) 'GP fundholding – a financial management perspective', in Malek, M., Vacani, P., Rasquinna, J. and Davey, P. (eds) *Managerial Issues in the Reformed NHS*, Chichester: Wiley.

Robinson, R. (1994) 'Introduction', in Robinson, R. and Le Grand, J. (eds) *Evaluating the NHS Reforms*, London: King's Fund Institute.

Robinson, R. (1996) 'Hopes and fears', *The NHS Fundholding and Commissioning Guide 1996/97*, London: Medical Information Systems.

Robinson, R. and Le Grand, J. (1995) 'Contracting and the purchaser-provider split', in Saltman, R. and von Otter, C. (eds) *Implementing Planned Markets in Health Care*, Buckingham: Open University Press.

Robinson, R. and Steiner, A. (1998) *Managed Health Care: US Evidence and Lessons for the National Health Service*, Buckingham: Open University Press.

Roland, M. (1991) 'Fundholding and cash limits in primary care: blight or blessing?', *British Medical Journal*, vol. 303, pp. 171-172.

Roland, M. (1992a) 'Hospital referral – the future', in Roland, M. and Coulter, A. (eds) *Hospital Referrals*, Oxford: Oxford University Press.

Roland, M. (1992b) 'Measuring referral rates', in Roland, M. and Coulter, A. (eds) *Hospital Referrals*, Oxford: Oxford University Press.

Roland, M. (1992c) 'Measuring appropriateness of hospital referrals', in Roland, M. and Coulter, A. (eds) *Hospital Referrals*, Oxford: Oxford University Press.

Roland, M. (1992d) 'Communication between GPs and specialists', in Roland, M. and Coulter, A. (eds) *Hospital Referrals*, Oxford: Oxford University Press.

Roland, M. (1996) 'The future of primary care', in Griffin, J. (ed.) *The Future of Primary Care*, London: Office of Health Economics.

Roland, M., Bartholomew, J., Morrell, D., McDermott, A. and Paul, E. (1990) 'Understanding hospital referral rates: a user's guide', *British Medical Journal*, vol. 301, pp. 98-102.

Russell, I. and Grimshaw, J. (1992) 'The effectiveness of referral guidelines: a review of the methods and findings of published evaluations', in Roland, M. and Coulter, A. (eds) *Hospital Referrals*, Oxford: Oxford University Press.

Rutten, F. (1993) 'Policy implications of the COMAC-HSR project', in Van Doorslaer, E., Wagstaff, A. and Rutten, F. (eds) *Equity in the Finance and Delivery of Health Care: An International Perspective*, Oxford: Oxford University Press.

Saltman, R. (1996) 'Thinking about planned markets and fixed budgets', in Schwartz, F., Glennerster, H. and Saltman, R. (eds) *Fixing Health Budgets: Experience From Europe and North America*, Chichester: Wiley.

Saltman, R. and von Otter, C. (1992) *Planned Markets and Public Competition: Strategic Reform in Northern European Health Systems*, Buckingham: Open University Press.

Saltman, R. and von Otter, C. (1995) 'Balancing social and economic responsibility', in Saltman, R. and von Otter, C. (eds) *Implementing Planned Markets in Health Care*, Buckingham: Open University Press.

Samuel, O. (1992) 'Fundholding practices get preference', *British Medical Journal*, vol. 305, p. 1497.

Sanders, D., Coulter, A. and McPherson, K. (1989) *Variations in Hospital Admission Rates: A Review of the Literature*, London: King's Fund.

Scheffler, R. (1989) 'Adverse selection: the achilles heel of the NHS reforms', *The Lancet*, vol. 1, pp. 950-952.

Schofield, D. and Hatcher, P. (1993) 'Implications of the NHS reforms for the future of primary health care in the United Kingdom', in Spurgeon, P. (ed.) *The New Face of the NHS*, Harlow: Longman.

Self, P. (1993) *Government by the Market? The Politics of Public Choice*, London: Macmillan.

Sen, A. (1992) *Inequality Re-examined*, Massachusetts: Harvard University Press.

Sheldon, T., Smith, P., Borowitz, M., Martin, S. and Carr-Hill, R. (1994) 'Attempt at deriving a formula for setting general practitioner fundholding budgets', *British Medical Journal*, vol. 309, pp. 1059-1064.

Silverman, D. (1990) 'Ceremonial order', in Pugh, D. (ed.) *Organization Theory*, London: Penguin.

Smee, C. (1995) 'Self-governing trusts and GP fundholders: the British experience', in Saltman, R. and von Otter, C. (eds) *Implementing Planned Markets in Health Care*, Buckingham: Open University Press.

Smee, C. (1996) 'Setting regional allocations and national budgets in the UK', in Schwartz, F., Glennerster, H. and Saltman, R. (eds) *Fixing Health Budgets: Experience from Europe and North America*, Chichester: Wiley.

Smith, P. (1973) *Groups Within Organizations: Applications of Social Psychology to Organizational Behaviour*, London: Harper and Row.

Smith, P., Sheldon, T., Carr-Hill, R., Martin, S., Peacock, S. and Hardman, G. (1994) 'Allocating resources to health authorities: results and policy implications of small area analysis of use of inpatient services', *British Medical Journal*, vol. 309, pp. 1050-1054.

Smith, R. (1998) 'New government, same narrow vision: it's time to move beyond the numbers on waiting lists', *British Medical Journal*, vol. 316, p. 643.

Spurgeon, P. (1993a) 'Purchaser-provider relationships: current practice and future prospects', in Peck, E. and Spurgeon, P. (eds) *NHS Trusts in Practice*, Harlow: Longman.

Spurgeon, P. (1993b) 'Regulation or free market for the NHS?: A case for coexistence', in Tilley, I. (ed.) *Managing the Internal Market*, London: Paul Chapman.

Spurgeon, P. (1993c) 'Resource management: a fundamental change in managing health services', in Spurgeon, P. (ed.) *The New Face of the NHS*, Harlow: Longman.

Spurgeon, P., Smith, P., Straker, M., Deakin, N., Thomas, N. and Walsh, K. (1997) 'The experience of contracting in health care', in Flynn, R. and Williams, G. (eds) *Contracting for Health*, New York: Oxford University Press.

Starkey, K. (1992) 'Time and the consultant: issues of contract and control', in Loveridge, R. and Starkey, K. (eds) *Continuity and Crisis in the NHS*, Buckingham: Open University Press.

Starkey, K. and Hodges, R. (1993) 'Of trusts and markets – accountability and governance in the new National Health Service', in Malek, M., Vacani, P., Rasquinna, J. and Davey, P. (eds) *Managerial Issues in the Reformed NHS*, Chichester: Wiley.

Starkweather, D. (1993) 'Profit making by nonprofit hospitals', in Hammack, D. and Young, D. (eds) *Nonprofit Organizations in a Market Economy*, San Francisco: Jossey-Bass.

Steele, G. (1993) *The Economics of Freidrich Hayek*, London: Macmillan.

Stewart, J. and Walsh, K. (1992) 'Change in the management of public services', *Public Administration*, vol. 70, pp. 499-518.

Stewart-Brown, S., Surender, R., Bradlow, J., Coulter, A. and Doll, H. (1995) 'The effects of fundholding in general practice on prescribing habits three years after the introduction of the scheme', *British Medical Journal*, vol. 311, pp. 1543-1547.

Stott, R. (1993) 'Everyone a trust?: trust status in the experience of the Guy's and Lewisham NHS trust', in Tilley, I. (ed.) *Managing the Internal Market*, London: Paul Chapman.

Strong, P. and Robinson, J. (1990) *The NHS under New Management*, Buckingham: Open University Press.

Subner, S. and Bruce, N. (1993) 'Social deprivation, health status and their relationship on a ward basis in Camden and Islington', in Malek, M., Vacani, P., Rasquinna, J. and Davey, P. (eds) *Managerial Issues in the Reformed NHS*, Chichester: Wiley.

Surender, R., Bradlow, J., Coulter, A., Doll, H. and Stewart-Brown, S. (1995) 'Prospective study of trends in referral patterns in fundholding and non-fundholding practices in the Oxford region, 1990-4', *British Medical Journal*, vol. 311, pp. 1205-1208.

Taylor, M. and Hoggett, P. (1994) 'Quasi-markets and the transformation of the independent sector', in Bartlett, W., Propper, C., Wilson, D. and Le Grand, J. (eds) *Quasi-markets in the Welfare State*, Bristol: SAUS.

Taylor-Gooby, P. and Lawson, R. (1993) 'Where we go from here: the new order in welfare', in Taylor-Gooby, P. and Lawson, R. (eds) *Markets and Managers: New Issues in the Delivery of Welfare*, Buckingham: Open University Press.

Tennison, B. (1992) 'The NHS review, 1988-1991: GPs and contracts for care', in Roland, M. and Coulter, A. (eds) *Hospital Referrals*, Oxford: Oxford University Press.

Thomas, K., Nicholl, J. and Coleman, P. (1995) 'Assessing the outcome of making it easier for patients to change general practitioner: practice characteristics associated with patient movements', *British Journal of General Practice*, vol. 45, pp. 581-586.

Thompson, D. (1993) 'Developing managers for the 1990s', in Spurgeon, P. (ed.) *The New Face of the NHS*, Harlow: Longman.

Thompson, G. (1990) *The Political Economy of the New Right*, London: Printer.

Tilley, I. (1993) 'Approaching the internal market: the nature and scope of the book', in Tilley, I. (ed.) *Managing the Internal Market*, London: Paul Chapman.

Timmins, N. (1995) *The Five Giants: A Biography of the Welfare State*, London: Harper Collins.

Toth, B., Harvey, I. and Peters, T. (1997) 'Did the introduction of general practice fundholding change patterns of emergency admission to hospital?', *Journal of Health Services Research and Policy*, vol. 2, pp. 71-74.

Townsend, P. (1987) 'The geography of poverty and ill-health' in Williams, A. (ed.) *Health and Economics*, London: Macmillan.

Tremblay, M. (1993) 'Of confidence and identity: the doctor in management', in Spurgeon, P. (ed.) *The New Face of the NHS*, Harlow: Longman.

Tuckman, H. (1993) 'How and why nonprofit organizations obtain capital', in Hammack, D. and Young, D. (eds) *Nonprofit Organizations in a Market Economy*, San Francisco: Jossey-Bass.

Tuckman, H. and Chang, C. (1993) 'Accumulating financial surpluses in nonprofit organizations', in Young, D., Hollister, R., Hodgkinson, V. and Associates (eds) *Governing, Leading and Managing Nonprofit Organizations*, San Francisco: Jossey-Bass.

Van Doorslaer, E. and Wagstaff, A. (1993) 'Equity in the finance of health care: methods and findings', in Van Doorslaer, E., Wagstaff, A. and Rutten, F. (eds) *Equity in the Finance and Delivery of Health Care: An International Perspective*, Oxford: Oxford University Press.

Wagstaff, A. and Van Doorslaer, E. (1993a) 'Equity in the finance and delivery of health care: concepts and definitions', in Van Doorslaer, E., Wagstaff, A. and Rutten, F. (eds) *Equity in the Finance and Delivery of Health Care: An International Perspective*, Oxford: Oxford University Press.

Wagstaff, A. and Van Doorslaer, E. (1993b) 'Equity in the delivery of health care: methods and findings', in Van Doorslaer, E., Wagstaff, A. and Rutten, F. (eds) *Equity in the Finance and Delivery of Health Care: An International Perspective*, Oxford: Oxford University Press.

Wagstaff, A., Van Doorslaer, E. and Rutten, F. (1993) 'Introduction', in Van Doorslaer, E., Wagstaff, A. and Rutten, F. (eds) *Equity in the Finance and Delivery of Health Care: An International Perspective*, Oxford: Oxford University Press.

Wall, A. (1993) 'Trusts: the reasons to be cautious', in Peck, E. and Spurgeon, P. (eds) *NHS Trusts in Practice*, Harlow: Longman.

Walsh, K. (1995) *Working with Contracts*, Paper to the ESRC quasi-markets research seminar on 20-21 March, Bristol: SAUS.

Warden, J. (1997) 'Hospital waiting lists grow by 13% in England', *British Medical Journal*, vol. 315, p. 501.

Warden, J. (1998a) 'Warning issued over hip implants', *British Medical Journal*, vol. 316, p. 650.

Warden, J. (1998b) 'NHS waiting lists grow under Labour', *British Medical Journal*, vol. 316, p. 650.

Warden, J. (1998c) 'Labour talks tough on waiting lists', *British Medical Journal*, vol. 316, p. 956.

Warden, J. (1998d) 'Waiting lists respond to cash boost', *British Medical Journal*, vol. 317, p. 618.

Warden, J. (1998e) 'UK waiting lists grow longer', *British Medical Journal*, vol. 316, p. 1627.

Weisbrod, B. (1988) *The Nonprofit Economy*, Massachusetts: Harvard University Press.

West, P. (1988) *Understanding the NHS: A Question of Incentives*, London: King's Fund.

West, P. (1997) *Understanding the National Health Service Reforms: The Creation of Incentives?*, Buckingham: Open University Press.

West, R. (1993) 'Joining the queue: demand and decision-making', in Frankel, S. and West, R. (eds) *Rationing and Rationality in the National Health Service: The Persistence of Waiting Lists*, London: Macmillan.

Whitehead, M. (1994) 'Is it fair? Evaluating the equity implications of the NHS reforms', in Robinson, R. and Le Grand, J. (eds) *Evaluating the NHS Reforms*, London: King's Fund Institute.

Wilensky, G. (1988) 'Filling the gaps on health insurance: impacts on competition', *Health Affairs*, vol. 7, pp. 133-149.

Wilkin, D. (1992) 'Patterns of referral: explaining variation', in Roland, M. and Coulter, A. (eds) *Hospital Referrals*, Oxford: Oxford University Press.

Wilkin, D. and Roland, M. (1993) *Waiting Times for First Outpatient Appointments in the NHS*, Manchester: University of Manchester.

Wilkin, D. and Smith, T. (1987) 'Explaining variation in general practitioner referrals to hospital', *Family Practice*, vol. 4, pp. 160-169.

Williams, A. (1987) 'Health economics: the cheerful face of the dismal science?', in Williams, A. (ed.) *Health and Economics*, London: Macmillan.

Williams, A. (1990) 'Ethics, clinical freedom and the doctors' role', in Culyer, A., Maynard, A. and Posnett, J. (eds) *Competition in Health Care: Reforming the NHS*, London: Macmillan.

Williams, A. (1993) 'Equity in health care: the role of ideology', in Van Doorslaer, E., Wagstaff, A. and Rutten, F. (eds) *Equity in the Finance and Delivery of Health Care: An International Perspective*, Oxford: Oxford University Press.

Williams, S., Calnan, M., Cant, S. and Coyle, J. (1993) 'All change in the NHS? Implications of the NHS reforms for primary care prevention', *Sociology of Health and Illness*, vol. 15, pp. 43-67.

Williamson, O. (1975) *Markets and Hierarchies: Analysis and Antitrust Implications*, New York: Free Press.

Williamson, O. (1986) *Economic Organization: Firms, Markets and Policy Controls*, Brighton: Wheatsheaf.

Willis, A. (1993) 'General practice – a force for change', in Spurgeon, P. (ed.) *The New Face of the NHS*, Harlow: Longman.

Willis, J. (1996) 'End of beginning for NHS changes', *Pharmaceutical Marketing*, vol. 7, pp. 30-31.

Wisely, I. (1991) 'General practitioner fundholding: experience in Grampian', *British Medical Journal*, vol. 303, pp. 171-172.

Wisely, I. (1993) 'General practitioner fundholding: experience in Grampian', *British Medical Journal*, vol. 306, pp. 695-697.

Wright, J. (1993) 'Fundholding practices get preference', *British Medical Journal*, vol. 306, p. 206.

Yates, J. (1987) *Why are we Waiting: An Analysis of Hospital Waiting Lists*, Oxford: Oxford University Press.

Young, D. (1983) *If Not for Profit, for What?: A Behavioural Theory of the Nonprofit Sector Based on Entrepreneurship*, Massachusetts: Lexington.

Young, D. (1987) 'Executive leadership in nonprofit organizations', in Powell, W. (ed.) *The Nonprofit Sector: A Research Handbook*, New Haven: Yale University Press.

Young, D. (1993) 'Emerging themes in nonprofit leadership and management', in Young, D., Hollister, R., Hodgkinson, V. and Associates (eds) *Governing, Leading and Managing Nonprofit Organizations*, San Francisco: Jossey-Bass.

Index

For Product Safety Concerns and Information please contact our EU representative GPSR@taylorandfrancis.com Taylor & Francis Verlag GmbH, Kaufingerstraße 24, 80331 München, Germany

T - #0100 - 160425 - C0 - 216/150/15 - PB - 9781138634343 - Gloss Lamination